MANAGEMENT PRACTICES
FOR THE HEALTH PROFESSIONAL

fourth edition

MANAGEMENT PRACTICES
FOR THE HEALTH PROFESSIONAL

fourth edition

Beaufort B. Longest, Jr., Ph.D.
Graduate School of Public Health
Joseph M. Katz Graduate School of Business
University of Pittsburgh
Pittsburgh, Pennsylvania

APPLETON & LANGE
Norwalk, Connecticut

Copyright © 1990 by Appleton & Lange
A Publishing Division of Prentice Hall
© 1984, 1980, 1976 by Reston Publishing Company, Inc.

92 93 94/10 9 8 7 6 5 4 3

Prentice Hall International (UK) Limited, *London*
Prentice Hall of Australia Pty. Limited, *Sydney*
Prentice Hall Canada, Inc., *Toronto*
Prentice Hall Hispanoamericana, S.A., *Mexico*
Prentice Hall of India Private Limited, *New Delhi*
Prentice Hall of Japan, Inc., *Tokyo*
Simon & Schuster Asia Pte. Ltd., *Singapore*
Editora Prentice Hall do Brasil Ltda., *Rio de Janeiro*
Prentice Hall, *Englewood Cliffs, New Jersey*

Library of Congress Cataloging-in-Publication Data

Longest, Jr. Beaufort B.
  Management practices for the health professional/Beaufort B. Longest, Jr.—4th ed.
      p.   cm.
  Includes bibliographies and index.
  ISBN 0-8385-6123-3
  1. Health services administration. 2. Management. I. Title.
  [DNLM: 1. Health Services—organization & administration—United States. WA 540 AA1 L8m]
  RA971.L663 1989
  362.1′068—dc20   89-6795
  DNLM/DLC   CIP
  for Library of Congress

PRINTED IN THE UNITED STATES OF AMERICA

ISBN 0-8385-6123-3

90000

9 780838 561232

For Brant and Courtland, my beloved sons, who have taught me the pleasures of continuity and the importance of revision.

CONTENTS

PREFACE

When the first edition of this book was published in 1976, its intended audience was those health professionals who found themselves in, or were preparing for, positions of mangerial responsibility. This important group of people remains the intended audience for the fourth edition. My purpose for writing this book was and remains to provide a sophisticated, yet readable, book that builds solidly upon the foundation of research on the practice of management, especially as it is practiced in health services organizations.

Increasingly, health services are provided in the context of organizations which combine—sometimes quite elaborately—human skills and talents, technology, and financial and other physical resources into the means of providing vital health services. Within these organizations, selected health professionals are called upon to play management roles. This might include, among others, the physician who heads a clinical department or becomes the vice president for clinical affairs; the nurse who heads a clinical unit or becomes the vice president for nursing; or the pharmacist, therapist, or social worker who leads a department. All such people are health professionals who must not only be proficient in their professional areas of expertise, but who must also understand the complexities of organizational life and management as they work in the context of the *organized* delivery of health sevices.

The basic format of this edition remains unchanged. The chapters, however, have been rewritten substantially and updated to reflect changes that have occurred in the health field and in the knowledge base upon which effective management practice is built. The vignette that opens each chapter is intended to illustrate the nature of management problems toward which the information in each chapter is directed. The vignettes all pertain to the untimely death of a fictitious patient in a hypothetical hospital. Even so, the problems contained in the vignettes are common to a great many health services organizations and provide a frame of reference for the reader.

A note of appreciation is due Mr. Edgar N. Duncan, Associate Dean of the Graduate School of Public Health at the University of Pittsburgh, who provided valuable support in updating source material for this revision. He has made a special effort to collect and organize the best management literature and he shared it generously with me.

Most importantly, I would like to thank my wife, Carolyn H. Longest, a health professional who became a manager, for providing valuable insights into both roles. Beyond this, her presence in my life has made many things possible—and doing them seem worthwhile.

Beaufort B. Longest, Jr.

ONE

Modern Health Services in an Organized Setting

March 2
7:10 A.M.

The brightly lit cafeteria, filled with the smell of fresh coffee, was like a little island to the day-shift employees of Memorial Hospital as they shook off the chill of a March wind and drank their first cup of coffee before the work day began.

At one table, several people were talking about the circumstances surrounding the death of Mr. Luther J. Fillerey.

"It's a mystery to me," the chief resident (who had led the resuscitation team) said between gulps of coffee. "I was called around 2 A.M. and told that he was going sour. His fever spiked to 104° and his breathing was very labored."

"What time did he arrest?" asked the head nurse for the day shift on the unit where Mr. Fillerey had been a patient.

"A little after three o'clock. I'm not sure exactly, but we declared him dead at 3:54 this morning. We worked on him for almost an hour. For a while there it looked like he might make it—but in the end we couldn't bring him around," the chief resident replied, his eyes never leaving his coffee.

"It's a shame," murmured one of the student nurses who had been assigned to Mr. Fillerey's floor.

"Sure it's a shame," the head nurse shot back, "but people die in hospitals!"

The student nurse glanced toward the head nurse and said, "But he was a young man, early thirties maybe, and quite pleasant to be around—at least up until the last few days—it seems so senseless. We have all this technology and all these people here, and still people die."

One of the medical technologists who had been sitting at the table stood up quickly saying, "Look at the time—we'd better get down to the lab and pick up our requisitions and get some blood drawn!" She and another technologist left together.

The head nurse touched the student's hand and said, "We'd better go, too." They left the chief resident still staring into his coffee. It was 7:25 A.M.

INTRODUCTION

The past half century of unparalleled progress in the scientific and technological base of medicine has brought a fundamental change in the way health services are delivered. This change, which affects every health professional in every developed country on earth, is that so much of the delivery of health services must now occur within the context of an organization. These organizations serve to bring together the human, technological, and physical resources that make the practice of modern medicine possible. Thus, it is critically important that those who are, or plan to be, health professionals understand not only their professional areas of expertise but also the nature of the organizations in which they will practice their professions.

Further, since many health professionals are, or will be, managers in these organizations, it is necessary for them to understand the practice of management. The purpose of this chapter is to describe the organizational context of health services. Then we turn our attention, in the remaining chapters, to the practice of management within these organizations.

The description of the organizational context of modern medicine is a complex task. The scope of the subject is broad and dynamic. In essence, we must describe the U.S. health care system. Before we do, three definitions are needed. First, *health* has been defined by the World Health Organization as a state of complete physical, mental, and social well-being and not merely the absence of disease. This definition of health describes an ideal state—one that is impossible to measure; yet it represents a target that permits a definition of a second important term.

Dictionaries generally define *service* as "an act of helpful activity." Thus *health services,* in their simplest terms, are acts of helpful activity specifically intended to maintain or improve health. Health services can be divided into three basic types: public health services, which are activities that must be conducted on a community basis, such as communicable disease control and the collection and analysis of health statistics; environmental health services, which often overlap with public health services and include such activities as radiation control and air pollution control; and personal health services, which are activities provided to individuals and include promotion of health, prevention of illness, diagnosis, treatment (sometimes leading to a cure), and rehabilitation. Helpful activities as diverse as the delicate corneal transplant performed on a 60-year-old patient, the drainage of a swamp in Louisiana during mosquito season, the dietary counseling of an obese member of a health maintenance organization, and the prohibition of smoking on a commercial airliner are all health services.

Building on these definitions, it is possible to define the *health care system* as the resources (money, people, physical plant, and technology) and the organizational configurations necessary to transform these resources into health services. It is the acts of helpful activity specifically intended to maintain or improve health that form the ultimate purpose of the health care system. The accessibility, quality, appropriateness, and efficiency of these health services constitute the basis of fair and rational judgments about the health care system.

It is important to note that the health care system and the services it provides are only one of a set of factors that affect health status. Health or health status in a human being is a function of many factors, including the basic biological characteristics and processes that comprise human biology (some diseases are inherited); the conditions external to the body (some diseases are caused by or exacerbated by environmental conditions); and the behavior patterns that constitute life-style (some diseases result from the pattern or style of life). Figure 1–1 represents, through the relative size of the arrows, assumptions about the relative importance of these determinants of health status. Thus, for example, the death of a person with a family history of (genetic tendency toward) cancer who smokes heavily, lives in a polluted urban environment, and sees a physician long after symptoms emerge is not a fair and rational basis upon which to judge the health care system. On the other hand, the death of an infant whose mother could not get good prenatal care (accessibility), unnecessary surgery performed by a less than fully qualified surgeon (appropriateness and quality), and the payment by a patient of a grossly inflated price for a diagnostic procedure because the technology necessary to conduct the procedure is owned by a hospital in a community where too much such technology exists (efficiency) are fairer and more rational bases upon which to judge the health care system.

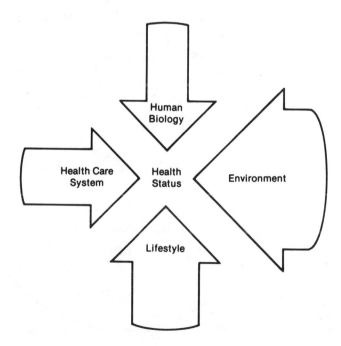

Figure 1–1. Determinants of health status. (Adapted from Blum HL: Planning for Health; Development and Application of Social Change Theory. New York: Human Sciences Press, 1973, p 3. with permission.)

Ironically, expenditures on health services, especially at the federal level, are not at all consistent with the view of the determinants of health status represented in Figure 1–1. Figure 1–2 depicts a rough estimate of the distribution of federal health expenditures by these determinants. The imbalance between determinants of health and expenditures for health is paradoxical and is not likely to change dramatically in the years immediately ahead. The historical causes of the paradox are far too complex to explore in detail here. Yet, it serves to put the discussion of the health care system in the United States in proper perspective. The health care system absorbs the vast majority of dollars spent to affect health status, but it is increasingly seen to be very limited in terms of future positive impact on the status of health of the population.

This is not to say that the health care system is not important to health status. It is, after all, the source of intervention when illness or disease occurs, even though the roots may lie in environmental, biological, or behavioral determinants. In this sense, the health care system can be viewed as a line of defense against the awful toll of untreated environmentally, biologically, and sometimes behaviorally caused illness and disease. It is largely because preventive measures in the areas of environmental, biological, and behavioral determinants have not been sufficient that the health care system is so vital to maintaining, to say nothing of improving, the health status of the population. With this perspective as background, we can turn to a description of the health care system.

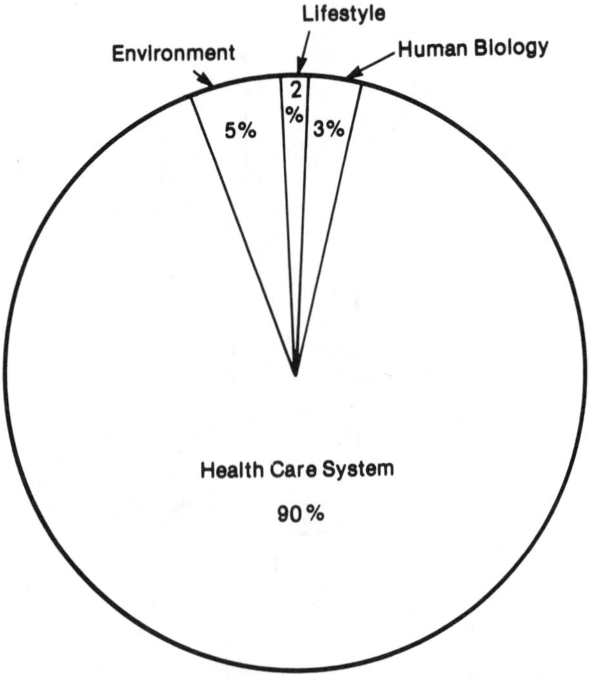

Figure 1–2. Federal health expenditures by health determinant (estimated).

THE DYNAMICS OF THE HEALTH CARE SYSTEM

The resources—money, people, physical plant, and technology—and the organizational configurations necessary to transform them into health services are described in the sections that follow. In addition, consideration will be given to the problems confronting the system as it attempts to provide services that are simultaneously of high quality, appropriate, efficiently produced, and accessible to all who need them. First, however, it is important to recognize the dynamic nature of the U.S. health care system. The dynamics are nowhere more explicit than in numbers of dollars spent. In 1990, total annual health expenditures are climbing past the $650 billion level. They are expected to reach more than $1.5 trillion and be about 15% of gross national product (GNP) by 2000. This is up from about $250 billion in 1980 and only $75 billion in 1970.[1] These dramatic increases reflect not only inflation and increased utilization, but also growth and change in the system.

The changes in the health care system reflect social change, different priorities, new technology, changes in disease trends, new delivery methods, and new approaches to paying for health care. All of these factors contribute to the dynamic state of the health care system. For example, there have been significant increases in drug addiction (particularly alcoholism) and sexually transmitted disease in recent years. Increasingly, these problems are viewed as health problems rather than social or criminal problems and thus bring concomitant increased expectation that the health care system should provide solutions. Furthermore, these factors affecting the health care system are often interactive. For example, we "marvel at new drugs, devices and scientific research, and recognize the miracles they can produce. But these innovations are expensive, and third-party payers must help determine the proper distribution and financing of these technologies."[2] When the effects of the other factors noted above are considered, the dynamic nature of the health care system begins to come into focus.

RESOURCES IN THE HEALTH CARE SYSTEM

The U.S. health care system, ultimately devoted to the provision of health services, requires an enormous quantity and variety of resources. *Resources* are defined here simply as the basic building blocks of the system: money, people, physical plant, and technology.

Money

As already noted, the health care system requires a total expenditure of about $650 billion dollars annually and consumes about 12% of the nation's GNP. Figure 1–3 illustrates the trend of this growth in total expenditures, and Figure 1–4 illustrates the trend in share of GNP. As Figure 1–5 illustrates, a substantial part of the nation's health expenditures are for hospital care and

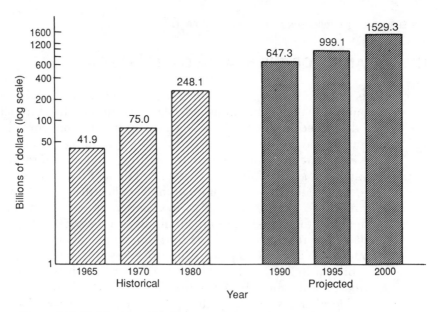

Figure 1–3. Total national health expenditures, selected years 1965 to 2000. *(From Division of National Cost Estimates, Office of the Actuary, Health Care Financing Administration: National health expenditures, 1986–2000. Health Care Financing Review 1987; 8:24.)*

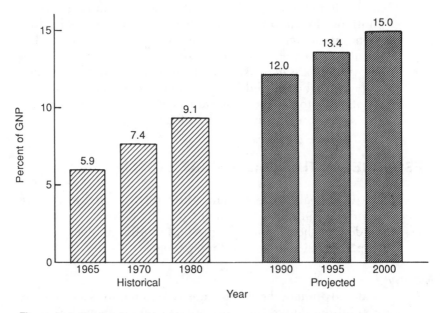

Figure 1–4. Total national health expenditures as a percent of GNP, selected years 1965 to 2000. *(From Division of National Cost Estimates, Office of the Actuary, Health Care Financing Administration, "National Health Expenditures, 1986–2000,"* Health Care Financing Review, *1987; 8:24.)*

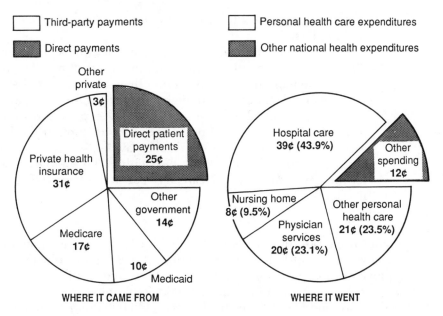

☐ Third-party payments   ☐ Personal health care expenditures

▨ Direct payments   ▨ Other national health expenditures

WHERE IT CAME FROM   **WHERE IT WENT**

Figure 1–5. The nation's health dollar: 1986. *(From Division of National Cost Estimates, office of the Actuary, Health Care Financing Administration: National health care expenditures, 1986–2000. Health Care Financing Review 1987; 8:3.) Almost three-quarters of national health expenditures were channeled through third parties. Nearly two-thirds were channeled through private hands. The bulk of that expenditure was for patient care, and the remaining 12% was spent for research, construction, administration, and government public health activity.*

physicians' services. These and other forms of personal health services are paid for in one of four basic ways:

1. Direct, or "out-of-pocket," payment in which an individual pays for care directly from personal funds.
2. Private insurance in which an individual or someone on the individual's behalf, such as an employer, enters into a contractual arrangement with an insurer who agrees to pay for a specified set of services under specified conditions in return for premium payments; or a prepayment is made to a provider such as a health maintenance organization or an organization such as Blue Cross who then contracts with providers to provide services to subscribers.
3. Government programs, principally Medicare, in which the federal government pays for health care services provided to Social Security recipients over age 65, and Medicaid, in which federal funds are combined with state funds to pay for health care services received by welfare recipients and other people defined by state law to be medically indigent. Payments under both Medicare and Medicaid are made to providers of service on behalf of program beneficiaries.
4. Although the relative amount is decreasing, some care is paid for through charitable contributions, endowment funds, or revenue gen-

erated by providers from other sources of income such as hospital parking lots.

All but the first of these mechanisms of payment are termed "third-party payments" because the providers of health care services receive payment from a source other than directly from the individual who received the care. Although direct, out-of-pocket payment now accounts for only about one fourth of total expenditures for personal health care services; all monies necessary to support the U.S. health care system, whether from direct payments, taxes or job-related benefits, ultimately come from the public. The complex flow of funds for the payment for health care services in the United States is shown in Figure 1–6.

People

Another basic building block of the health care system is human resources. The Department of Labor lists more than 225 categories of workers who are employed primarily in the health care system. Over 5 million people work in this sector. There are now about 534,000 active physicians, 1,600,000 registered nurses and 560,000 practical nurses, 143,000 dentists, 160,000 pharmacists, and over 1.2 million other allied health personnel at work in the U.S. health care system.[3]

Whereas as recently as 1976, almost two thirds of all health workers worked in hospitals, today only about 55% of the U.S. health care work force is employed in this setting. This increasing trend toward employment of health professionals in alternative settings is indicative of a growing diversification of health services beyond the traditional bounds of the acute care hospital.

Just as locales of employment are varied, so too are the settings in which health personnel are trained and educated. Whereas physicians and dentists are characteristically educated in universities or academic health centers, a large proportion of nurses and allied health professionals undergo training in hospital-based programs or in the community college setting.

Supplementing the entry and graduation requirements of these educational programs is an extensive array of credentialing regulations designed to ensure the competence of health care workers. *Credentialing* is a broad term referring to the recognition of individuals who have met certain predetermined standards attesting to their occupational skill or competence. There are two primary forms of credentialing in the health fields: licensure and certification.

Licensure is the process whereby a governmental agency grants permission to an individual to practice a given occupation after verification that the applicant has demonstrated the *minimum competency* necessary to protect the public's health, safety, or welfare. Since licensure is one of the "police powers" delegated to the states, licensure laws are normally enacted by state legislatures and regulated by a specific state agency, such as a medical or nursing board. In states where licensure laws govern an occupation, prac-

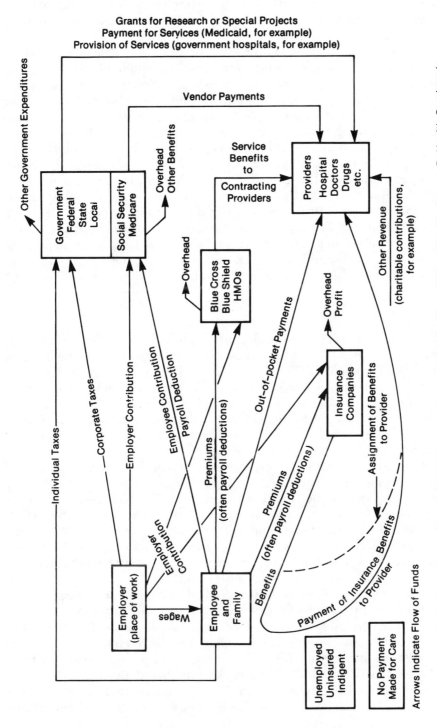

Figure 1–6. *Flow of funds for payment of health care services in the U.S. (From Wilson, FA, Neuhauser D: Health Services in the United States [Cambridge, MA: Ballinger Publishing Co., 1974], p 91. Reprinted with permission from Health Services in the United States, Copyright 1974, Ballinger Publishing Company.)*

ticing in that field without a license normally is considered a crime, punishable by fines or even imprisonment. The exception to this rule are so-called "permissive" licensure regulations, which do allow unlicensed individuals to maintain employment in the given field.

Certification is a voluntary process whereby a nongovernmental, or private, agency or association grants recognition to an individual who has met certain predetermined qualifications, including graduation from an approved educational program, completion of a given amount of work experience, and acceptable performance on a qualifying examination or series of such examinations. The term *registration* is often used synonymously with certification, but may simply imply an official listing of credentialed persons maintained by either a private or public agency. As a voluntary process, certification standards can and often do exceed the minimum standards deemed necessary for entry-level competency. However, certification generally does not exclude others from working in that occupation, as do most forms of licensure.

Ideally, both certification and licensure help to ensure the availability of appropriate numbers of health care workers with acceptable levels of preparation. However, certification and licensure can restrict the supply of human resources, thereby driving up the cost of this critical resource of the health care system.

Physical Plant

Another building block of the health care system is the nation's investment in the "bricks and mortar" of physical facilities required to meet health care needs. There are about 6,800 hospitals in the U.S. health care system, with almost 1.3 million beds. On any given day, about 880,000 people are patients in the nation's hospitals, and more than 300 million outpatient visits occur annually.[4] It is important to recognize that there is substantial variation in U.S. hospitals in terms of size, scope of service, ownership, and other characteristics.

There are about 20,000 nursing homes with 4 million beds in the United States. There are three categories of nursing homes, based on the type of service they provide: skilled nursing facilities (SNF), which provide continuous nursing service on a 24-hour basis; and intermediate care facilities (ICF), which provide care that is less intensive than that provided in SNFs; and resident care facilities that provide supervised living accommodations for residents who do not routinely require nursing care. About 8% of the national health expenditures are for nursing home care.

Another major category of physical plant resources in the health care system is represented by the facilities necessary for the office practices of the nation's physicians. A great deal of personal medical care is rendered in physicians' offices. About 80% of physicians are engaged in the direct care of patients as their primary activity. Of these, approximately 70% are engaged in office-based practice and 30% are in hospital-based practice. While the majority of office-based physicians are in solo practice, that is, independent practice by a physician usually with his or her own facilities and equipment, many physicians are in group practices (three or more physicians formally organized to provide medical care, consultation, diagnosis, and treatment through the joint use of equipment and personnel and with income from medical practice distributed in accordance with methods previously determined by members of the group). These groups may be organized as general-practice, single-specialty, or multispecialty groups. The physical facilities necessary to support physicians in office practices represent a substantial investment in physical plant.

While all of the physical plant resources of the health care system are too numerous to even mention here, some of its other components include about 13,000 ambulance services and 2,800 medical laboratories independent of those in physicians' offices and hospitals. In addition, there are about 9,000 commercial dental laboratories, and about 90% of the nation's active dentists are in private office practices.

Technology

The technological base of modern medicine is quite remarkable and must be viewed as one of the building blocks of the health care system. It has made organ transplants and microscopic surgery possible; many diseases have been eradicated and treatment for others has been greatly improved; and early diagnosis for many diseases has been possible. These advances have had a marked impact on the health care system. Societal expectations of the health care system have risen (often unrealistically) as technology has advanced, and the costs of health care have risen dramatically as expensive new technology has been adopted.

The paradox of technological advance is that as people benefit from it (live longer), they are then in a position to need and utilize other health services. The net effect is to drive up total health care expenditures. This phenomenon becomes important, even critical, when it occurs in a context of limited dollars for health care expenditures. The result is complex and frustrating. As has been noted: "As technological advances continue, we will increasingly be confronted with difficult decisions related to coverage of (payment for) new technology by insurers and the federal government. These decisions will become even more difficult as resources for health care become more limited, forcing tradeoffs between providing basic primary health care service and providing new, potentially expensive, but quality-enhancing technology."[5] This is precisely the problem that technology presents to the health care system today. It is likely now that as new technology is developed its adoption will be carefully weighed in terms of its relative cost against projected benefits—a new *modus operandi* for the health care system.

It is clear that the health care system is structured from building blocks that include vast sums of money, many different kinds of people with specialized training, an impressive investment in physical plant, and a growing technology. In the next section, we turn our attention to some of the organizations that these resources have been used to build and maintain, which, in turn, convert these resources into health services.

ORGANIZATIONS IN THE HEALTH CARE SYSTEM

The organizations within it are the most visible component of the health care system. There are thousands of organizations, and they give form and substance to the system. The variety of these organizations defies easy categorization. Figure 1–7, however, can serve as a starting point for their description. The shortcomings of such a categorization become apparent quickly when one considers, for example, that Blue Cross plans, which are essentially secondary providers of a basic resource (payment for services rendered to their subscribers), sometimes *require* hospitals that receive payment from them to prove the need for expansion of services, and typically have representatives on statewide planning boards. These activities could qualify Blue Cross plans as planning and regulating organizations. Or consider the case of a hospital, whose primary purpose is the provision of health services, but which also operates a school of nursing or is heavily involved in medical education. It is not always easy to categorize organizations in the health care system.

Organizations That Provide Health Services

This category of primary providers includes the following kinds of organizations: hospitals, nursing homes, physicians' offices, health maintenance organizations, home care programs, clinics, and local health departments, among others. Their distinguishing characteristic is that they provide the physical plant where the delivery of health care services is made directly to consumers, whether the purpose of those services is curative, preventive, or rehabilitative. Four of these primary provider organizations are described in some detail below.

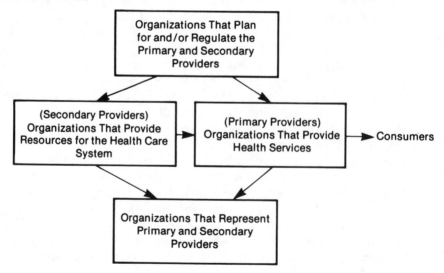

Figure 1–7. Organizations in the health care system.

Hospitals

Hospitals are perhaps the most complex organizations in the health care system. They come in many types and sizes, but by definition a hospital is a

> health care institution with an organized medical and professional staff and with inpatient beds available round-the-clock, whose primary function is to provide inpatient medical, nursing, and other health-related services to patients for both surgical and nonsurgical conditions, and that usually provides some outpatient services, particularly emergency care.[6]

There are two primary categories of hospitals: community and noncommunity.[7] *Community hospitals* include all nonfederal short-term general and other special hospitals whose facilities and services are available to the public. *Noncommunity hospitals* include federal hospitals, long-term hospitals, hospital units of institutions, psychiatric hospitals, hospitals for tuberculosis and other respiratory diseases, chronic-disease hospitals, institutions for the mentally retarded, and alcoholism and chemical-dependency hospitals.

Hospitals may be further categorized according to how they are controlled. The two primary types of hospital control are *governmental,* or publicly controlled, and *nongovernmental,* or privately controlled. Governmental hospitals may be further divided according to level into those controlled by federal, state, or municipal governments. Likewise, nongovernmental or privately controlled hospitals may be organized as either not-for-profit or investor-owned (for-profit) institutions.

A general hospital will usually be organized along the lines shown in Figure 1–8, although the reader should be cautioned that hospitals will almost invariably differ in details of their organization. The functions of the general hospital have been described as follows:

> First, there are diagnostic and treatment services to inpatients. Within this broad function are many subdivisions of medical, surgical, obstetrical, pediatric, and other special forms of care. Psychiatric service and rehabilitation may be included. Involved in all of these inpatient services are various modalities, including nursing, dietetics, pharmaceutical skills, laboratory and x-ray services, and varying refinements of diagnosis and therapy. Second, there are services to outpatients, with an equally wide range of specialties and technical modalities. A third hospital function concerns professional and technical education, for many classes of health personnel must work in hospitals and thereby receive training. A fourth function is medical research, since the accumulation of patients in hospitals provides the basis for scientific investigation into the causes, diagnosis, and treatment of diseases. A fifth function concerns prevention of diseases or health promotion in the surrounding population; there are many ways that hospitals, as centers for technical skill, can offer services to people before they are sick or can protect patients from the hazards of disease beyond that for which they have come to the hospital.[8]

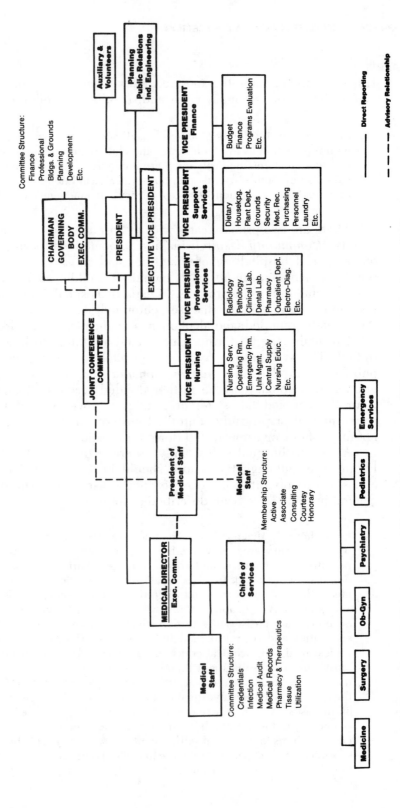

Figure 1–8. Hospital organizational structure. *(From Rakich JS, Longest BB Jr., Darr K:* Managing Health Services Organizations, *ed 2. Philadelphia: W.B. Saunders Company, 1985, pp 179.)*

The emphasis given to these different functions will vary from hospital to hospital, depending largely upon the basic objectives and goals of the particular hospital. For example, the large medical center may emphasize education and research to a much greater extent than the small general hospital.

The hospital is a very complex social system with substantial conflicts among the participants—patients, physicians, trustees, administrative staff, and other personnel. The diversity of the organization can create major problems. The governing board has the legal authority over, and responsibility for, the organization. The medical staff possesses the technical knowledge to make decisions regarding patient care and treatment. The management staff is responsible for day-to-day functioning of the hospital. These three elements, sometimes referred to as the *organizational triad,* share the same basic objectives. However, people within each element of the triad may interpret the means for meeting these objectives in terms of their own values and personalities, which are not necessarily identical. This makes the hospital one of the most complex institutions in modern society.

Nursing Homes

Since the enactment of the Social Security Act of 1935, which made public assistance funds available for the needy aged, the nursing home industry has flourished in the United States. Several other factors have exacerbated the need for institutional care for the aged. Among them, and perhaps most important, are the increased percentage of older people (65+) in the population and changes in the family structure. For these reasons, expenditures for nursing home care are projected to be among the most rapidly increasing categories of health care costs, rising from their current level of some $38 billion to about $129 billion in the year 2000.[9] The nursing home is defined as a

> health facility with inpatient beds and an organized professional staff that provides continuous nursing and other health-related, psychosocial, and personal services to patients who are not in an acute phase of illness but who primarily require continued care on an inpatient basis.[10]

The typical organization pattern of the nursing home is similar to that given for the hospital, the main difference being that the nursing home offers a much narrower range of services. A second major difference is a less complex medical staff organization in the nursing home, where medical staff are not as involved in day-to-day patient care. A typical nursing home organization is shown in Figure 1–9. The reader is cautioned that, as with hospitals, there are many alternative patterns of organization.

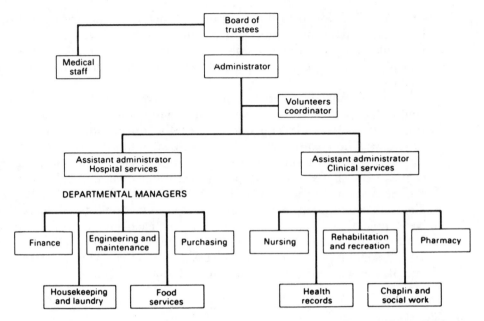

Figure 1–9. Nursing home organizational structure. *(From Leatt P, Shortell SM, Kimberly JR: Organization Design, in Shortell SM, Kaluzny AD (eds):* Health Care Management: A Text in Organization Theory and Behavior, *ed 2. New York: John Wiley and Sons, 1988, p 321. Reprinted with permission.)*

Health Maintenance Organizations—HMOs

While the hospital and the nursing home represent two of the most important traditional health service provider organizations, there are new types of organizations that fit this category. Few subjects have aroused more interest or generated more discussion in the health care community during the past few years than the concept of health maintenance organizations—or, as they are more commonly called, "HMOs."

There are five essential features of an HMO. Each single component or feature does not make the HMO special but, taken together, the five components make the HMO a unique form of health care delivery. An HMO is an *organized system* providing a comprehensive range of health care services to a *voluntarily enrolled* consumer population. In return for a *prepaid, fixed fee*, the enrollee is guaranteed a defined set of *benefits*. This fixed fee is usually the same for all members (enrollees) of the HMO regardless of the extent of services utilized. The prospective enrollee usually has a dual choice of joining either an HMO delivery system or another form of health insurance (e.g., Blue Cross/Blue Shield or commercial insurance policy). Enrollees join the HMO primarily on a year-to-year (contractual) basis and have the option of changing their choice once a year.[11]

Home Health Care

Unlike the primary provider organizations previously described, home health care is more a concept than a discrete organizational stucture. Home health care represents "the provision of health services such as nursing, therapy, and health-related homemaker or social services in the patient's home."[12] Such services are provided to aged, disabled, or sick or convalescent individuals who do not need institutional care.

Given this broad definition, it is not surprising that home health care currently is provided by a great variety of organizations, including home health agencies, visiting nurse services, hospitals, outpatient facilities, durable medical equipment (DME) companies, charitable organizations, hospice groups, and other private concerns.

Although total activity in this sector of health services is difficult to project, it is estimated that total expenditures for home health care currently range from $4 to $5 billion and that between 1973 and 1984, expenditures for home health services increased annually by an average of about 31%.[13] Recently, however, stricter federal regulations and reporting requirements have slowed this rapid growth rate to about 10% annually.

Organizations That Provide Resources for the Health Care System

This category of secondary providers includes educational institutions, financing mechanisms, and drug and equipment suppliers, among others. Their distinguishing characteristic is that they provide resources needed for the direct provision of health services.

Educational Institutions

Space does not permit a complete description of the tremendous variety of educational organizations that supply human resources to the health care system. Medical schools and nursing schools are the dominant examples, but a great variety of educational organizations make an impact on the health care system.

Physicians, still the key personnel in the health care system, are trained in the nation's 126 medical schools, or in foreign medical schools. Foreign medical graduates (FMGs) now represent about 20% of the total active physicians in the United States. While there is considerable variation among U.S. medical schools in terms of curriculum, they generally provide four years of postbaccalaureate training consisting of two years of preclinical, or basic sciences work, and two years of clinical and practical experience.

The present mold for medical education was largely cast in the 1910 document written by Abraham Flexner, *Medical Education in the United States and Canada, A Report to the Carnegie Foundation for the Advancement of Teaching*, which criticized (a well-deserved criticism) extant medical schools and led to major improvements. Following medical school, physicians enter a period of graduate medical education called *residency.* This education lasts two to seven years, depending upon the specialty chosen.

The physician who wishes, after specialty training, can apply to be certified in that specialty by a specialty board. After meeting the requirements (which generally include completion of an approved residency, written and oral examination, and varying years of experience), the physician becomes a board-certified specialist. This certification is in addition to licensure, which is granted by each state and which requires graduating from an approved medical school and passing an examination as set forth in each state's medical practice act. Many states have reciprocity agreements with other states through which a physician may move his or her license from one state to another. The arduous path through a medical education serves not only to impart necessary knowledge but also to instill a distinctive group identity and, for many physicians, a rather homogeneous set of values.

Professionally licensed nurses, usually called registered nurses (RNs), are trained in three different types of organizational settings: baccalaureate programs, which are 4- or 5-year university-based programs leading to a bachelor of science degree; associate degree programs, which are two-year programs usually based in junior or community colleges; and diploma programs, which usually provide three years of training past high school and are based in hospital-operated schools of nursing. Following completion of one of these approved programs, the nurse can become a registered nurse by passing a state licensure examination. There are also master's degree programs that provide nurses with advanced training in education, administration, or such clinical nursing specialties as public health, medical-surgical nursing, mental health, maternal and child health, and cardiovascular nursing. Other specialty training includes nurse anesthetists, nurse-midwives, and pediatric and family nurse practitioners. A pediatric nurse practitioner, for example, is a registered nurse who has received additional training permitting an expanded role in the care of children.

Organizations That Pay for Care

A second important category of organizations that provide resources for the health care system are those that pay for care. Except for "out-of-pocket" payments by individuals, health care in the United States is largely paid for through third parties. The current maze of third parties has been created fairly recently and has grown largely in response to the rising cost of health care and the concurrent financial risk that individuals run if they make no provision through insurance or prepayment for protection against their potential health care costs. More than half the third-party payments now come from two sources: Blue Cross plans and the federal government (principally Medicare and Medicaid).

The Blue Cross organization began as a prepayment plan for hospital expenses for school teachers in Dallas, Texas, in 1929. The original plan provided 21 days of hospitalization for a prepayment of 50 cents a month. Today, there are 77 Blue Cross organizations covering almost 78 million subscribers. Blue Shield plans provide for prepayment of physician fees in a similar manner. The Blue Cross and Blue Shield plans are linked together as members of the Blue Cross and Blue Shield Association.

One of the most important dates in history, in terms of understanding the U.S. health care system, is July 1, 1966. On that date the federal government initiated two programs that had their basis in the 1965 amendments to the Social Security Act. These amendments (Title XVIII—Health Insurance for the Aged and Title XIX—Grants to the States for Medical Assistance Programs), more commonly known as Medicare and Medicaid, were the culmination of many years of national debate. Although substantial changes have been made in the Medicare and Medicaid programs in the intervening years, they were at their inception and still are insurance mechanisms to help pay for the health care of the elderly and the poor. Together, these programs account for about 40% of the revenues that flow into the nation's hospitals.

Medicare provides health care benefits to over 30 million aged and disabled enrollees, and is the largest single purchaser of hospital and physician services in the nation. The program currently consists of two parts: Part A, which is compulsory insurance for hospital care and related services for the U.S. population over age 65, and Part B, which is voluntary supplementary insurance to partially cover the costs of physician and surgeon fees, clinic visits, diagnostic and laboratory tests, and home health visits. Part A, constituting about two-thirds of the total expenditures, is financed through Social Security payroll taxes. Part B, which accounts for the remaining outlays, is financed through premiums paid by enrollees and matching general revenues.

In 1983, under amendments to the Social Security Act, the mechanism of hospital reimbursement under Part A of the Medicare program underwent a dramatic change. Up until that time, reimbursement to hospitals for Medicare patients was based on the actual cost of providing services (cost-based reimbursement). Generally, under this original system, a hospital could expect to be reimbursed for whatever it spent on patient care.

The 1983 amendments switched the mechanism for reimbursing hospitals to a *prospective* payment system, based on *Diagnosis Related Groups*, or DRGs. A DRG is simply a predefined category of patient illness, as identified by the admitting diagnosis, nature of care (surgical vs. nonsurgical), patient age, and presence or absence of complicating factors.

For each DRG, the Health Care Financing Administration (HCFA) of the U.S. Department of Health and Human Services has established a fixed rate of reimbursement. Since the DRG amount remains fixed for a given admitting diagnosis, hospitals that provide care for less than the fixed rate can keep the difference, thereby realizing a "profit." On the other hand, hospitals whose cost of care exceeds the fixed rate must absorb the cost difference, thereby taking a financial loss.[14]

By placing hospitals at risk financially, prospective reimbursement by DRGs has provided a powerful incentive for cost-efficiency in the provision of inpatient hospital services. Since the cost of a patient's care is directly related to length of stay, most hospitals have focused their cost-containment efforts on minimizing the duration of inpatient care, while simultaneously attempting to reduce or prevent "needless" admissions, that is, cases that could be handled effectively on an ambulatory or outpatient basis.

Medicaid is a program through which the federal government provides a subsidy to the states, 50% to 80% of the total cost depending on per capita income in the state, to help participating states provide health insurance to their poor and near-poor population. Each state administers its own Medicaid program under certain federal requirements. Certain basic services must be provided, including: inpatient and outpatient hospital care, laboratory and X-ray services, skilled nursing services, home health care, physician services, and family planning services. Originally intended to provide medical services mainly to low-income women and children, Medicaid has evolved over time to be the largest third-party financer of long-term care in the U.S., with nearly a third of its total expenditures going to nursing home care.

The private, or commercial as they are often called, insurance companies represent another component of the third-party payors. There are several hundred private insurance companies in the United States, including some major ones like Prudential, Equitable, Aetna, Metropolitan, and Connecticut General. These companies, through their policies, provide "protection by written contract against the hazards (in whole or in part) of the happenings of specified fortuitous events."[15] Although private insurance companies were initially reluctant to enter the health insurance market, the market created by the large industrial unions that grew up during World War II provided a sufficient stimulus for their entry, and by carefully experience-rating the various groups they serve, the private companies have been successful.

Pharmaceutical and Medical Supply Industries

A third category of resource-providing organizations to be described briefly here are those found in the pharmaceutical and medical supply industries. Currently, the national expenditures for pharmaceutical and medical supplies total more than $40 billion annually. Research and development (R&D) costs in developing new drugs are themselves quite large due to the complexity of the search for new, effective drugs and the nature of the process of obtaining approval from the Food and Drug Administration before the new drug can be placed on the market. Even with high marketing and R & D costs, the pharmaceutical industry has consistently earned high profits. The pharmaceutical manufacturers who make and sell prescription drugs are represented by the Pharmaceutical Manufacturers Association.

The organizations that manufacture and distribute medical supplies are as diverse as their products, which range from cotton balls to computerized axial tomography (CAT) scanners costing hundreds of thousands of dollars each and capable of producing remarkably informative "pictures" of the inside of the human body. There are more than 1,100 medical supply organizations in the United States, ranging from very large firms such as Baxter Health Care Corporation to relatively small firms that specialize in a few products.

Interestingly, up until 1976, most medical devices, unlike prescription drugs, could be designed, marketed, and used in the United States without any federal controls.[16] However, with implementation of the Medical Device Act of 1976, all medical devices fell under a comprehensive regulatory framework, currently administered by the United States Food and Drug Administration.

While space has not permitted a comprehensive view of all the organizations, the reader can see that a diverse and diffuse set of organizations provide the resources necessary to sustain the U.S. health care system.

Organizations That Plan for or Regulate the Primary and Secondary Providers

It is important to note that the title of this subsection does not include "the health care system." This choice of title was made to emphasize the point that no one, to date, plans for or regulates the health care system. Instead, planning and regulating occur for many components of the system, but not the system as a whole. This fact is, if nothing more, consistent with the pluralism that characterizes the system itself. While there is a good deal of internal self-regulation and self-planning in health care organizations—for example, hospitals can regulate their own performance through organizational policies and procedures—we shall look mainly at external regulation and planning; that is, those organizations that are separate from, but that regulate, the primary and secondary providers or plan for the provision of health services.

Voluntary Regulating Groups

Regulation of health care provider organizations has historically been on a voluntary basis. The voluntary regulatory process sets standards, but does not carry the mandate of law. The best example of voluntary regulation, among many possible choices, is the Joint Commission on Accreditation of Healthcare Organizations (JCAHO), which can trace its origin to a 1915 program of the American College of Surgeons and whose board now includes representation from the American Medical Association, American Hospital Association, American College of Surgeons, American College of Physicians, and, more recently, both the American Association of Homes for the Aging and the American Nursing Home Association. The JCAHO through established standards, accredits health care organizations that voluntarily seek such accreditation and thus guides and directs (regulates) much of the operation of these providers. The JCAHO accrediting standards include requirements for health care organizations as a whole, and for each of their key service departments.[17]

The voluntary regulation of organizations that educate health personnel is also extensive. The following partial list of education programs and the agencies that accredit them, and thus regulate their activities to a large extent, illustrates this:

Educational Program	Accrediting Agency
Cytotechnology	Council on Medical Education of the American Medical Association (AMA) and the American Society of Clinical Pathologists
Dentistry	Commission on Accreditation of the American Dental Association
Dietetics	American Dietetic Association
Hospital Administration	Accrediting Commission on Education for Health Services Administration
Medical Records	Council on Medical Education of the AMA and the Committee on Education and Registration of the American Medical Record Association
Medical Technology	Council on Medical Education of the AMA and the American Society for Medical Technology
Medicine	Council on Medical Education of the AMA and the Association of American Medical Colleges
Professional Nursing	National League for Nursing
Pharmacy	American Council on Pharmaceutical Education
Physical Therapy	Council on Medical Education of the AMA and the American Physical Therapy Association
Radiologic Technology	Council on Medical Education of the AMA, American College of Radiology, and the American Society of Radiologic Technologists

As was described above for health care organizations, this process is called *accreditation.* Educational accreditation represents the process whereby a private, nongovernmental agency grants public recognition to an institution or specialized program of study that meets certain established qualifications and educational standards.[18]

We can use the accreditation of programs for the education of respiratory care personnel as an example. They are accredited by the Committee on Allied Health Education (CAHEA), in collaboration with the Joint Review Committee for Respiratory Therapy Education (JRCRTE). A quasi-independent, broadly representative agency, CAHEA is sponsored, in part, by the American Medical Association. In addition to respiratory care, CAHEA currently oversees the accreditation process for some 25 other allied health occupations, through an umbrella review committee structure.[19]

The Joint Review Committee for Respiratory Therapy Education is the review committee responsible for assuring that respiratory therapy educational programs comply with the accrediting standards, or *essentials,* adopted by the American Medical Association. Representatives of the JRCRTE visit educational programs for respiratory care personnel to evaluate applications for accreditation and perform periodic reviews. In cooperation with CAHEA, the JRCRTE publishes an annual listing of accredited programs for the education of respiratory therapy technicians and respiratory therapists.

The JRCRTE is collaboratively sponsored by the American Association for Respiratory Care (AARC), the American College of Chest Physicians (ACCP), the American Society of Anesthesiologists (ASA), and the American Thoracic Society (ATS). Along with a public member, representatives from these organizations serve as members of the committee, which, with the support of an executive office staff and cadre of volunteer site visitors, assumes responsibility for reviewing accreditation applications, conducting on-site evaluations of programs, and making accreditation recommendations to CAHEA.[20]

Federal Regulating Efforts

Although the level of voluntary regulation in the health care system has been and continues to be high, governmental involvement in planning for and regulating the quality, cost, availability, and delivery of health care services in the United States has increased dramatically in the past 25 years, especially since the enactment of the Medicare and Medicaid programs in the mid-1960s. With the enactment, in 1974, of the National Health Planning and Resources Development Act (PL 93-641) and its subsequent implementation, governmental efforts to regulate the health care system perhaps reached their zenith.

This legislation created Health Systems Agencies (HSAs), which were intended to assume responsibility for health planning at the local level. Their responsibilities included forecasting demand and developing areawide plans for services and facilities. In addition, PL 93-641 called for the establishment of State Health Planning and Development Agencies (SHPDAs), which were to develop state health plans. The single strongest element in PL 93-641 was the requirement that all states enact certificate-of-need (CON) legislation that meets federal standards. In concept, this feature permitted tighter control (regulation) of capital expenditures for many existing health care providers and restricted the addition of new capacity in places where it was not needed.

Although elements of this structure still exist, particularly the state health planning agencies and the certificate-of-need requirements, the concept of the local HSA has generally failed. The general inability of HSAs to contain costs, the politicization of the process, and federal funding cutbacks have spelled the demise of many of these local planning agencies.

More recently, the federal government has actually sought to *decrease* its regulation of the health care industry, in hopes that increased competition among health care providers will help stem the extraordinary rises in costs characterizing this sector of the economy. This deregulation has been largely responsible for the increased number and diversity of health care providers now populating the landscape of the health care system, and the concomitant increase in the health care options available to the American public.

The overall federal involvement in the health care system is largely centered in the massive (with a budget second only to the Department of Defense) Department of Health and Human Services (DHHS). Established in 1953, DHHS has undergone several major reoganizations. Figure 1–10 represents a highly abbreviated view of DHHS as it is currently structured.

State Regulating Efforts

State government (and those aspects delegated to counties, cities, and towns) involvement in the health care system is made through a very complex and ever-changing variety of organizations and agencies that vary from one state to another. Some of this involvement is lodged in a department of public health but ranges from assurance of water quality to education of physicians in state-supported medical schools. State governments are also heavily involved in planning for and regulating the health care system. Their involvement in planning is extensive; many states now have certificate-of-need legislation through which they control the investment in various components of the health care system. The regulatory involvement by the states includes licensing of many categories of health care workers and provider organizations and the establishment and enforcement of insurance laws and health and safety codes. A final, and potentially very important, example of state regulatory involvement is rate review, already enacted in a number of states and being seriously considered in others. Under these programs the rates charged by providers for health services rendered are subject to review and approval by rate review agencies.

Organizations that Represent the Primary and Secondary Providers

The providers of health services, whether groups of individual professionals, such as physicians, nurses, and the many other categories of personnel, or the provider organizations, such as hospitals and nursing homes, are almost invariably represented by an association whose main purpose is to represent the interest of its constituency. In addition to national associations, such as the American Medical Association and the American Hospital Association, there are usually state associations, such as the Hospital Association of Pennsylvania and the Pennsylvania Medical Society, and frequently local organizations that represent the interests of members, such as the Allegheny County Medical Society and the Hospital Council of Western Pennsylvania.

The American Association for Respiratory Care (AARC) is a good example of an organization representing individual professionals. With some 27,000 members nationwide, the AARC represents the profession of respiratory care. The AARC strives to facilitate cooperation between respiratory care personnel and the medical profession, hospitals, health care organizations, service companies, and governmental organizations. In addition, the AARC serves as a focal point for guidance and assistance to its members in the practice of

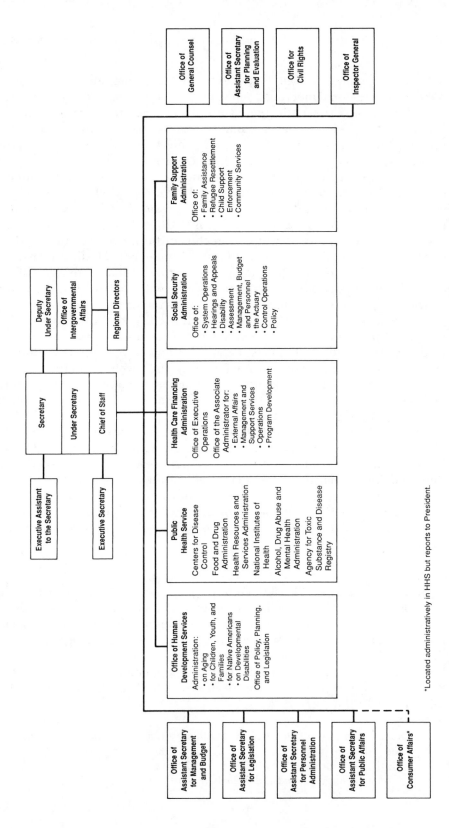

Figure 1–10. Summary of organization, Department of Health and Human Services. *(From U.S. Department of Health and Human Services.)*

*Located administratively in HHS but reports to President.

respiratory care. This role is achieved, in part, through the provision of national and regional meetings, and via various publications. Current periodical publications of the AARC include its official scientific journal, *Respiratory Care,* and the *AARC Times,* a monthly professional interest magazine. The association also acts as a center for communication with other health professions, institutions, and state and federal agencies.

The AARC functions under the direction of a voluntary board of directors, elected by and accountable to the membership as a whole. An executive committee of the board, chaired by the president of the association, is responsible for the oversight of the AARC central office, including its executive director. The executive director, in turn, oversees the day-to-day operations of the central office and its full-time staff. Medical oversight of Association affairs is provided through its Board of Medical Advisors (BOMA), a broadly representative group of physicians with expertise in the clinical, educational, or research aspects of pulmonary medicine.

According to its bylaws, decision making within the AARC occurs at two complementary levels. Major policy and budgetary decisions are normally made by the Board of Directors. Other elements of operation are under the control of the general membership, either by direct vote (as in the election of officers), or through the Association's representative body, called the House of Delegates. Representation to the AARC House of Delegates is via affiliated state chapters of the Association.

State chapters of the AARC share a purpose and structure similar to those of the national association, but delimit their activities to respiratory care practitioners within their geographic locale. In some large states, such as New York and California, the state society is broken into regional components, allowing better communication and coordination of services to meet local needs. In combination with the national AARC, these state affiliates provide a rich network of resources to promote and advance the practice of respiratory care.

Consumers

Perhaps the largest, and least organized, component of the health care system are those people who consume its services. Potentially at least, the ultimate consumers of health care services include everyone in the United States. In reality, not all consumers have equal access to health care services, nor do they utilize services in the same way. There have been gaps in access to health care among various segments of the population for some time. Trend analysis of the results of two major national surveys in the early 1980s bears this out.[21,22] In the early 1980s:

1. Some 28 million Americans had difficulty obtaining health care when they needed it, including:
   1 in 4 poor people (9 million)
   1 in 3 unemployed individuals (2.3 million)

1 in 5 Hispanics (2.6 million)
1 in 6 Blacks (2.5 million), and
1.5 million elderly;
2. 6.5 million families included at least one member with a serious or chronic illness. Of these families, about 1 in 4 reported that the chronic illness represented a "major" financial burden;
3. Nearly 1 in 20 Americans who had a medical emergency had difficulty getting emergency care;
4. Although 20% of adults believed the US health care system worked "pretty well," nearly 1 in 3 believed the system "has so much wrong with it that we need to rebuild it completely."

In recent years, these access problems have worsened, especially for some segments of society. For example, there are indications suggesting that obtaining necessary health care is becoming more difficult for the poor and uninsured.[23] Several surveys have been funded by the Robert Wood Johnson Foundation in recent years to determine American satisfaction with and access to the health care system. Results of the 1986 survey[24] indicate that 16% of the survey respondents (the equivalent of 38.8 million Americans) had difficulty obtaining needed health care. Over half of these reported that the reason for the difficulty was financial. The results also indicated that access to care (measured as the number of ambulatory visits during the prior 12 months) for the uninsured and the poor has declined since 1982. Despite their generally poorer health and greater likelihood of chronic disease or serious illness, between 1982 and 1986 the number of ambulatory visits for poor adults (ages 17 to 64) declined 30 percent. In addition, the number of ambulatory visits for the poor in fair or poor health declined almost 8% between 1982 and 1986 (from 9.1 visits to 8.4 visits). In comparison, the number of visits for the nonpoor in fair or poor health increased 42% during the same period (from 9.1 visits to 11.5 visits). Differences between the uninsured and the insured in fair or poor health are also striking. In 1986, the uninsured in fair or poor health had only six visits annually, compared to 10 visits for the insured.

In spite of such disparity in access, on the whole, consumers are remarkably satisfied with the *quality* of health care they receive—almost 80% of Americans express satisfaction with the health care they personally receive. Yet, at the same time, an equal proportion believe the health care system requires fundamental change.[25] Moreover, demand for a larger voice in the decision-making processes that exist in the health care system (a phenomenon termed "consumerism") has never been stronger than today.

Perhaps the most obvious reason for the paucity of active participation in the health care system by consumers, except of course as consumers, is the difficulty any individual faces in relating to large complex systems. (What impact does an individual citizen have on the banking industry, for example?) Although critical questions remain about the knowledgeability and relative persuasive strength of consumers, few seriously question that the consumer, who directly or indirectly pays for the services provided by the health care system, is any longer willing to leave the decision-making power in the health care system entirely in the hands of the other components of the system.

PROBLEMS CONFRONTING THE HEALTH CARE SYSTEM

The health care system faces a dizzying array of problems. The more complex of these problems are not transitory and will not be solved soon or easily. Full enumeration of the set of problems is not possible, for the set developed by one individual or group will differ, frequently in content and almost always in priority, from those developed by someone else. There are even those, although their number has diminished to a naive few, who claim there are no serious problems.

One of the most encouraging signs that the health care system can resolve many of its problems, and perhaps the single greatest strength of the system, is that central components of the system spend considerable energy in identification of its problems and efforts to develop solutions to these problems. For example, one of the most comprehensive examinations of problems confronting the health care system in the 1980s came from a symposium of leading experts convened by the American Hospital Association with support from the National Center for Health Services Research. A book reporting the deliberations of this symposium and summarizing its results sets forth the following set of questions (problems) facing the U.S. health care system.[26]

1. *Cost.* How should society establish means for determining limits on the quantity of resources to be expended on health care services?
2. *Entitlement.* How should society establish a guaranteed minimum set of health care services available for all citizens?
3. *Technology.* How should society establish methods for evaluating the development and use of new medical technologies?
4. *Decision Making.* How should society achieve better decision-making capability by individuals who are not providers of health care services in matters concerning the appropriate allocation, distribution, and use of these services?
5. *Structure.* How should society exert substantial pressures for the reorganization and restructuring of the health care, education, financing, and delivery system to make it more efficient, effective, or economical?

More recently, 172 organizations with varying perspectives on problems confronting the health care system collaborated in developing a consensus for addressing them.[27] Termed "The Health Policy Agenda for the American People: Framework for the Future," this agenda includes 195 specific recommendations to address such problems as:

- The cost of health care in the United States is now more than $1 billion a day.
- Millions of Americans cannot afford or gain access to needed health care professionals and facilities.
- New technologies are raising questions about the ethical and moral consequences of many health care decisions.
- Consumers lack adequate information to make informed choices among the many options in health care.

Finally, the Institute for the Future, with support from the Robert Wood Johnson Foundation and the Commonwealth Fund (both are large foundations with health care interests), has projected the key public policy issues that will affect the health care system between now and the year 2000. Their prediction is that eleven issues will dominate the national health care agenda during the 1990s:[28]

1. Controlling costs: continuing contentiousness and conflict between various actors in health care; tough choices by government, business, labor, and families; acrimonious public debate
2. Uninsured and underinsured: continuing problem with uninsured and underinsured requires federal, state, and local governments to develop more coherent policies for high-risk groups
3. Long-term care: expanding debate over public/private insurance roles and responsibilities, limiting progress on financing and delivering long-term care
4. Mother-child: continuing health needs of this group require increased coordination and cooperation of both medical and social interventions
5. AIDS: emerging health crisis raises fundamental questions about the role of government in health care insurance, financing, and regulation
6. Quality in a competitive environment: measuring, managing, and assuring quality supplanting cost as key issues in the next decade
7. Health personnel: raising questions about adequacy of the flow of trained personnel to meet future health care needs
8. Health R&D: requiring sustained research and development focusing on potential high-impact areas
9. Redeploying capital: increasing reliance on market forces to determine where new facilities will be located and who will get new equipment
10. Tort liability: increasing role of courts in setting standards for care at all levels
11. Ethics: raising a host of questions on roles and responsibilities as well as conflicts of interest for individual practitioners, the professions, and society

The premier position of cost concerns in all three lists of problems reflects the staggering level of total health care expenditures and the continuing steep increases in those expenditures in recent years. But the other problems are important as well. These sets of problems serve to demonstrate the complexity, breadth, and interrelatedness of problems facing the health care system. They will probably be solved in the years ahead because they are so important; but as solutions emerge, we can be sure that other equally thorny and important problems will replace them. That is the price of society's effort to achieve a goal so important and so elusive as "complete physical, mental, and social well-being." We can also be sure that managers in health services organizations will play a crucial role in their solution.

SUMMARY

Increasingly, health services are being delivered in a wide variety of organizational settings. At a time when medical knowledge and clinical capability are at an all-time high, there are continuing problems with health services delivery. This reflects the fact that the organization and management of the means of delivering health services and the development of financial resources and mechanisms to pay for the services have not kept pace with clinical advances. Since so many aspects of the health services organizations described in this chapter are managed by health professionals, it is imperative that they develop management skills. The remainder of the book will deal with the practice of management in the health services organizations in which so many health professionals find themselves. Although we will concentrate on organizations that provide health services, many of the practices described are also applicable to the other types of organizations that comprise the health care system.

REFERENCES

1. Division of National Cost Estimates, Office of the Actuary, Health Care Financing Administration: National health expenditures, 1986–2000. *Health Care Financing Review*, 1987; 8:1–36.
2. *The Health Policy Agenda for the American People: Framework for the Future.* Chicago, The Health Policy Agenda for the American People, 1987, p 8.
3. U.S. Department of Health and Human Services, Public Health Service, Health Resources and Services Administration: *Report to Congress on the Status of Health Personnel in the United States.* U.S. Department of Health and Human Services publication No. HRS-P-OD 84-4. Washington, D.C., Government Printing Office, 1984.
4. American Hospital Association: *Hospital Statistics.* Chicago, American Hospital Association, 1988, p 2.
5. Rubin RJ, Moran DW, Jones KS, Hackbarth MA: *Critical Condition: America's Health Care in Jeopardy.* Washington, DC, Lewin/IFC, 1988, pp 8–9.
6. American Hospital Association: *Hospital Administration Terminology*, ed 2. Chicago, American Hospital Association, 1986, p 27.
7. American Hospital Association: *Hospital Statistics*, p xi.
8. Roemer MI, Friedman JW: *Doctors in Hospitals.* Baltimore, Johns Hopkins Press, 1971, pp 1–2.
9. Health Care Financing Administration: National health expenditures, 1986–2000.

10. American Hospital Association: *Hospital Administration Terminology*, p 41.
11. U.S. Department of Health and Human Services: *A Student's Guide to Health Maintenance Organizations*. Washington, DC, U.S. Department of Health and Human Services, 1978, p 5.
12. American Hospital Association: *Hospital Administration Terminology*, p 26.
13. Health Care Financing Administration: National health expenditures, 1986–2000.
14. Scanlan CL: The prospective payment system: What you see is what you get. *Pulmonary Medicine Technician*, 1984; 1:19–34.
15. Health Insurance Association of America: *Source Book of Health Insurance Data*. Washington, Health Insurance Association of America, 1985, p 95.
16. Godwin GG: Governmental regulation of medical devices. *Respiratory Care*, 1988, 33:251–257.
17. Joint Commission on Accreditation of Healthcare Organizations: *Accreditation Manual for Hospitals*. Chicago, Joint Commission on Accreditation of Healthcare Organizations, 1988.
18. American Medical Association: *Allied Health Education Directory*. Chicago, American Medical Association, 1988.
19. American Medical Association: *Allied Health Education Directory*.
20. DeKornfeld TJ, Scanlan CL: Education of respiratory care personnel, in Burton GG, Hodgkin JE (eds): *Respiratory Care: A Guide to Clinical Practice*, ed 2. Philadelphia, Lippincott, 1984.
21. Aday LA, Anderson R, Fleming GV: *Health Care in the U.S.: Equitable for Whom?* Beverly Hills, Calif, Sage Publications, 1980.
22. Center for Health Administration Studies, University of Chicago: *Updated Report on Access to Health Care for the American People*. Princeton, NJ, The Robert Wood Johnson Foundation, 1983.
23. Rubin RJ, Moran DW, Jones KS, Hackbarth MA: *Critical Condition: America's Health Care in Jeopardy*, pp 8–9.
24. *Access to Health Care in the United States: Results of a 1986 Survey*. Princeton, NJ, The Robert Wood Johnson Foundation, 1987.
25. Blendon RJ: The public's view of the future of health care. *JAMA*, 1988; 259:3587–3593.
26. Philips DF: The public policy issues facing hospitals in the 1980's, in American Hospital Association, *Hospitals in the 1980's*. Chicago, American Hospital Association, 1977, pp 215–234.
27. *The Health Policy Agenda for the American People: Framework for the Future*.
28. Amara R, Morrison JI, Schmid G: *Looking Ahead at American Health Care*. Washington, D.C. Health Care Information Center, McGraw-Hill, 1988, pp 14–15.

*T*WO
The Practice
of Management

April 12
9:40 A.M.

The hospital president's brow furrowed more deeply than usual as he read the letter from the attorney for Mrs. Luther J. Fillerey. When he had finished the letter, he let it drop to his desk and swiveled his chair around to face the window. Clasping his hands tightly behind his head, he rocked the chair back and stared out the window at the grounds of Memorial Hospital.

He had known the letter was coming, and he was not surprised that it requested access to certain hospital records in preparation for the suit the attorney was preparing.

His mind was cluttered with thoughts:

"How could Luther Fillerey, a young and healthy man, come into this hospital for a bit of routine surgery and develop an infection serious enough to kill him?"

"If we are at fault, how much is this going to cost Memorial, and what effect will it have on our already astronomical malpractice insurance premiums?"

"I never even saw Luther J. Fillerey while he was a patient here and yet, as the manager of this hospital, I must bear the burden for whatever went wrong in our treatment of him."

"It's too bad when a young man, in the prime of his life, is taken away from his family."

"I wish I knew what went wrong; the board of trustees will want to know."

"We do our best to set up an organization that can deliver good medical care to everyone who comes here seeking it, but sometimes things just don't work out the way we planned."

"I had better try to find out what went wrong this time."

As he made himself a note to tell the medical records administrator to get Luther Fillerey's medical record in good order, he thought to himself, "Sometimes I wish I managed a factory making televisions. The mistakes could be replaced—nobody can replace Luther J. Fillerey."

At 9:50 A.M., the president picked up some papers from the corner of his desk and hurried off to a Budget Committee meeting.

INTRODUCTION

Many aspects of health organizations are managed by health professionals. The physician who, as chief of staff, is in charge of and responsible for many activities of several hundred other physicians needs management skills; the physician in charge of a laboratory or a radiology department needs management skills; the nurse who, as vice-president for nursing, is responsible for the largest department in the typical health services organization must be an effective manager; the head nurse, directly responsible for supervising the nursing care of a group of patients, needs management skills; the pharmacist who is responsible for a critical area of the health services organization needs management skills; the medical social worker's effectiveness can be greatly increased by the proper practice of management; medical or radiology technologists in charge of a major department need management skills; the physical or respiratory therapist in charge of a department is a manager; the list could go on and on. The point is that, in many cases, the health professional is also a manager in a health services organization.

Making decisions is a natural human endeavor—to make them in a rational way and to make them when they involve other people requires management skill. To take action is a normal human activity. But action can be more effective and efficient if management skills are exercised, especially when other people are involved in that action. In reality, management is in many ways merely an extension of certain rather routine aspects of human life. Yet, to manage effectively is a very great challenge indeed! This chapter is about the nature of ways to meet this challenge and about the science of management that has grown up around them. It is an *overview* of the things one must do to manage successfully. Other chapters in this book treat the topics in more detail. The purpose here is to set out a framework for understanding the process of management and to provide a mechanism for viewing that process as a coherent, integrated whole.

Although management is an extension of certain rather common human activities, it is a complex extension. There is no widely agreed upon set of principles that can be applied rigidly to every situation. There is not even a universally accepted definition of the management process. Management is not an exact science. Researchers and managers have come to realize that the search for universal principles of management is a frustrating one. Sweeping, generalized principles cannot be developed because what works in one setting or under one set of circumstances may not work in another. This phenomenon has been termed the *contingency approach* to management. The contingency approach suggests that the selection of management practices that should be applied to a given set of circumstances and the manner in which they should be applied are contingent upon the particular situation at hand.

This means that, because health services organizations are in many ways unique, management principles and practices should be chosen to be consistent with that uniqueness. For example, health services organizations have a number of features that should influence the approach taken to managing them. Among these features are: the absolute necessity for a high level of quality in the work performed; a high-technology base; the utilization of a wide range of human resources—a range that runs from some of society's most highly trained professionals and scientists to manual laborers; and the coexistence of automated and manual work methods. We shall take the contingency approach in this chapter by defining management in terms of the process in health services organization and by providing an overview of principles of management that are particularly appropriate for situations confronting the manager in that setting.

MANAGEMENT: THE SCIENCE AND THE ART

Management is an art, with a scientific base. People can learn the science of management in terms of how best to make decisions, establish objectives, structure an organization or some part of it, select among job applicants, or motivate people. But management is also an art and for the most part "the art of management is learned on the job."[1]

Like so many complex things, management is interpreted differently by different people. As a result, one may find many definitions of the term *management*. A common thread in most of these is that when studying management as an academic field, or when discussing its relationship to a real work situation, we find it necessary to think of management as a process. Since a process can be thought of simply as a series of actions directed to some end, we can, by thinking of management as a process, examine in some detail the actions or functions that comprise it.

As a beginning point, we will define management as follows: *Management is a process, with both interpersonal and technical aspects, through which the objectives of the health services organization are specified and accomplished by utilizing human and physical resources and technology.* This process can be viewed as a simple input-output relationship in which inputs (human and physical resources and technology) are transformed, under the influence of management, into desired outputs (accomplishment of the objectives of the organization or some part of it). See Figure 2–1.

Thus the manager is concerned with achieving objectives and, as we shall see, with first setting objectives. The effective manager is many things—a practical historian learning from past successes and failures; a psychologist who must understand the way people act in and react to group situations; a theoretician who can develop new ways to achieve desired objectives and apply them in a manner contingent upon the situation at hand. The manager in the health services organization must do two essential things to manage: specify objectives and then see that they are accomplished. The scope of managerial work "includes acquiring and deploying resources, monitoring

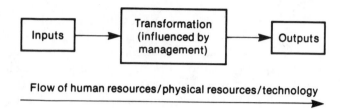

Figure 2–1. Input-output relationship.

Flow of human resources/physical resources/technology

and interacting with elements in the environment, and facilitating the performance of work"[2] done by a vast array of other people.

THE WORK OF MANAGERS: FUNCTIONS, SKILLS, ROLES

It is possible to take several approaches to an explanation of the work of managers. In this section, three basic approaches—functions, skills, and roles—are described.

The Functions That Comprise the Management Process

In the practice of mangement, the manager must take a number of actions. One way to examine the work of the manager is to group these activities into basic categories. Although different authorities categorize these actions in different ways, they may be conveniently viewed as follows: *planning*, which involves the determination of objectives and the means of accomplishing them; *organizing*, which is the structuring of people and things to accomplish the work required to fulfill the objectives; *directing*, which is the stimulation of members of the organization toward meeting the objectives; *coordinating*, which is the conscious effort of assembling and synchronizing diverse activities and participants so that they work harmoniously toward the attainment of objectives; and *controlling*, in which the manager compares actual results with objectives to provide a measure of success or failure.

These actions (planning, organizing, directing, coordinating, and controlling) are usually referred to in the management literature as the *functions* of the management process. Perhaps a word of caution is in order here. In discussing the process of management it is convenient, indeed necessary, to separate the functions. So it may seem that the management process is a series of separate functions to be treated as discrete components of the whole. This is not the case at all. In practice, a manager performs each of these functions simultaneously and as part of a continuum. This can be visualized by referring to Figure 2–2. Thus, the separation of management functions is necessary for purposes of discussion, but it is an artificial treatment of the reality of the management process. It does permit us, however, to examine some of the ways that have emerged through research and practice as to how the various functions should be carried out.

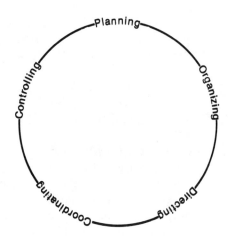

Figure 2–2. The
management functions as a
continuum.

Skills Needed in the Practice of Management

Another way to examine the work of managers is to think about the skills that
an effective manager must utilize. Katz has identified three types of skills:[3]

1. *Technical skill* is the ability to use the methods, processes, and
   techniques of a particular field. It is easy to visualize the technical
   skills of a surgeon or a physical therapist, but in a similar way,
   counseling a subordinate or making out a departmental budget also
   requires a considerable amount of technical skill.
2. *Human skill* is the ability to get along with other people, to understand
   them, and to motivate and lead them in the workplace.
3. *Conceptual skill* is the mental ability to visualize all the complex
   interrelationships that exist in a workplace—relationships among
   people, among departments or units of an organization, and even
   among a single organization and the environment in which it exists.
   Conceptual skill permits the manager to understand how the various
   factors in a particular situation fit together and interact with one
   another.

Katz suggests that not all managers will need to utilize these skills to the
same degree, although every manager must rely on all three types of skills in
performing his or her work. For example, if one examines the managerial
work that goes on in a hospital nursing service, one finds that the vice-
president for nursing must rely heavily on conceptual skill because the
vice-president is vitally concerned about how nursing service fits into the
total picture of the hospital's operation. However, the vice-president can rely
on staff specialists to take care of much of the technical work. In contrast, a
nursing supervisor whose main function is to "troubleshoot" an entire nursing
staff on one shift in the hospital may be constantly required to make decisions
on the basis of technical knowledge of nursing while rarely having time to
think about the relationship of nursing service to other hospital departments.

A head nurse may need a considerable amount of technical skill because in addition to being a manager, this individual also must practice nursing. The head nurse may also, however, be required to exhibit greater human skill on the job than either the vice–president or nursing supervisor, since almost all of the head nurse's work involves direct contact with other human beings. This variation in the degree of utilization of these three types of skills may be visualized (Fig. 2–3).

Roles Played by Managers

A third way to examine the work of managers is to think about the different roles they play. Mintzberg has defined roles as "organized sets of behavior" and compared managerial roles to those of actors on a stage. Just as the actor plays a role, the manager, simply because he or she is a manager, must adopt certain patterns of behavior when filling a managerial position.[4] Mintzberg points out that all managers share the common bond of formal authority over the organizational units they manage and that this authority leads to *interpersonal roles* as figurehead, leader, and liaison with other units of the organization. These interpersonal roles provide the manager with the opportunity to gather information. This fact, along with what the manager does with the information, permits a second set of roles. These *informational roles* include monitor, disseminator, and spokesperson roles. Finally, the authority granted to managers, supported by their interpersonal and informational roles, requires that they play *decisional roles*. These include disturbance-handler, resource-allocator, and negotiator roles. In addition, a key decisional role for every manager is that of entrepreneur, in which the manager functions as an initiator and designer of changes intended to improve the unit over which he or she has authority. These ten managerial roles are summarized in Figure 2–4. These roles cannot really be separated. "They are tightly linked together

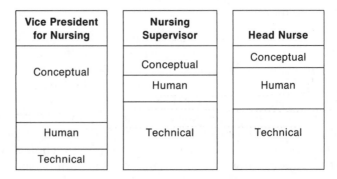

Figure 2–3. Relative skills needed for effective managerial performance in nursing service.

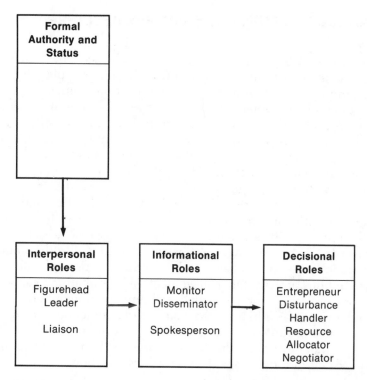

Figure 2–4. The manager's roles. *(From Mintzberg H: The manager's job: folklore and fact,"* Harvard Business Review, *July-August 1975, p 55, Copyright © 1975 by the President and Fellows of Harvard College. Reprinted with permission.)*

in what the psychologist would call a gestalt, an integrated whole. The manager's job is not simply the algebraic sum of these ten roles, but much more—the whole that results when these roles are linked together in the managerial job."[5]

We can see that the work of managers can be viewed from three perspectives: the functions they perform, the skills they need, and the roles they play. In the remaining chapters of this book, we will integrate all three viewpoints. However, for purposes of providing a framework for the book, we will take a functional approach. That is, we will examine the functions of planning, organizing, directing, coordinating, and controlling as they are carried out by the manager in the health services organization. In the remaining sections of this chapter, we will describe each of these functions briefly and look at some of the special aspects of practicing management in the health services organization.

THE MANAGERIAL FUNCTIONS BRIEFLY DESCRIBED

Planning

In essence, *planning* means deciding in advance what is to be done—charting a course of action for the future. The aim of planning is to achieve a coordinated and consistent set of operations aimed at desired objectives. Without planning, random activities prevail. Planning is basically an intellectual process and as such is easy or difficult for individuals depending upon their capacities. It is so basic to management that planning must be done by all managers whether they find it easy or not. Logically, planning is the first of the management functions. It lays the foundation for organizing; an organization structure is designd to help carry out plans. It dictates those activities to which others are directed. It facilitates coordination and, in the absence of good planning, coordination becomes much more difficult. Finally, during the planning activity, standards are set, against which actual performance can be measured when management carries out the controlling function. As conditions change, plans have to be constantly revised and updated. It is a continuous activity for management. While planning can be discussed as a separate function of management, it must be remembered that it intertwines and overlaps with the other managerial functions. There is no clear-cut sequence of functions that managers perform one after another.

A number of reasons, listed below, explain why planning is so critically important in today's health services organizations:

1. *Planning focuses attention on objectives.* Good planning yields reasonable organizational objectives and develops alternative approaches to meeting these objectives. In this way planning provides a means of unifying the actions of all organizational participants toward common ends. Health services organizations of all kinds are undergoing a serious reevaluation, both internally and in the eyes of many interested parties external to the organizations, in terms of their roles in health delivery and the manner in which they operate. Planning is the function that allows organizations to decide where they should be going and literally forces a determination of the means to get there.

2. *Planning offsets uncertainty and chance.* The only thing certain about the future is uncertainty. No one knows what changes will occur even one day in advance. The further into the future one looks, the less the certainty. However, if the manager thinks about the future and plans for those contingencies that can be imagined or foreseen, this will greatly reduce the chance of being caught unprepared. Uncertainty or chance cannot be eliminated, but it can be prepared for through planning. The means of delivering health services are undergoing significant changes. These changes require that health services organizations be adaptable and flexible; planning is critical to organizational flexibility.

3. *Planning enhances economical operation.* The costs of health services,

particularly those provided in organized settings, are rising at a very fast rate. While many aspects of cost are beyond the manager's control, some can be minimized through planning for efficient operation and consistency. Planning substitutes integrated effort for random activity, controlled flow of work for uneven flow, and careful decisions for snap judgments. As the delivery of health services becomes more and more an organized effort, the managerial function of planning becomes increasingly important as a means of containing service costs.

4. *Planning facilitates control.* Control implies comparing actual results with some predetermined desired result and correcting deviations when they occur. The planning function yields information that can be used to set standards against which actual results can be compared. As third parties, principally the government through Medicare and Medicaid, have assumed a greater share of the health care financial burden, they have required significantly more accountability from health services providers. This accountability goes beyond cost to include both the quality of care and the manner in which it is delivered. The trend toward more accountability and the concurrent necessity for control that it implies will become increasingly important in health services organizations in the years ahead. From the manager's perspective, the effect of planning on the effort to control those activities for which he or she is responsible is one of the most important reasons for effective planning.

Organizing

Once objectives have been established through planning, management concern can turn to developing an organization that is capable of carrying them out. The basic objective of the organizing function is development of a structure or framework called the *formal organization structure.* Organizing can be defined as relating people and things to each other in such a way that they are combined into a unit capable of being directed toward the organization's objectives. The most basic premise of organization is that division of work is essential for efficiency. Work activities required for organizational performance are separated through the process of vertical and horizontal differentiation (i.e., dividing the organization into operational units). Vertical differentiation establishes the hierarchy and the number of levels in the organization. Horizontal differentiation comes about because of the need to group similar activities for more effective and efficient performance. This usually results in the formation of departments within the organization.

The formal organization depends on two basic relationships: (1) responsibility and (2) authority. Responsibility can be thought of as the obligation to execute functions of work. The source of responsibility is one's superior in the organization. By delegating responsibility to a subordinate, the superior creates a relationship based on obligation between superior and subordinate. The basis for dividing responsibility in organizations is functional similarity.

The total work load of an organization is divided among available personnel by grouping functions that are similar in objectives and content. This should be done in a manner that avoids overlaps and gaps as much as possible. Responsibility may be continuing, or it may be terminated by the accomplishment of a single action.

When responsibility is given to a person, he or she must also be given the authority to make commitments, use resources, and take the actions necessary to carry out their responsibilities. Authority and responsibility must be commensurate. If authority exceeds responsibility, a misuse of authority can occur. Conversely, a person who is delegated responsibility without adequate authority to fulfill it is in a most frustrating and often embarrassing position. The tangible product of the delegation of authority and responsibility is a formal organization structure.

Directing

Once plans have been made and an organization has been created to put them into effect, the next function of management is to stimulate the effort needed to perform the required work. This is done through the *directing* function, which includes the following activities:

1. Order giving
2. Supervising
3. Leading
4. Motivating
5. Communicating

At some point managers have to indicate what they want done. The order is the technical means through which a manager conveys to a subordinate what is to be done. Supervision is the activity of management that ensures proper execution of orders. It is also therefore, a part of the control function, which will be discussed later. Supervising is a required function for every manager from the top of the health services organization on down.

Leadership is the ability to inspire and influence others to contribute to the attainment of objectives. It is obviously necessary for getting work done through and by others, which is the manager's central task. Traditionally, success in leadership was thought to be dependent on traits of the leader. However, more recently, it has been shown that successful leadership is the result of interaction between the leader and his or her subordinates in a particular organizational situation. This means that a single pattern of leadership behavior used without discretion is not likely to be successful in a wide variety of managerial situations. Thus, the successful leader is not a blind follower of particular leadership methods but chooses the method that he or she considers most appropriate for a given situation. The leader reaches a choice by considering the overall situation, especially the subordinates themselves, and what effect his or her actions will have on them.

The manager must always keep in mind that getting an employee to carry out a directive is *caused* behavior. In that sense, the manager must *motivate*, or cause, the employee to follow directives. The importance of motivation skill for the manager cannot be overemphasized. There is a growing body of sound empirical evidence that the best motivator is a challenging job—one that allows a feeling of achievement, responsibility, growth, advancement, enjoyment of the work itself, and earned recognition. This is especially true with professional and high-skill-level workers. Jobs that have these characteristics do not just happen. They must be created by, and carefully nurtured by, the manager.

Communicating with workers is the final activity of the effort to direct their work performance. In a sense it is the key to directing because unless a manager can effectively communicate what is to be done, how it is to be done, by whom it is to be done, and when it is to be done, the chances of adequately carrying out the directing function are greatly reduced. *Communication* in highly complex organizations such as those providing health services is a multidirectional process requiring movement downward, upward, and in all directions necessary to reach superiors, subordinates, and peer-level positions. It is a process of people relating to one another. As they do so in performing work and solving problems, they communicate facts, ideas, feelings, and attitudes. If this communication is effective, the work gets done more effectively and the problems are solved more efficiently.

Coordinating

Coordinating is the act of synchronizing people and activities so that they function smoothly in the attainment of organization objectives. The importance of this managerial function cannot be overemphasized. Fulmer has said, "Coordination is perhaps the closest thing to a true synonym for management."[6] Koontz and Weihrich have said, "It is the essence of managership, for the achievement of harmony of individual efforts toward the accomplishment of group goals is the purpose of managing."[7]

Different kinds of organizations require different amounts of coordination. In some organizations it is possible to separate activities in such a way as to minimize these requirements. In other organizations, particularly those such as health services organizations, which are departmentalized functionally and where the interactions among the departments are so important, coordination is more important. One must recognize the interaction between the need to specialize activities and the requirements for coordination. The more differentiation of activities and specialization of labor, the more difficult are the problems of coordination. Hospitals, for example, are among the most complex organizations in modern society in terms of differentiation of activities and specialization of labor. They are characterized by a detailed division of labor into a number of technical skills. The work of the institution is so specialized and performed by such a variety of workers that very significant problems of coordination often arise. Furthermore, in the hospital, organizational activities are often contingent on one another. It is this condition of functional interdependence among organizational parts and activities that makes coordination so important in hospitals.

The essential challenge of coordination stems from the fact that individuals often perceive objectives differently and also favor various methods of accomplishing those objectives. This means that coordinating, in a very real sense, means managing conflict. Conflict may be between various functional groups in the health services organization, such as between the medical staff and management, or between nursing service and the laboratory. But it may also be conflict between subordinate and superior, between the individual and the organization, or between two peers. Any one of these and other relationships is a potential source of conflict. As we shall see later, not all conflict is bad, but even such low levels of conflict as are evidenced by "disliking" and "difficulty in getting along with" are often associated with reduced effectiveness. In a very real sense, coordination is a preventive managerial function concerned with heading off conflict and misunderstanding.

Controlling

Controlling can be defined as the regulation of activities in accordance with the requirements of plans. By definition, control is directly linked to the planning function. This may be stated in another way: the managerial function of control consists of measuring and correcting activities of people and things in an organization to ensure that objectives and plans are accomplished. It is a function of all managers on all levels, and its basic purpose is to ensure that what is intended to be done is what is done. Control techniques are based upon the same basic elements regardless of whether people, quality of care, money, or morale is being controlled. The control process, wherever it is applied, involves four steps: (1) establishing standards, (2) measuring performance, (3) comparing actual results with standards, and (4) correcting deviations from standards.

THE NEED FOR MANAGEMENT OF HEALTH PROFESSIONALS

Provision of high-quality health services is the basic objective of health professionals. Determination of the need for, and the development of, organizations through which these services can be provided would be a formidable management task even without the constraints of scarce resources. However, given these constraints and the fact that consumers must expend an increasingly large portion of their incomes on health services, another objective has become important in the operation of health services organizations. That is the responsibility to provide needed services of high quality as efficiently as possible. Health services organizations must now be concerned not only with the scope and quality of their services but also the efficiency with which these services are provided. The dual concern for quality and efficiency places a tremendous burden on health professionals and those who manage them. Yet it is a burden they must bear if we are to have high-quality health care that is both available and affordable.

Managers in the health services organization must be concerned with both quality and productivity at the same time. They cannot emphasize one to the detriment of the other. Figure 2–5 illustrates this dual concern. The diagram shows that the (1,1) manager would have low concern for both quality and productivity in providing health services. Hopefully, this is a hypothetical case. The (10,1) manager would be highly concerned with quality but would lose his or her effectiveness because he or she is unconcerned about productivity. A health services organization can tolerate some managers of this type (many of them do), but if everyone were this way, the organization in all likelihood could not function in today's environment of economic constraints. The (1,10) position is not desirable because, although a manager who takes this approach is concerned about productivity, this individual has a low concern for quality—an intolerable position for one who provides vital health services. The (5,5) position indicates a median but balanced concern for both quality and productivity. It is a desirable position from the perspective of its balance but undesirable in that it represents a halfhearted concern for both quality and productivity. It is a "getting-by" position and, as such, does not represent a best effort toward which everyone should strive. The (10,10) position—maximum concern for both quality and productivity—may also be hypothetical, given the nature of human effort, but it is clearly the most desirable position for a manager to occupy. There are, of course, a limitless number of other managerial positions on this diagram. The point is that the

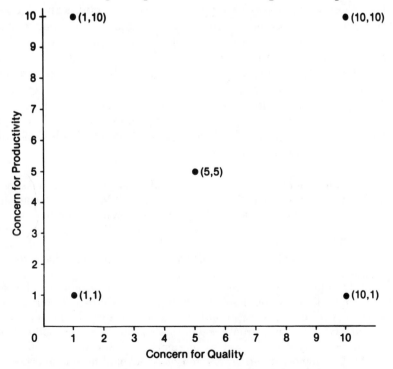

Figure 2–5. Concerns of the health professional.

manager should strive for the (10,10) position to maximize effectiveness in terms of both quality and costs.

It has frequently been argued that the quality of health services is a basic determinant of the cost of delivering health services. That is, if the manager focuses too much on containing costs, then quality will suffer. Clearly, severe attempts to curtail costs could reduce quality of care if they resulted in inadequate staffing or lack of certain necessary equipment and supplies. Of more practical interest, however, is the relationship between quality and costs that does not represent extremes. In a study conducted by the author using four measures of quality and two measures of productivity, it was found that hospitals able to provide services in an efficient manner tend to produce services of higher quality than those that operate less efficiently (where costs are higher). This suggests that the ideal objective of high-quality services at the lowest possible cost is not only desirable but pragmatic and consistent. The two go hand in hand and are strongly influenced by effective management.[8] Other researchers have also shown that there is apparently no need to make trade-offs between costs and quality, and between efficiency and effectiveness.[9]

ETHICS AND THE MANAGER

Increasingly, ethical issues have an impact on actions and decisions in health services organizations in both the biomedical and managerial spheres of activity, and some that overlap. All decisions and actions in health services organizations contain ethical dimensions, whether they are clinical or managerial or both. Managers, to behave ethically, must first recognize ethical issues and then act on them.

It is probably most useful to think of these issues in terms of those that involve: individuals, institutions, and communities. A few examples under each heading should suffice to show the extent of ethical issues facing the health services manager:[10]

Questions of ethics focusing on the individual address such issues as: What are the limits of the patient's right to privacy? Under what circumstances can a patient refuse treatment? Who is competent to refuse treatment on a patient's behalf? Should life be extended by artificial means when that life holds little or no promise of normal function or the treatment causes acute suffering? What is the proper balance between survival and the quality of life?

Institutional issues include: Given limited resources, who should be admitted? Who should not? Is ability to pay the critical factor? How does the manager deal with inappropriate use of scarce goods and services when in effect, use for one purpose makes it impossible to serve another? As a health services manager, how does one cope with the proper balance between health promotion and cure when one gets paid for one and not the other? How does one balance provider versus patient rights in deciding whether to provide home care services to residents of dangerous neighborhoods? Under what circumstances does the manager "blow the whistle" when physicians charge excessive fees? What about excessive hospital fees? In advertising, to what degree is the truth rationalized? In investor-owned institutions, what are the relative rights of the patient and the stockholder? Does the physician as well as the chief executive officer and board member have a conflict of interest? What does the manager do when medical staff needs are inconsistent with community needs?

Ethical issues under the community heading include: How do communities deal with matters of distributive justice? If all persons seeking all the health services they want outstrip community resources to provide these services, do one and all get smaller-but-equal shares, or is a minimum standard of service offered, with variation above it based on ability to pay? How does the community balance demand and need? How does one balance provider rights versus patient rights, in the community interest, when both are legitimate? What is the community's obligation under areawide planning: simply to promulgate the plan? To screen applications for buildings and services? Or, further, to accept responsibility when there are gaps, such as in nursing home services or home care services, that are not being filled, or when the underprivileged lack access to care because of institutional flight to the suburbs? Who are the community's agents; is the president of a nonprofit hospital a community agent? When organs or given procedures are in short supply, who gets the transplant or service?

In addition to the vast array of ethical issues facing managers in health services organizations, they face an ethical imperative not shared by managers in other settings. This is that, as moral agents for patients, they have an independent duty to protect patients and further patients' interests. In health services organizations, all actions and decisions—both clinical and managerial—must be measured against the duty to protect patients and further their interests.

In concept, ethics generally refers to "the rules and principles that define right and wrong conduct."[11] It is important to distinguish between law and ethics. Managers who aspire to ethical behavior face considerably more ambiguity than those who aspire to do only that which is legal.[12] Laws provide the minimum standard of performance for the manager. Ethical standards imply higher standards, those involved in moral conduct and judgment. Figure 2–6 presents a matrix of the possible combinations of legal, illegal, ethical, and unethical characterizations of decisions or actions. As can be seen, actions taken or decisions made by managers can be legal but, at the same time, unethical.

As we saw above, managers make decisions and take actions that have consequences for individuals, the health services organizations in which they work, and for the communities their organizations serve. In making decisions and taking actions, a manager needs a well-developed personal ethic, which must be applied in the context of the philosophy and culture of the health services organization in which the manager works. Compatibility between the two is important, but the manager's personal ethic (that is, the principles of

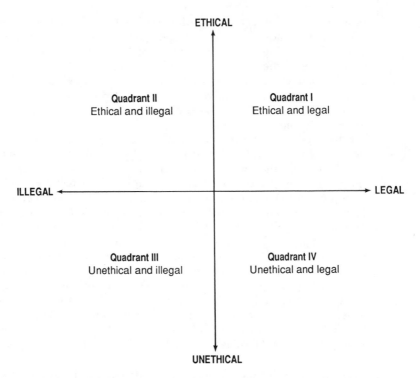

Figure 2–6. A matrix of legal and ethical decisions. *(Henderson VE: The ethical side of enterprise.* Sloan Management Review *1982; 23:37. Reprinted with permission.)*

behavior he or she uses to distinguish between good, bad, right, and wrong) is paramount because managers, by virtue of their positions, face many consequential decisions. They control resources that can be used for good, bad, right, or wrong purposes.

There is a school of thought that says that "ethics can't be taught, instead it is *caught*."[13] That is to say that ethics are primarily a function of character formation, a process that begins very early in life. However, an understanding of ethics can be learned, and one's personal ethic can be enhanced by thoughtful consideration of some key elements in ethics. Fortunately, a solid literature base is emerging for the manager interested in ethics.[14] For example, inherent in any personal ethic adequate to guide personal behavior toward patients are four principles: autonomy, beneficence, nonmaleficence, and justice.[15]

Autonomy means that the wishes of self-legislating (competent) patients are followed, that they are involved in their own care to the extent they choose to be, and that when patients are not self-legislating because they are children or of diminished competence, the organization has special procedures for surrogate decision making or substituted judgments. Autonomous patients are treated with respect; it is unethical to lie to them. The principle of autonomy is especially important in terms of consent and use of confidential patient information.

Beneficence requires a positive duty to contribute to the patient's welfare. This principle has a long and noble tradition in the health professions and is equally applicable to the organization.

Nonmaleficence is a duty that obliges managers to refrain from inflicting harm. This harm can be mental as well as physical and is readily extended into an organizational setting to issues such as patient privacy. While beneficence is a positive duty, nonmaleficence is negative—refraining from doing something that harms. Beneficence and nonmaleficence affect managers in issues such as fiduciary duty, use of confidential information, and conflicts of interest.

Justice is the final principle important to a personal ethic. A major problem is defining what is just or fair. Egalitarians say that it is just to provide like amounts of services to all with similar needs. Libertarians stress merit and achievement as measures of what is just. Aristotle asserted that "equals" should be treated equally, "unequals" unequally. An interpretation of Aristotle's view means that most medical care should go to those in greatest need, since in terms of health they are situated unequally. There is broad latitude in developing the specific content of the principle of justice, but there are limits, nonetheless. Considerations of justice have most apparent application in resource allocation.

Whether managers act ethically or unethically is a function of the interaction between the managers' personal ethics *and* the philosophy and culture of the health services organization in which they work. Cultures that minimize ambiguity and continuously remind managers to make ethical decisions and take ethical actions will encourage more ethical behavior than those that do not do these things.[16] Ambiguity can be reduced by such actions as developing codes of ethics. It can also be reduced by rewarding ethical behavior and by creating a climate in which managers are free to challenge standards or practices they consider unethical, or even questionable, and have them changed. Finally, health services organizations can encourage ethical behavior by providing training in applied ethics. Such programs can enhance achievement of the purposes for which health services organizations exist, increase the awareness of the ethical dimensions of managers' decisions and actions, encourage critical evaluations of values and priorities, and help managers integrate ethical considerations into their decision making and actions.

SPECIAL ISSUES IN MANAGING HEALTH PROFESSIONALS

The basic contribution of health professionals is intellectual in nature. They provide knowledge to be used in meeting the objectives of health services organizations. These organizations employ large numbers of professionals who produce, apply, preserve, and communicate knowledge. So the challenge facing managers in health services organizations is one of integrating management authority and the knowledge brought in by the health professionals.

In order to manage these professional human resources, it is useful to understand those characteristics that set health care professionals apart from other occupational groups. This is not to say that they are completely different from other members of the work force. They do, however, exhibit certain rather unique characteristics, as do the organizations in which they work. Organizations that are professionally dominated exhibit certain characteristics. Among them are[17]:

1. A large number of jobs are classified as *professions*.
2. Work satisfaction is based on enjoyment of one's *profession*.
3. Learning how to do the job is based essentially on *professional* training.
4. On-the-job training is intended primarily for *professional* development.
5. Long hours due to *professional* commitment are typical.
6. Important day-to-day communications are always with fellow *professionals* and clients.
7. Individual efforts are devoted to *professional* goals.
8. The benefits of work go to clients or *professional* colleagues.
9. Relationships with clients are based on *professional* knowledge and trust.
10. Career development is oriented toward *professional* development.
11. Primary loyalty is to the *profession*.
12. Leaders are selected on the basis of *professional* competence.
13. The *professional* job is central to one's life and part of one's individual identity.
14. *Professional* knowledge is more important than any other type.
15. Status is based on *professional* and occupational competence.

Beyond their organizational characteristics, there are some characteristics of professionals, as individuals, that are useful to keep in mind as one manages them. For example, Miner has identified five such characteristics[18]:

1. *A desire to learn.* For the professional, it is essential that technical knowledge and expertise be developed, transmitted, and used in the service of patients.
2. *A desire to work independently.* Professionals have private and personally responsible relationships with patients that require independent action based on an individual's best professional judgement.
3. *A desire to acquire status.* For the professional, the provision of services to patients is predicated on the patient's recognition of the professional's expert status.
4. *A desire to help others.* For the professional, the relationship between the professional and the patient is central and involves the expectation that the professional will help the patient as much as possible.

5. *A value-based identification with the profession.* Professionals feel strongly committed to their profession and to its ethical norms.

There is always the danger of creating unwarranted stereotypes in generalizing about any group of people. Clearly, there are many health professionals who do not exhibit the characteristics described above—at least, there are varying degrees of the characteristics among health professionals. Yet these generalizations are widely applicable and can be helpful to the person who manages health professionals.

We have described management as a process made up of several functions. The reader, especially one who has been involved in complex health services organizations, no doubt realizes that management is not so simple as performing a set of functions. Perhaps the one thing we can say with complete confidence about management is that there is *no one best way* to organize and manage a health services organization or any part of it. What works best for one group in one setting may not work best for another group in another setting. Several writers have formalized this concept, calling it the Contingency Theory of Management.[19]

For the manager to impose sameness dictatorially on those he or she manages is not effective management. The art and the science of the practice of management is to draw out the strengths of those who are managed and to direct them toward the achievement of objectives—by whatever methods that work. A key point for the manager of health professionals is that effective management is an essential ingredient in the effective delivery of health services. It is no longer desirable or possible to completely separate clinical and managerial activities in the delivery of health services.

SUMMARY

The art and science of the practice of management is a process, with both interpersonal and technical aspects, through which the objectives of an organization, or that part of it being managed, are established and accomplished by utilizing human and physical resources and technology. The functions of management (planning, organizing, directing, coordinating, and controlling) have been briefly described. The need for management of health professionals in today's organizational setting has been emphasized. We have described the dual responsibility of health professionals to provide needed services of high quality but in an efficient manner. Attention has also been given to some of the special characteristics of health professionals.

With this background on the management process, we are ready to turn our attention to an examination of specific aspects of the management functions—especially as they apply to the management of health professionals.

REFERENCES

1. Robbins SP: *Management: Concepts and Applications,* ed 2. Englewood Cliffs, NJ, Prentice-Hall, 1988, p 16.
2. Charns MP, Schaefer MJ: *Health Care Organizations: A Model for Management.* Englewood Cliffs, NJ, Prentice-Hall, 1983, p 11.
3. Katz RL: Skills of an effective administrator. *Harvard Business Review,* September–October 1974, pp 90–100.
4. Mintzberg H: The manager's job: folklore and fact. *Harvard Business Review,* July–August 1975, pp 49–61.
5. Lorsch JW, Baughman JP, Reece J, Mintzberg H: *Understanding Management.* New York, Harper & Row Pub., 1978, p 221.
6. Fulmer RM: *The New Management,* ed 4. New York, Macmillan, 1988, p 39.
7. Koontz H, Weihrich H: *Management,* ed 9. New York, McGraw-Hill, 1988, p 18.
8. Longest BB Jr: Hospital services: An empirical analysis of their quality-cost relationship. *Hospital and Health Services Administration,* Fall 1978, pp 20–35.
9. Scott WR, Flood AB: Costs and quality of hospital care: a review of the literature. *Medical Care Review,* Winter 1984, pp 213–261; and Scott WR, Shortell SM: Organizational performance: managing for efficiency and effectiveness, in Shortell SM, Kaluzny AD (eds): *Health Care Management: A Text in Organization Theory and Behavior,* ed 2. New York, Wiley, 1988, pp 418–457.
10. McNerney WJ: Ethics in health care, in Anderson GR, Glesnes-Anderson VA (eds): *Health Care Ethics: A Guide for Decision Makers.* Rockville MD, Aspen Publishers Inc, 1987, p 6.
11. Davis K, Frederick WC: *Business and Society: Management, Public Policy, Ethics,* ed 5. New York, McGraw-Hill, 1984, p 76.
12. Roberts J: The moral character of management practice. *J Management Studies,* July 1984, pp 286–302.
13. Colian CS: Whose responsibility is it to teach ethics? *Managing,* Spring 1988, p 5.
14. Darr K: *Ethics in Health Services Management.* New York, Praeger Publishers, 1987; and Anderson GR, Glesnes-Anderson VA (eds): *Health Care Ethics: A Guide for Decision Makers.*
15. Darr K, Longest BB Jr, Rakich JS: The ethical imperative in health services governance and management. *Hospital and Health Services Administration,* March/April 1986, pp 56–57.
16. Trevino LK: Ethical decision making in organizations: a person-situation interactionist model. *Academy of Management Review,* July 1986, pp 601–617.
17. Oliver JE: *Scoring Guide for the Oliver Organization Description Questionnaire.* Buffalo NY, Organizational Measurement Systems Press, 1981, pp 4–15.
18. Miner JB: *Organizational Behavior: Performance and Productivity.* New York, Random House Business Division, 1988, p 168.
19. Kast FE, Rosenzweig JE: *Organization and Management: A Systems and Contingency Approach,* ed 4. New York, McGraw-Hill, 1985.

T HREE
Planning: The Beginning of Management

April 29
1 P.M.

"Will the meeting come to order?" the president of Memorial Hospital asked. "We have a long agenda." The fourteen department heads settled into their seats around the conference table, anticipating another lengthy round of planning committee deliberations.

Before anyone else could speak, the medical records administrator cleared her throat and said: "Listen, while we're all together I'd like to ask that everyone have all the documentation on the treatment of Mr. Luther J. Fillerey, patient number 3222-004, forwarded to Medical Records if you haven't already done so. As you may know, his family is bringing suit against the hospital, and I have to get his medical record in good order."

The vice-president for nursing asked, "What's missing? He died over two months ago!"

The medical records administrator responded, "Some of the lab reports are not in, and I'm pretty sure that there is some radiology work that is not yet in the record." Her voice reflected irritation as she added, "And some of the nurses' notes haven't been signed."

The president leaned forward in his chair and interrupted by saying, "I know how important this suit is to all of us, and I know that it is upsetting . . . but this meeting is supposed to be devoted to long-range planning for the hospital; not these day-to-day problems." He slumped back and looked at the ceiling as he continued, "This planning committee meets once a month for the purpose of setting long-range planning recommendations that I can pass on to the board of trustees. Yet, every month we have a new crisis on our hands, and we end up devoting the meeting to it. Last month it was our accreditation site visit, this month it's the suit . . . who knows what it will be next month." The department heads sat motionless and silent as the president admonished them, "If we always spend our time fighting fires, we'll never get around to long-range planning!"

The director of the Social Service Department used a pause in the president's speech to exclaim, "The most important thing facing Memorial Hospital is this suit. It affects everything from patient confidence in us to the financial stability of the hospital."

The vice-president for finance supported her view: "This suit is for a million dollars. If we lose it, our insurance premiums are going to go through the ceiling!"

For the next hour and twenty minutes, the topic never varied from the suit brought against the hospital by the family of Luther J. Fillerey.

The meeting adjourned at 2:40 P.M.

INTRODUCTION

Health services organizations operate in an environment of change. They must be able and prepared to accept change as the inevitable consequence of operating in a dynamic world. Continued success and further development demand innovation and adaptation to the changing political, social, economic, and technological environment in which health services are delivered. In such an environment, effective planning ability is a necessary tool for the effective manager.

Health services organizations face a future that no one can predict with certainty. Effective planning can reduce the impact of this uncertainty. Managers must plan for means of carrying out the tasks of acquisition, allocation, and utilization of resources; striking the balance between formal and informal organizational patterns; coordinating diverse but interdependent efforts; developing suitable reward and incentive programs; integrating organizational requirements with the needs and goals of participants; developing suitable leadership and supervisory skills at all levels of the organization; and anticipating all of the other operational problems they will face. They must also plan for appropriate responses to the set of demands stemming from the "external" relationships of the organization, to the needs and demands of the community it serves, and to other relevant outside groups that have an interest in or a relationship to the organization. The viability and effectiveness of health services organizations depend upon the ability of their managers to plan for the impact of these and other factors on the organization.

PLANNING DEFINED

Planning can be defined as *deciding in advance what is to be done and how it is to be done.* The "what" decisions lead to the establishment of objectives, and the "how" decisions lead to the determination of methods for achieving those objectives. The determination of what is to be done and how it is to be done at the level of an organization, such as a hospital, results in a statement of objectives and corresponding methods for the entire organization. The development of these objectives and methods is the responsibility of top-level managers, although they need the participation and involvement of managers at middle and lower levels to develop them fully. The manager of each department or unit within the organization must determine what is to be done and how it is to be done in his or her unit. We can think of this as the determination of objectives and methods that will guide the actions of those people being managed as well as the use of resources that are available to the manager. While both levels of planning are important in the overall scheme of health services delivery, we are primarily concerned with the second level— planning within the health services organization at the level of departments or subparts. We will focus our attention on the determination of what is to be done (setting objectives) and how it is to be done (developing methods). Before we examine these aspects of planning, however, it will be useful to set the stage by describing planning at the level of the health services organization (at this level, planning is often referred to as strategy formulation) and by describing several key elements that pertain to the management function of planning.

STRATEGY FORMULATION

Strategy is the set of decisions that determine the character (size, scope, and mix of services) of a health services organization and give it direction in the marketplace. From this definition, it is obvious that a great many individual decisions make up the strategy of a particular health services organization at a particular time. However, it is possible to characterize the strategy of a health services organization in general ways such as a "growth strategy" or a "reputation enhancement strategy" or a "stabilization strategy," to mention only a few possibilities.

The strategy of an organization does not simply emerge by chance. It is formulated by people for an organization that exists in relationship to an external environment upon which the organization is highly dependent.[1] Appreciating this external dependency phenomenon is quite important in order to understand what strategy is and how it is formulated. The external dependency relationship between a hospital, for example, and its environment can be outlined as follows:

1. Hospitals find themselves dependent, in varying degrees, on elements (competitors, suppliers, labor markets, consumers, and regulators) in their external environments.
2. Hospital managers, because of this dependence on the external environment, must constantly view the external environment as a series of opportunities and/or threats.
3. Those responsible for managing hospitals must try to capitalize on the opportunities and defend their organizations against the threats that face them.
4. Managers' efforts to respond to the opportunities and threats from the external environment heavily influence and are directly reflected in the strategy elaborated for the hospital.

Figure 3–1 illustrates the strategy formulation process and shows the relationship between the external environment of the health services organization and the strategy elaborated for it. Mintzberg has suggested that strategy formulation in an organization facing a complex, demanding, and constantly changing environment will be an adaptive process.[2] As Figure 3–1 illustrates, the strategy of a health services organization will be an adaptation by managers to perceived opportunities and threats presented to their organizations by their external environments and influenced by extant strengths and weaknesses of their organization. The dependence of health services organizations on their external environments is so great that their strategic responses to particular environmental circumstances are largely predictable.[3]

As Lefko has suggested, "strategic planning will form the foundation for those institutions that can effectively manage their resources and their changing internal and external environments.[4] Figure 3–2 provides a more detailed look at the strategic planning process in health services organizations. Some of the changes hospitals will face in the next few years as well as a look at how dramatic changes in the past two decades have been are reflected in Table 3–1.

KEY ELEMENTS IN THE PLANNING FUNCTION

Any consideration of the basic elements in planning as they relate to management of a health services organization, or any part of it, should center around four points: evaluation of present conditions; the time factor; collection and analysis of data; and a hierarchy of plans within the health services organization.

Evaluation of Present Conditions

Perhaps the central element in the planning function is recognizing in present conditions any inadequacies that require change. Once these undesirable conditions have been identified, the question arises of what to do about them. It is the existence of alternative answers to this question that gives rise to planning. Earlier in this chapter we outlined some of the internal operational

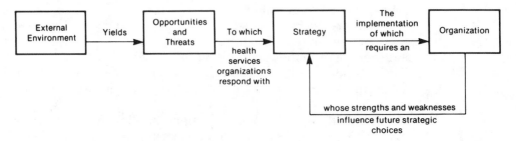

Figure 3–1. The strategy formulation process.

Current Business Assessment
- Key internal trends (marketing, medical staff, finance, product lines, diversification businesses, other)
- Key external trends (markets, competitors, insurers, other)
- Strengths/weaknesses
- Opportunities/threats

↓

Goal Setting
- Goals and objectives
- Strategic objectives (which broad strategies, and what specific initiatives within the broad strategies?)

↓

Options Evaluations
- Potential options
- Relationship of options to strategic objectives
- Costs/risks
- Implications for key constituencies (physicians, trustees, other)
- Consistency with capabilities

↓

Strategy Development
- Overall strategy
- First action plan (actions, responsibilities, costs)
- Strategic initiatives budget
- Revised action plan

↓

Implementation
- Selling to trustees, physicians, other constituencies
- Monitoring
- Changing
- Reselling

Figure 3–2. Strategic planning process. *(From Coddington DC, Moore KD: Market-Driven Strategies in Health Care. San Francisco, Jossey-Bass Publishers, 1987, p 239. Reprinted with permission.)*

TABLE 3–1. THE DYNAMIC HOSPITAL PLANNING ENVIRONMENT

Change	1973	1983	1993
"Snapshot" characterization	• Freestanding hospitals providing primarily acute care with growing inpatient demand • Focus on encouraging use of inpatient hospitalization and expanding hospital beds	• Discouragement of inpatient hospital care • Increased competition for a dwindling, stabilized inpatient demand and revenue base • Diversification efforts aimed at seeking out new markets and income sources	• Closed hospital systems selectively determining health niche in an openly competitive, "bottom-line"-oriented patient market • Inpatient utilization only by those requiring hospitalization; others treated outside hospitals in a variety of noninstitutional settings
Hospital role and mission	• Singular in purpose • Oriented to acute inpatient care • Informally identified	• Plurality of purpose • Oriented to both acute and ambulatory care • Documented and formally identified	• Multidimensional purposes • Multitude of businesses, both hospital- and non-hospital-related • Specifically delineated and enunciated
Hospital link to external environment	• Relatively independent of external environment	• Generally dependent on external environment	• Intimately dependent on external environment
Financial reimbursement and structure	• Mounting concern over increasing hospital costs • Commencement of federal regulations to control costs • Retrospective cost- or charge-based reimbursement for hospital services • Sufficient available capital for expansion or renovation • Limited price consideration in purchase of hospital services	• Emphasis on payment system reform to control costs • Reduced federal- and state-sponsored reimbursement of health care services • Limited and expensive capital to fund growth and development • Case-mix orientation • Increasing competition and price sensitivity in marketplace • Declining availability of traditional capital sources	• Provider reimbursement based on institutional competencies, resources, and prices • Federally controlled lid on hospital costs • Use of imaginative and creative payment approaches • Hospital reorganization to allow for limited capital sources • Uniform payment for patient diagnosis

(continued)

TABLE 3–1. (Cont.)

Change	1973	1983	1993
Hospital/ medical staff relationships	• Provision of all necessary institutional resources for medical staff • Close working alignment between hospitals and medical staffs	• Competition between hospitals and physicians to undertake traditional hospital services • New interest in corporate and financial physician/hospital arrangements	• Corporate grouping of physicians and hospitals • Innovative arrangements and joint ventures involving hospitals, physicians, and investors
National health planning initiatives	• Transition from planning agencies to regulatory agencies • Beginning of Certificate of Need (CON) legislation	• National health planning in state of flux • Shift from federal to state jurisdiction • Continued control of capital expenditures and health resource supply	• Health planning continuing but at state, not local level. • Federal efforts regulate health resource supply aided by limited capital sources
New technology	• Rapid implementation of advanced technology	• Reduced implementation of advanced technology • Priorities shift to limited capital resources and increased CON constraints	• Selective implementation of new technology
Hospital organization and governance	• Dominated by freestanding independent hospitals with autonomous governing boards	• Plethora of multihospital arrangements • Board control increasingly geographically and organizationally separate from institutions	• Multi-institutional arrangements to be more predominant • Centralized governance through fewer and more geographically disparate boards
Institutional management	• Generalist approach to hospital management • Facility and bed orientation • Knowledge of computer assistance in financial operation	• Multidisciplinary specialist approach to management • Emphasis on strategic and market-based planning • Knowledge of computer application in medical and management information systems	• More sophisticated and specialized management expertise required • Multidisciplinary techniques required for program initiatives • Pressing need for integrating clinical, administrative, and financial decision making

TABLE 3–1. *(Cont.)*

Change	1973	1983	1993
			• Need for sophisticated strategic management in hospitals • Knowledge of complex computer-assisted decision-making techniques

(Adapted from Jeffrey J. Lefko, "A Portfolio of Progress," Hospitals, 57:11 June 1, 1983, pp 78–82. Used with permission from Hospitals, American Hospital Publishing, Inc., June 1, 1983, 57:11. Adapted with permission.)

problems and external demands faced by health services managers. Given the complexities of meeting these challenges, it would be extremely naive of any manager to feel that there is nothing more that could be done to improve the activities for which he or she is responsible.

The Time Factor

The issue of timing of events is very important in planning. Perhaps this is nowhere more apparent than in relation to patient care. Suppose a person is admitted to a hospital, for example, to have a certain surgical procedure performed. Many decisions have to be made about this patient far enough in advance to allow the procedure to go smoothly and provide the patient an opportunity to get maximum benefit from the hospital stay. This is known as *lead time*. Different activities associated with this patient's surgical episode require different amounts of time. If we wish to coordinate events with different lead times, we must analyze the points at which we want coordination to take place and schedule events accordingly. To further complicate this, there is usually a sequence in which events have to take place; hence we must make provision for sequential lead times. The surgical episode is only one example. Indeed, most activities in health services organizations are related to and dependent upon other activities, often in other departments or units, and must be considered in light of this fact.

It is essential to grasp another aspect of the time factor in relation to planning—that short-range and long-range planning are aspects of the same continuous activity. Success in planning depends on the ability of managers to understand that short-range planning can be successful only if it is carried out in the context of adequate long-range planning.

Collection and Analysis of Data

Effective planning depends on the quality and quantity of data available to the manager. Consideration must be given to pertinent data from the present and the past, and an assessment must be made of probable future events. The assessment of probable future events is more than peering into a crystal ball. It is the establishment of assumptions or forecasts of the future that bear upon present actions. For example, how many tests of a certain type are going to be performed by the laboratory in the coming year? How many person-hours will be required? What equipment and supplies will be needed? The answers to these and similar questions will provide the premises upon which planning will take place in the laboratory. Similar premises can be established for other units in the health services organization. The fact that premises cannot be established with certainty makes it essential that plans contain built-in flexibility.

Planning premises include three types of information: estimates of factual data, policies of the organization, and future plans of the organization as a whole. Perhaps examples of each type of premise will help clarify them. To continue with the laboratory example, its manager can estimate that the laboratory will perform 2,000 tests of a certain type. This is an example of an estimate of factual data. An organization policy that should be considered a planning premise for human resources needs is a situation in which the organization has a policy of requiring some minimum level of experience for certain jobs. Another might be a policy of promoting from within wherever possible. An example of the plans of the entire organization serving as a planning premise for a department would be a plan to open a new wing during the next year. This must be taken into account in plans of each department in the health services organization. Premising is the assessment of the future. For the institution as a whole, and to only a slightly smaller extent for individual departments or units within the organization, it is becoming necessary to forecast further and further into the future.

A Hierarchy of Plans Within the Health Services Organization

It is important to realize that plans exist in a hierarchy that covers all levels of the organization and, to some extent, are related to what is going on in other competing health services organizations in the area. The key thought is that all of the plans within a health services organization are interrelated. It is imperative that plans along this hierarchy be compatible and mutually supportive.

Proper attention to these four points should result in plans that are objective, structured, and yet flexible. It is very likely that the extent to which plans are developed with these elements in mind is a measure of their probable success. People share a common inclination to react negatively to pressures. These negative reactions invariably create blocks to effectiveness. Many pressures can be avoided by good planning that provides an orderliness that is the antithesis of pressure.

With these thoughts as background, we can turn our attention to the two things that the manager must accomplish in planning: setting objectives and developing methods for achieving them.

SETTING OBJECTIVES

By definition, the initial step in planning is the determination of objectives. Unless one knows *what* is to be accomplished it makes no sense to worry about *how* to accomplish it. Objectives can be, and are, set for the entire health services organization, but they are also established for units within the organization. In a very real sense the key to the entire management process (as well as the planning function) is the establishment of meaningful objectives. The management process begins with the specification of objectives and ends with an evaluation of how well they were accomplished.

In setting objectives at the level of the health services organization, the institution must have a basic philosophy. To establish it, certain questions must be asked and answered. Examples include: What are the health needs of the citizens in our community? Who should receive health services, to what extent, and from whom? Building on this philosophical outlook, health services organization managers can then determine their own particular objectives by asking and answering such questions as: Which of the general health needs should this organization meet? What group or groups should it serve? What health care services and programs will best meet the needs selected? What special or combined programs are most appropriate? What human abilities, knowledge, and skills are required to carry out the selected programs and activities? What quantities and types of resources are necessary to carry out the programs and activities? And on and on.

When these questions are satisfactorily answered, managers can set objectives to serve as guides to thought and action for each unit within the organization. Knowing the objectives of the entire health services organization permits the managers of the various departments and units within it to establish compatible and supportive objectives. It is important to remember that no manager can effectively plan in a vacuum. The objectives and methods set for each unit must be related to those of other units and to those of the entire organization. This can be visualized in Figure 3–3. The reader can see that each set of objectives is related to those above them in the sense that they must be supportive and to those below them in the sense that objectives at lower levels depend on higher-level objectives to give them an appropriate sense of direction. It is also clear in Figure 3–3 that objectives down at the level of the individual eventually affect those at the highest level of the organization.

By examining the studies that have been made on setting objectives, a number of conclusions can be drawn that are relevant to the manager in the health services organization:

1. *Individual and departmental objectives must blend with the objectives of the organization.* Theoretically, everyone in the organization should have specific work objectives that are part of the larger plan of the department or unit and ultimately the organization as a whole.

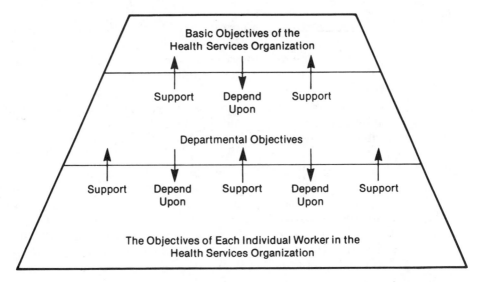

Figure 3-3. Levels of objectives.

2. *Objectives should be progressive if possible.* It is desirable that there be continuity from period to period in setting and achieving objectives.
3. *Objectives should be jointly determined.* This means that a manager must work with his or her subordinates in setting their objectives; he or she must also work with the next manager up the line in determining objectives for the organizational unit. Participation in setting objectives will mean that those who work to achieve them will have a better understanding of their importance and relevance and will therefore be much more likely to exert maximum effort toward their achievement.
4. *Objectives should be measurable whenever possible.* Health professionals are aware of the difficulties in measuring certain aspects of their work, particularly evaluation of the quality of patient care. Nevertheless, many aspects of the work done in health services organizations are measurable in such terms as person-hours, dollars, satisfaction, and ratios of various types. Such measures permit many objectives to be stated in specific, quantifiable terms that allow a realistic evaluation of progress toward the objectives.
5. *Provision must be made for formal accountability.* Objectives imply accountability. When objectives are stated in measurable terms, progress toward their achievement can be directly evaluated. The main reason for making objectives specific is to pinpoint accountability. Every organizational participant who has specific objectives and who is given the resources to accomplish them should be held accountable for the results.

6. *Methods are not as important as objectives*. Such a statement must be qualified somewhat when applied in a health care context. There are methods in the radiology department, for example, that define the way in which a certain procedure will be performed. The method may have been found to be the best way to perform the procedure. Allowing deviation from such methods is not what is intended here. The reader should realize that methods are only means to an end. Those responsible for getting a job done should be allowed to alter the means if it will get the job done in a better way. This kind of attitude stimulates everyone's creativity and makes work much more satisfying.

7. *Flexibility must be built into objectives*. Circumstances change and, on occasion, the objectives must change with them. For example, nursing service may have an objective of holding payroll expenditures below a certain level. However, if patient load goes above that which was projected when the objective was set, then the objective will have to be altered to reflect the new circumstances.

Even though the establishment of objectives is the critical first step in the planning function, some managers do not effectively establish meaningful objectives for their areas of responsibility. Stoner and Wankel have suggested five main reasons for this:[5]

1. *Unwillingness to give up already established alternative objectives*. The decision to establish specific objectives and commit resources to their achievement requires that other alternatives be foregone. Each of us will at times find it difficult to accept the fact that we cannot achieve *all* of the objectives that are important to us. We may be reluctant to make firm commitments to specific objectives in order to avoid the painful task of giving up other desirable objectives.

2. *Fear of failure.* Whenever someone sets a definite, clearcut objective, that person takes the risk that he or she will fail to achieve it. Managers, no less than other people, see failure as a threat to their self-esteem, to the respect that others have for them, and even to their job security. Thus, their fear of failure keeps some managers from taking unnecessary risks and establishing specific objectives.

3. *Lack of organizational knowledge*. In order to set effective objectives, a manager needs a good working knowledge of three areas of the organization: (1) the organization as a whole, (2) other subunits of the organization, and (3) his or her own subunit.
   No manager can establish meaningful objectives for a subunit without understanding the broad objectives and strategies of the organization. The objectives of the subunit must contribute to the broader objectives of the total organization. A manager who is new in the organization or who does not keep informed about its latest plans will be understandably hesitant to set new objectives because they might conflict with those established by higher-level management.

Similarly, the manager must be aware of the objectives of other subunit managers to avoid establishing objectives that conflict with or duplicate theirs. A manager with an undeveloped or faulty information system may therefore try to avoid objective setting altogether, and, instead, fall back on already established subunit objectives.

4. *Lack of knowledge of the environment.* In addition to understanding the organization's internal environment, the manager needs to understand the external environment—the competition, clients, suppliers, government agencies, and the general public. The opportunities that an organization needs to fulfill its major objectives, as well as the pitfalls it must avoid in order to survive, are in the external environment. Without knowledge of the external environment, managers are apt to become confused about which direction to take and are reluctant to set definite objectives.

5. *Lack of confidence.* To commit themselves to objectives, managers must feel that they and the subunit or organization have the ability to achieve those objectives. Obviously, if the manager lacks self-confidence or confidence in the organization, he or she will hesitate to establish difficult objectives.

These obstacles to the effective formulation of objectives can be overcome. For example,

Managers who lack knowledge of the organization or its external environment need assistance in developing a viable information system. This assistance can be given in a variety of ways. For example, one of the important benefits of management development programs (offered within the health services organization) is that they help participants establish informal contacts with people from different departments, divisions, and locations. These contacts help managers find things out and get things done. This, in turn, raises their confidence in others and in themselves.

The barriers due to fear of failure and unwillingness to give up attractive alternative goals are reduced in health services organizations that have effective and well-communicated systems for planning. Where planning is a well-understood process, it is easier for each individual to develop his or her own goals—and to obtain help in developing plans to achieve those goals. Where effective decision-making techniques are widely used, it is easier to determine which are the more attractive alternatives and to recognize the necessity of forgoing some alternatives in order to achieve others.

Fear of failure and lack of confidence are also reduced by setting realistic goals and achieving them. The individual's immediate superior plays a key role in creating a climate in which difficult but attainable goals will be set. Providing training and guidance in ways to achieve such goals is one important step. Recognition and reward for successful goal achievement is a second step; and providing constructive and supportive responses when targets are occasionally missed is a vital third step.[6]

DEVELOPING METHODS

We have defined planning as deciding in advance what the objectives are and what methods should be developed to achieve them. Objectives are the *ends* toward which the manager must get people to work, and the methods are the *means* of achieving those ends. The manager's planning efforts, once objectives are established, must be turned to the development of methods to accomplish them. In many ways, the work of the manager is a constant search for effective methods to use in achieving objectives. The fact is that it is the methods that largely account for both quality of work and the efficiency with which it is done.

The dilemma facing managers who must develop methods for achieving objectives is the existence of what can be a very wide range of alternative methods. The manager's task thus becomes establishing a list of possible methods and then choosing from among them. As the experienced manager knows, and as the student will quickly learn, only rarely is there an obvious "best" method. Therefore, decisions have to be made—most often, tough decisions. Decision making is such an important part of developing methods (and also necessary in the performance of all the management functions) that we will devote all of Chapter 4 to this topic. Suffice it to say here that as managers choose from among the various methods available to accomplish a particular objective, they must consider the cost of a particular method and weigh this against the probable benefits that will result from it. These costs and benefits are not simply the dollars involved but the social and psychological costs as well. Upon considering the costs and benefits of alternative methods, relative to each other, the manager can choose from among alternative methods in an informed manner.

MANAGEMENT BY OBJECTIVES

Peter Drucker, a noted authority on management, coined the phrase "management by objectives" (MBO) to illustrate the central importance of objectives to the effective management of any undertaking.[7] The "management by objectives" concept is simply that every person in an organization should have specific, attainable, measurable objectives that mesh with those of the organization and that each person's performance should be assessed against achievement of these objectives. It is important to note the word *mesh*. This does not mean that all objectives have to be the same. They must, however, be compatible with one another.

In the MBO process, superior and subordinate pairs periodically establish objectives for the subordinate; these objectives usually cover a specific time period and there is periodic review to see how well the subordinate has achieved the objectives. The MBO process can be viewed schematically in Figure 3–4.

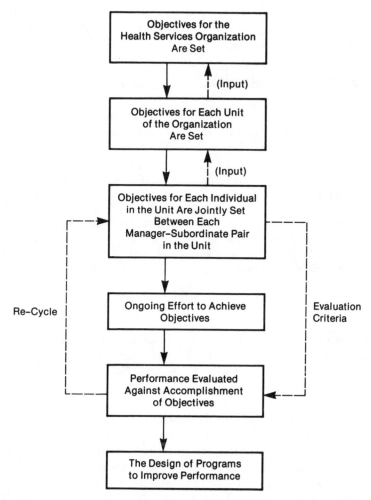

Figure 3–4. The MBO process.

While MBO is not a panacea for managers, it does provide a number of benefits. A survey of managers found the following benefits to be associated with its use:[8]

1. It lets individuals know what is expected of them.
2. It aids in planning by making managers establish objectives and target dates.
3. It improves communication between managers and subordinates.
4. It makes individuals more aware of the organization's objectives.
5. It makes the evaluation process more equitable by focusing on specific accomplishments. It also lets subordinates know how well they are doing in relation to the organization's objectives.

This last benefit, making evaluation more equitable, suggests that individuals' performance can be evaluated by their impact on the achievement of predetermined objectives.

THE IMPACT OF SUCCESSFUL PLANNING

When managers are successful at the planning function, their efforts are of considerable benefit to their organizations. For example, Peters and Tseng have noted, in regard to planning in hospitals, that it forces managers

> To scrutinize what they do and why they do it. It has broadened the horizons of hospital authorities by encouraging them to look beyond their institutional walls. Planning generates new data on internal operations and environmental trends and involves more people in long-range thinking. It also imposes a rationality, too often lacking, on institutional decision-making. And, planning provides hospitals with long-term goals and short-range objectives against which progress may be charted and measured.[9]

SUMMARY

Planning is the determination of objectives and the methods for achieving them. It is important to think of planning in one unit of a health services organization as part of a larger whole. For example, the plans of the health services organization to expand must be taken into account in the human resources planning done by the organization's various departments. No departmental plan should be made that does not contribute to the objectives set out in the plans of the entire health services organization. It is the responsibility of top-level management in the organization to ensure that all other managers understand the objectives of the organization. It is the joint duty of all managers to determine whether or not their plans are compatible with all other plans in the organization. If this is done initially, a great deal of trouble can be avoided.

If planning is to be successful, it is essential that plans be properly and effectively communicated to all who are affected by them. All too frequently there is a gap between the knowledge of top management and lower levels of management with respect to plans. The very essence of planning is informed anticipation of the future. Planning must take place against a background of information and assumptions regarding future conditions that have a bearing on the health services organization.

REFERENCES

1. Pfeffer J, Salancik GS: *The External Control of Organizations: A Resource Dependence Perspective.* New York, Harper & Row Pub., 1978.

2. Mintzberg H: Strategy-making in three modes. *California Management Review* 1973; 26:44.
3. Longest BB Jr: An external dependence perspective of organizational strategy and structure: The community hospital case. *Hospital and Health Services Administration,* Spring 1981, pp 50–69.
4. Lefko JJ: A portfolio of progress. *Hospitals,* June 1, 1983, p 82.
5. Stoner JAF, Wankel C: *Management,* ed 3. Englewood Cliffs, NJ, Prentice-Hall, 1986, pp 93–94.
6. Stoner and Wankel: *Management,* p 94.
7. Drucker PF: *The Practice of Management.* New York, Harper & Brothers, 1954.
8. Tosi HL, Carroll SJ: Managerial reaction to management by objectives. *Academy of Management Journal,* December 1968, pp 415–426.
9. Peters JP, Tseng S: Managing strategic change. *Hospitals,* June 1, 1983, p 65.

FOUR

Decision-making Tools for the Practice of Management

April 29
3 P.M.

The operating room supervisor and the chairman of the department of surgery sat together, as was their custom, for a few minutes after the last procedure for the day was completed. They usually discussed the operating schedule for the next day during this time, but today they were on a different subject.

"You know," the chairman mused, "I've got to find a way to convince our penny-pinching board of trustees to expand the surgical intensive care unit."

The supervisor responded, "I don't see what their problem is. We could fill up twice as many SICU beds as we have—and they charge more than $1,000 a day for them. I would think they could make a lot of money for the hospital by expanding the SICU."

"They could," the chairman replied, "but they are on this cost-benefit kick, and the numbers showed that they could get a bigger bang-for-the-buck by spending money on expanding the outpatient clinic."

"Since when have the decisions on life and death been made on the basis of money?" the supervisor questioned.

"I guess since money became so scarce."

"Well, this is no way to run a hospital. The word around the nursing service is that if this fellow, Luther Fillerey, had been in SICU where he belonged, he wouldn't have died."

"We'll never know for sure about that," the chairman cautioned, "but you probably have a point."

"I know I have a point! When we start making decisions on the basis of bang-for-the-buck around here, quality flies out the window."

"Maybe I can use that argument to get the SICU expanded. The board has to listen when I tell them that Fillerey died because the SICU was too full to take him. That lawsuit is going to cost them plenty."

At 3:10 P.M. the chairman reached for the operating schedule for the next day and said, "Well, let's see what's on the schedule for tomorrow."

INTRODUCTION

Decision making is a central element of planning. Yet it is not limited to the planning function. It permeates all the management functions—planning, organizing, directing, coordinating, and controlling. It is difficult to think of anything a manager might do that does not have a relationship to a decision made somewhere. Some authorities believe that decision making is a synonym for management. Charns and Schaefer have concluded that the work of management is to increase the degree to which decisions made by members of the health services organization are organizationally rational.[1]

There have been a number of attempts to describe how practicing managers make decisions. Two views of this have dominated the literature: the *economic-person* model and the *administrative-person* model. The classic economic-person model makes the underlying assumptions that the decision maker will know the alternatives available in a given situation and the consequences that they will bring, and that he or she will always behave rationally. Under the economic-person model, the decision maker will always make a choice so as to maximize some desired value.

Herbert Simon has described a more realistic model of the decision maker, calling him or her the *administrative person*. Under the administrative-person model, decision-making behavior may be summarized as follows:[2]

1. In choosing between alternatives, the decision-makers attempt to satisfice or look for the one which is satisfactory, or "good enough."
2. The decision-makers recognize that the world they perceive is a drastically simplified model of the real world. They are content with this simplification because they believe the real world is mostly empty anyway.
3. Because they satisfice, rather than maximize, they can make their choices without first determining all possible behavior alternatives and without ascertaining that these are in fact all the alternatives.
4. Because they treat the world as rather empty, decision makers are able to make decisions with relatively simple rules of thumb or tricks of the trade, or from force of habit. These techniques do not make impossible demands upon their capacity for thought.

Simon developed the administrative-person model as a more valid model of reality than the economic-person model. He argued that the decision maker was never completely informed and was seldom able to maximize anything. Because of these physical limitations of the decision maker, Simon introduced his principle of bounded rationality:[3]

> The capacity of the human mind in formulating and solving complex problems is very small compared to the size of the problem; it is very difficult to achieve objectively rational behavior in the real world . . . or even a reasonable approximation to such objective rationality.

Because maximizing is viewed as too difficult for humans, Simon suggested that "satisficing" was a more realistic and typical procedure. The satisficer considers possible alternatives until one that meets minimum standards of satisfaction is found. Instead of searching a haystack to find the sharpest needle in it, the decision maker is content with a needle sharp enough to sew with. Satisficing is not as complimentary to the decision maker as maximizing, but it is much closer to reality.

DECISION MAKING DEFINED

Decision making is almost universally defined as *making a choice between two or more alternatives.* This definition has the advantages of being brief and of focusing attention on the essential element of decision making—making a choice. However, to really grasp the nature of decision making, one must understand that making a choice is only one of several sequential steps that must occur as part of an intellectual process. These steps include:

1. Becoming aware that a decision must be made
2. Defining the problem
3. Analyzing available information
4. Developing relevant alternative solutions
5. Choosing the alternative
6. Converting the chosen alternative into action—execution of the decision. (This step is not technically a part of the decision-making process, but attention must be given to it if management decisions are to be effective.)

We will examine each of these steps in detail below and then describe several decision-making tools that can be of help to the health professional who must make management decisions.

Awareness

The most difficult step in decision making, in many cases, is being aware that a decision needs to be made. Effective managers must be sensitive to situations in their areas of responsibility that do not meet standards and expectations. This sensitivity can be termed *perceptual skill*, and it enables managers to collect and interpret cues from their surroundings. When no triggering cues are picked up by managers, no decisions will be made. The manager with limited perceptual skills goes along oblivious to potential problems until they blossom into full-blown crises. This sort of manager lives her or his life reacting instead of acting. Perceptual skills cannot really be taught by textbook and lecture. They are developed through experience and are thus one of the main reasons that managers usually become more effective with experience.

Definition

The effective manager must be able to distinguish between cause and symptom. As in medicine, failure to make this distinction will inevitably lead to a relapse. Defining the real problem is not always an easy task because what appears to be the problem might only be a symptom. For example, a head nurse might believe he or she is confronted with a problem of conflicting personalities when two staff nurses are continually disagreeing and cannot get along with each other. Upon checking into this, the head nurse might find that the real problem is that he or she has never clearly outlined the functions and duties of each staff nurse, specifying where their duties begin and end. Therefore, what appeared to be a problem of personality conflict was actually one of organization.

Defining a problem is usually a time-consuming task, but it is time well spent. There is no need for a manager to go any further in the decision-making process until the problem has been clearly defined, because nothing is as frustrating as the right solution to the wrong problem. A simple, but effective, way of getting behind the symptom and to the underlying problem is to ask *why?* Thus, the crucial step in decision making is an awareness of the real problem that requires a decision.

Analysis

After the problem—and not just the symptoms—has been defined and there is reasonable assurance that its satisfactory solution will provide a means to a desired end, the manager can take the next step in decision making—analyzing available information. This means assembling the facts that are *relevant* to the decision that must be made. Judgment must be used in deciding what information is to be used as well as what information is available. Great care must be exercised to be as fair and objective as possible in gathering and examining the facts that are used in making a decision.

The most difficult "facts" to deal with are the intangible factors that may be involved and that can play a significant role. These intangible factors are such things as reputation, morale, discipline, and personal biases. It is difficult to be as specific about these facts as about those that are subject to physical measurement of some form. Nevertheless, they must be considered in the decision-making process.

In many situations, it is necessary to ferret out the relevant facts. However, the manager should also realize that many decisions can be based on information already at hand. First, there are those problems that clearly fall within the scope of existing procedures. One of the major functions of an established procedure is to provide a predetermined course of action, or, in other words, a solution to problems that keep demanding a decision over and over again. Secondly, there are many problems that fall within the decision maker's range of experience and, therefore, do not require the acquisition of additional information. The manager may possess, as the result of prior experience and training, the factual information and conceptualizations necessary to resolve the question and make a decision. The ability to sythesize past experiences into a cohesive network of information is useful in solving current problems.

The quality of decisions is directly proportional to the number of *relevant* facts that are gathered and analyzed in reaching a decision. Judgment is required in determining when additional facts are needed or whether it is advisable to make a decision even though all necessary facts have not been acquired or analyzed.

Development of Alternate Solutions

After having defined the problem and analyzed the available information, the decision maker's next step is to search for and develop alternate courses of action. One simple rule should guide the decision maker in this step: the greater the number of alternatives considered, the greater the chance of selecting a satisfactory one.

The decision maker should not always think in terms of "one best solution." More realistically, problems have several solutions that have both positive and negative characteristics. The task is to develop as many satisfactory solutions as possible and from these choose the one that seems "best." It is during this step in the decision-making process that creative and innovative solutions to problems come into being. Logic and experience play major roles in idea generation, but imagination can also make a significant contribution. The use of imagination, or creative thinking, is of great assistance in all functions of management, but it is particularly valuable in the development of relevant alternatives from which the decision maker can exercise choice.

A key point to remember is that creativity is latent within all people. Ordinary people under the proper circumstances may create new solutions to problems. These proper circumstances include being able to work in an atmosphere of freedom, trust, and security.

The creative process itself can be viewed as a series of steps including:

1. Personal need
2. Preparation
3. Incubation and illumination
4. Verification

The fact that a *personal need* to think creatively must exist emphasizes the individual aspect of the creative thinking process. It also implies that there must be a motivating force to initiate the creative thought process. This motivation may be a need for self-expression or the result of an externally imposed problem situation.

Contrary to what many people believe, very few creative ideas come as a "bolt from the blue." Rather, they usually grow out of an intensive period of *preparation* during which the decision maker becomes saturated with information and makes a concerted effort to perceive new and meaningful relationships. To a large extent, the originality of ideas depends upon the number of avenues explored and the extent to which all possible interrelationships and solutions are considered. This preparatory step represents the "work" of the creative process.

It is possible for an original solution to a problem to be found quickly as the result of a brief period of analysis. Sometimes this is necessary. However, there is a real need for the concept of *incubation*—a period of mulling the problem over, sometimes consciously and sometimes completely unaware of the thinking process. The value of an incubation period lies in the fact that a more fully developed or more fully illuminated idea may result. It is helpful to set a deadline for the incubation period so that problems do not go unsolved for unduly long periods of time while the manager hopes for an illumination. However, it is true that some period of incubation is usually necessary for original solutions to be developed.

The final step in the creative thinking process is *verification*. When a solution is first envisioned, especially through the insight of illumination, it is usually not in a polished and final form. The verification step is a period of refining an idea, changing it, and improving it. In effect, it represents the difference between an idea and a creative thought that can be implemented.

The foregoing discussion of the creative process emphasizes the individual's role in creativity, especially in regard to illumination. However, it should be pointed out that often the creative process is stimulated by group effort. This is the underlying basis for brainstorming as an effective method of solving problems.

Brainstorming can be a simple process, but certain guidelines may be useful:[4]

1. Hold the session to about 40–60 minutes in length.
2. Do not reveal the problem before the session begins.
3. State the problem clearly and not too broadly.
4. Use a conference table that allows the participants to communicate easily with one another.
5. If the matter discussed is a physical product, bring along a sample that can be used as a point of reference.

Relying upon the creative process, experience, perhaps brainstorming with others, and logic, the decision maker should try to visualize as many different solutions to a particular problem as possible; this increases the chance of selecting a good alternative.

Choosing the Alternative

After the decision-making manager has developed and evaluated the alternatives, he or she must select that alternative thought to be best. Although the assistance of specialized personnel and various decision-making aids such as those described later in this chapter can be used, the final choice is most often the manager's alone. If the other steps in the decision-making process have been properly carried out, the manager will usually have to choose from several alternatives. One choice that is always available is to do nothing. This should be the most carefully considered choice of all. The decision maker should visualize the consequences that would result from taking no action. Only if the decision to take no action will result in the most desirable consequences should it be selected as the best course of action. The manager should never view the no-action decision lightly or feel that things will remain unchanged as a result of it. After all, something necessitated the need for the decision-making process to take place.

Making the correct choice is not easy. Management decisions tend to be gray rather than black or white. They are usually made in the context of a constantly changing environment; this means that the correct choice now may not remain the most desirable choice. There are several bases upon which the choice can be made. Among them are: experience, intuition, advice from others, experimentation, and scientific decision making. The whole purpose of the choice is to select the alternative that has the greatest number of desired, and least number of undesired, consequences. Making the best choice is not easy, even when all the bases suggested above are considered. Aside from the element of change, which will affect any decision that is made, there is a problem of incomplete and unavailable information. Also, personal prejudice and bias can cripple the manager's effectiveness as a decision maker by forcing a choice of an alternative that fits some preconceived notion.

The largest stumbling block to making a choice among alternatives is indecisiveness. Often this stems from feelings of personal inadequacy and insecurity, and these feelings are reinforced by pressure from superiors in the organization. The opposite situation can exist and may be just as detrimental to the effectiveness of the decision maker. This is impulsiveness or a tendency to jump headlong into a situation without considering all factors. It is not uncommon for a young, inexperienced manager to be impulsive in his or her first decisions; however, if enough of them turn out to be wrong, then the manager may become indecisive. In either case the manager is of little value to the health services organization.

There is no simple way to ensure that decisions will be sound ones. However, if the manager asks three questions regarding the decision about to be made its quality can be considerably improved.

First, the decision maker should ask whether or not the decision contributes to the attainment of stated objectives. This implies that the decision is but a means to an end—an end that has been clearly thought out and stated in the form of an objective. If a potential solution does not support stated objectives, it should not be adopted.

Secondly, the decision maker should ask whether or not the decision represents a high degree of economic effectiveness. In other words, does the proposed solution make maximum use of available resources? There may be times, of course, when economics should not be used as a criterion for decision making, especially in a health services organization where quality considerations are so important. Usually, however, the economic consideration is a useful guideline.

Finally, the decision maker should ask whether or not a potential solution is feasible or capable of execution. In answering this question, the decision maker must think in the very practical terms of how a particular decision will be implemented in view of the resources available.

These considerations do not guarantee that the best decision—or even a good decision—will be made. They do, however, increase the chances for a good decision and are thus worth the effort.

Execution

The process of converting the selected decision into action is not technically a step in the decision-making process. However, the manager will be evaluated more on the outcome of the decisions made than on the decisions themselves. Managers must live with their decisions. The manager must also view each decision as part of a continuum. Once a decision is made and implemented, it will lead to other situations that require decisions. The good manager will use experience with executing decisions as a means of self-evaluation and self-improvement. He or she will learn from mistakes and successes. The important point is that a decision, from the manager's point of view, is not really complete until it has been executed and then finally appraised.

DECISION-MAKING TOOLS

One of the most striking changes in management practice has been a steady increase in the development and use of quantitative decision-making tools. We cannot cover all of them in detail. Yet it is important to be familiar with some of them; they can make decision making easier and more effective. The interested reader can find a good treatment of quantitative decision making in Warner and Holloway's, *Decision Making and Control for Health Administration* [5] and Warner and Luce's *Cost-benefit and Cost-effectiveness Analysis in Health Care: Principles, Practice and Potential.* [6]

Decision Grid

The most basic (and in many ways one of the most useful) decision-making tool is the *decision grid.* This is nothing more than a display of the possible alternatives in a decision along with the various elements that will affect it. Figure 4–1 illustrates a decision grid where the decision involves an addition of inpatient hospice beds. The alternatives are listed down the left-hand margin, with the elements affecting the decision making up the rest of the grid. The grid's main advantage is that all pertinent information can be displayed. This becomes especially important in complex decisions and when a committee or other group is working with the decision.

Payoff Tables

An advance over the decision grid can be made if probabilities can be determined for the various possible outcomes of each alternative in a decision. For example, suppose the operating room supervisor is concerned about how many disposable syringes of a certain type should be ordered and stocked each week. Assume the supervisor has determined that there is an 80% probability that 800 syringes will be needed and a 20% probability that 1,000 syringes will be needed in a week. (These estimates are most likely based on past usage patterns.) The supervisor can also assign costs to each of these two alternatives. In this case, storage space is allocated at $10 per 1,000 syringes. In addition, if too few syringes are ordered and stocked, an extra cost of $20 will result for special ordering and messenger pickup. Figure 4–2 illustrates the two alternatives (1,000 and 800 syringes) and the costs associated with each of the two outcomes.

For the first alternative, if 800 syringes are stocked and the usage during the week is 800, the costs will be $8 (see cell 1). If 800 syringes are stocked and 1,000 are needed that week, the costs will be $28 ($8 for storage and $20 for the special order [see cell 2]).

For the second alternative, if 1,000 syringes are stocked and the usage during the week is 800, the costs will be $10 (see cell 3). Also, if 1,000 syringes are ordered and stocked and 1,000 are used, the costs will be $10.

If the operating room supervisor orders and stocks 800 syringes, then 80% of the time this decision will be correct and only an $8 storage cost will be incurred; 20% of the time there will not be enough and the $28 storage and reorder costs will be incurred. Expected costs can be determined for each alternative as follows:

Expected costs if
800 are ordered $8 (0.8) + $28 (0.2) = $12

Expected costs if
1,000 are ordered $10 (0.8) + $10 (0.2) = $10

Thus, to minimize costs, 1,000 syringes would be ordered and stocked, although this number would be needed only 20% of the time. The reader might ask, "Is all this trouble necessary for a $2 saving?" There are many items to which this decision technique might be applied. The potential benefits go far beyond this single example.

Obviously, the basic difficulty in using this technique is in determining probabilities. When possible, the preferred procedure is to use historical data or experimental samples so that the probabilities have a clear basis in fact. Where this is not possible, judgment by people who are in the best position to estimate may have to suffice.

Alternatives	Patient/Family Preferences	Medical Staff Preferences	Relative Costs of Implementation	Financial Impact	Impact on Public Image	Relative Feasibility	Decision
1. Maintain status quo: continue to provide home health agency-based hospice service and permit terminal patients to die, either at home or throughout hospital, on services determined by their diagnosis (i.e., medicine, ICU, etc.).	Unacceptable	Unacceptable	No new costs	No change	Increasingly negative impact	Feasible, but problematic as consumers gain sophistication	Not recommended
2. Modify status quo: specify, on appropriate units, decentralized throughout the hospital, certain beds to be used for hospice patients.	Moderately acceptable	Acceptable	Modest new costs	Positive (new patients)	Positive	Feasible	Second priority

	Desirable	Desirable	Significant new costs	Positive (new patients)	Very positive (comprehensive, coordinated terminal care)	Feasible	First priority
3. Modify status quo: designate, remodel, and properly equip a permanent inpatient unit to be used by hospice patients.	Desirable		Significant new costs	Positive (new patients)	Very positive (comprehensive, coordinated terminal care)		First priority
4. Establish a referral agreement with another organization to provide inpatient care for hospice patients; refer patients as needed.	Moderately acceptable	Unacceptable (fear losing relationship to patients and reduced income for some physicians)	No direct costs; but loss of revenue	Negative (revenue follows patients)	Negative (disrupts relationship between doctor and patient; marks hospital as less than full service)	Highly feasible (assuming a nearby organization with appropriate facilities)	Not recommended

Figure 4–1. Decision grid for the addition of inpatient beds to an acute care hospital's hospice services. This grid can be used to help make a decision on any problem once alternatives are defined and elements selected. At option of the user, the elements may be weighted.

		Events and Results	
		800 (.8)	1,000 (.2)
Decision Quantity (Alternatives)	800	1 $ 8.00	2 $28.00
	1,000	3 $10.00	4 $10.00

Figure 4–2. Payoff table.

Decision Trees

The decision grid and the payoff table presented above give the manager techniques for improving decision making. Yet they suffer from a basic problem. In reality, decisions are seldom one-time affairs. They are more often linked to other decisions in the sense that one decision necessitates other decisions. Decision trees are very useful in evaluating decisions that are linked together over time with various possible outcomes. This technique is especially useful when probabilities can be determined for the possible outcomes.

For example, suppose a clinical laboratory director is faced with a 60% probability that the demand for a certain laboratory procedure will increase by 20% next year and a 40% probability that demand for the procedure will decrease by 10%. The decision is whether or not to buy a piece of automated equipment (at a cost of $50,000) or to pay existing employees overtime wages to do the increased work, should that be necessary. (We assume here that it would be cheaper to pay overtime than to hire an additional worker.) Because of the vital nature of the lab procedure, simply deciding not to do the increased work is not acceptable. Figure 4–3 illustrates a decision tree based on this decision. (Assume that quality is not an issue here because it will be the same whether the procedure is done manually or on the automated equipment.) Thus, the decision hinges on the objective of making the wisest expenditure of money.

Assume that revenue from this procedure is currently $100,000 per year. If the 60% probability of a 20% increase holds up, the revenue for the next year (and future years if everything stays the same) will increase to $120,000; if the 40% probability of a decrease in demand of 10% holds, then revenue will decrease to $90,000 in both cases (see column 3 of Figure 4–3).

The cost of the machine (installation and first year's operation included) is $50,000; the cost of overtime wages is figured at $10,000 if the increased work has to be done and at zero dollars if it does not (see column 4). Net cash flow can be determined in all events by subtracting costs from revenues (see column 5). The expected value at the end of the first year can be obtained in all events by multiplying net cash flow (column 5) by the probability of the event. Sixty percent chance of increase times $70,000 equals an expected value of $42,000 (see column 6). At the end of the first year the expected value of automation is $58,000 (42,000 + 16,000) and of paying the overtime is

(1) Alternative Actions	(2) Possible Events	(3) Revenue from Procedures	(4) Costs	(5) Net Cash Flow	(6) 1st Year Expected Value	(7) Costs	(8) Net Cash Flow	(9) 2nd Year Expected Value
Automate — Increased Demand (.6)		$120,000	$50,000	$70,000	$42,000	$2,000	$118,000	$70,800
Automate — Decreased Demand (.4)		90,000	50,000	40,000	16,000 / 58,000	1,500	88,500	35,400 / 106,200
Pay Overtime — Increased Demand (.6)		120,000	10,000	110,000	66,000	10,000	110,000	66,000
Pay Overtime — Decreased Demand (.4)		90,000	-0-	90,000	36,000 / 102,000	-0-	90,000	36,000 / 102,000

Figure 4–3. Decision tree.

$102,000. Clearly, at that point in time the decision should be to forego the machine and pay overtime. But, if the decision is projected out over additional years, this may not be the best decision. Even at the end of the second year (see column 9), the expected value is greater for the decision to automate. Of course, the reader must remember that the initial $50,000 outlay must still be overcome. It will not take many years to do this. By extending the computation the number of years can be determined, and when compared to the expected useful life of the machine, this information can form the basis of the final decision.

Cost-benefit Analysis

As we saw in Chapter 1, the cost of health care services has become very great—to the point that great care must be exercised in the use of health care resources. A tool offering considerable promise in this area, if used wisely, is cost-benefit analysis. This technique can be especially useful when trying to decide between alternative expenditures of money. A cost-benefit ratio (Z) is defined as the ratio of the value of benefits of an alternative to the value of the alternative's costs:

$$Z = \frac{\text{present value of economic benefits}}{\text{present value of economic costs}}$$

Several alternatives can be evaluated by comparing the ratios of their benefits and costs. Of course, this ratio is only one factor in the decision, but it can be helpful. It is relatively easy to determine the costs of an alternative. However, frequently in health care situations the value of benefits is much more difficult to determine. What is the value of a human life? What is the value of a higher level of health? Is it better to spend money on making old people more comfortable in their declining years, or is it better to spend the money on improving infant mortality rates?

Of course, there are many decisions where the costs and benefits of various alternatives can be determined rather easily. In those cases, cost-benefit analysis is a useful tool. For example, suppose the head of a radiology unit is interested in choosing between two pieces of equipment that do essentially the same work. Machine A costs $80,000 (installed) and requires a person to operate it at an annual cost of $24,000 plus $12,000 in nonlabor operating costs. The total cost for a year is $116,000. Machine A will produce revenues of $165,000 per year because of its rate of operation. Machine B will have a total cost of $128,000 but will permit revenues of $180,000 because of its rate of operation. Which should be purchased? Assume that they both have the same useful life expectancy and salvage value.

$$\text{Machine A:} \quad Z = \frac{\$165,000}{\$116,000} = 1.422$$

$$\text{Machine B:} \quad Z = \frac{\$180,000}{\$128,000} = 1.406$$

Obviously, if all other things are equal, the best decision is to purchase Machine A.

PERT

The *timing* of decisions is important—in some cases it is the most important aspect of the decision. A tool that is especially helpful in the timing of decisions (on complicated projects particularly) is the Program Evaluation and Review Technique (PERT).

The PERT approach represents a major advance in management practice. It was developed by Booz-Allen-Hamilton, management consultants, and the U.S. Navy as a method to plan and control weapons systems programs. The basic concept used in PERT is the network, or flow, plan. The network is composed of a series of related events and activities. *Events* are required sequential accomplishment points in the program or project. *Activities* are the time-consuming elements of the program and actually connect the various events.

For example, suppose a hospital is planning to establish an open-heart surgery unit. A number of events and activities will have to take place. Among them are: renovation of an existing operating room, installation of new equipment, hiring and training an open-heart surgery team, and many others. When many events and activities are involved, PERT can be very useful in planning and controlling (making decisions about) them. In a project of this type, the manager might begin by renovating the operating room, then purchasing and installing equipment, then hiring and training the team. Obviously, there is a basic weakness in this approach—namely, the events and activities will be strung out for an unnecessarily long time, thus delaying the project. The PERT tool can eliminate this problem.

Figure 4–4 illustrates a PERT network for the development of an open-heart surgery unit. Events are represented by boxes in the network; activities are represented by arrows connecting events. It should be noted that some events may depend on only a single prior event while, in other situations, there may be an interrelationship of several events leading to the accomplishment of an ultimate objective.

Figure 4–4 illustrates the three basic characteristics of a program or project that is amenable to the PERT approach. The first characteristic is that activities must be such that time estimates can be made. In the example, it is possible to estimate how long it will take to accomplish each activity. Second, there must be definite starting and ending points. Without them, there could be no events that are the beginning or ending of an activity. Finally, and this is the key to PERT's usefulness, there must be parallel activities. That is, several activities must be taking place simultaneously for PERT to be of any real value. This fact will become clear as we proceed.

To make the network understandable and usable, the time between the various events (activity time) must be computed. As anyone concerned with large-scale projects knows, it is not always possible to estimate accurately how long it will take to complete the various parts of the project. However, a method does exist whereby a fairly accurate estimated time between events can be determined. This approach involves estimating three different times for each activity:

1. *Optimistic Time*. This occasionally happens when everything goes right. The estimate is predicated on minimal and routine difficulties in the activity.
2. *Most Likely Time*. This represents the most accurate forecast based on normal developments. If only one estimate were given, this would be it.
3. *Pessimistic Time*. This is estimated on maximum potential difficulties. The assumption here is that whatever can go wrong will go wrong.

The characteristics of these three time estimates are best described by a beta curve as in Figure 4–5.

A formula based on the probability distribution of time involved in performing the activity is then used. The formula is:

$$\text{Activity Time} = \frac{O + 4M + P}{6}$$

Where O is optimistic time,
M is most likely time, and
P is pessimistic time.

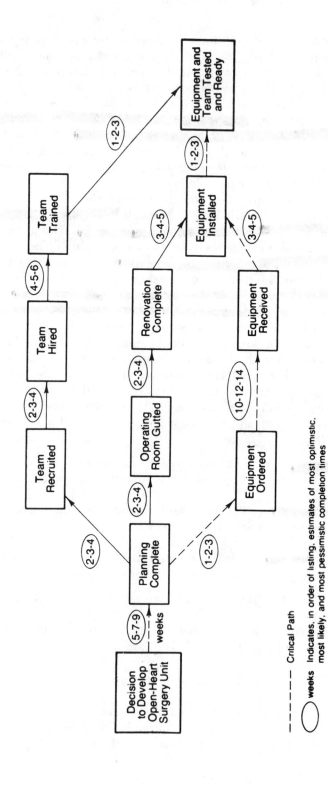

Figure 4-4. PERT network for development of open-heart surgery unit.

- - - - Critical Path

(weeks) Indicates, in order of listing, estimates of most optimistic, most likely, and most pessimistic completion times

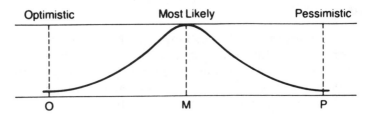

Figure 4–5. Beta curve for optimistic, most likely, and pessimistic time estimates.

Referring to Figure 4–4, we can see that time estimates between the first two events have been made as follows: optimistic = 5 weeks, most likely = 7 weeks, and pessimistic = 9 weeks. The estimated activity time would then be:

$$t_e = \frac{5 + 4(7) + 9}{6} = 7 \text{ weeks}$$

Using the resulting value, we could be reasonably certain that the activity time between events 1 and 2 will be 7 weeks. The process of calculating activity time must be completed for all activities in the network.

The next step in applying the PERT approach is to determine the *Critical Path.* The Critical Path through the network is the path that takes the longest period of time to complete. In Figure 4–4 the Critical Path is shown by the dashed line. Inasmuch as the Critical Path takes the longest time and is the determinant of project completion, other events that do not lie along the Critical Path may be completed before the time they are actually needed. The time differential between scheduled completion of these noncritical events and the time when they are actually required to be completed is called the *Slack Time.* Where excessive Slack Time exists in the project or program, a reevaluation should take place. It should be determined which resources, and in what amounts, could be transferred to activities along the Critical Path. This may permit the Critical Path, and thus the completion time, to be shortened.

In our example, for instance, it would do no good to speed up recruitment, hiring, or training of the team or the renovation of the operating room *unless* we could reduce time on equipment delivery and installation. The entire process can be speeded up only through those activities, since they form the Critical Path.

The PERT technique illustrates the interrelatedness of management functions (especially planning and controlling) and the basic role of decision making. It can be used to great advantage in any building or remodeling project, for the addition of new equipment, for physically moving a department or unit, as well as for many management jobs like budget preparation or policy manual development.

SUMMARY

We have viewed decision making as making a choice between two or more alternatives. In this sense it is critical to effective planning, but it also permeates all other functions of management. Some authorities have even suggested that decision making is a synonym for management.

The decision-making process has been viewed as a series of steps including:

1. Becoming aware that a decision must be made
2. Defining the problem
3. Analyzing available information
4. Developing relevant alternative solutions
5. Choosing the alternative
6. Converting the chosen alternative into action

Several decision-making tools, which can be helpful if properly utilized, were described in this chapter. Most basic is the decision grid, which is a display of the possible alternatives in a decision along with the various elements that will affect it. Payoff tables are an advance over the decision grid in those situations where probabilities can be assigned to various possible outcomes. The decision tree illustrates the necessity, in many cases, of realizing that decisions are not one-time affairs. They are more often linked in the sense that one decision necessitates future decisions. The decision tree is a tool that can be helpful in evaluating decisions linked together over time with various possible outcomes. Cost-benefit analysis is a tool with great potential for the decision maker so long as he or she recognizes the difficulty in determining the true costs and benefits of various alternatives. Finally, PERT is an important tool in the timing of decisions.

Many factors enter into decision making, including: experience, intuition, advice from others, experimentation, and scientific decision making. The effective manager will take advantage of all of these aids to make the vital decisions of what is to be done, by whom, where, and how.

REFERENCES

1. Charns MP, Schaefer MJ: *Health Care Organizations: A Model for Management.* Englewood Cliffs, NJ, Prentice-Hall, 1983, p 234.
2. Simon HA: *Administrative Behavior*, ed 3. New York, Macmillan, 1976, pp xxv–xxvi.
3. Simon HA: *Administrative Behavior*, p xxvi.
4. Hodgetts RM, Cascio DM: *Modern Health Care Administration.* New York, Academic Press, 1983, p 67.
5. Warner DM, Holloway DC: *Decision Making and Control for Health Administration*, ed 2. Ann Arbor, Mich, Health Administration Press, 1984.
6. Warner KE, Luce BR: *Cost-benefit and Cost-effectiveness Analysis in Health Care: Principles, Practice and Potential.* Ann Arbor, Mich, Health Administration Press, 1982.

FIVE
Organizing: The Framework for Management

April 30
9:30 A.M.

The president of Memorial Hospital stood up and extended his hand as the professor from a local university entered his office. They shook hands and exchanged brief pleasantries before they got down to the business at hand.

"The reason I've asked you to come in for this consultation," the president began, "is that I know about your reputation as an expert on organization design, and I've talked with some of my colleagues you've helped. I think some of my problems with managing here at Memorial Hospital result from our organization structure, and I'd like your advice on how we should be set up."

The professor, whose research had centered on organization design for many years, listened intently. After the president had described the organizational set-up at Memorial and showed her a copy of the organization chart, the professor asked, "What kinds of problems are you having with this organization design—or, more precisely, what kinds of problems do you think it causes for you?"

"For one thing," the president replied, "everyone brings their problems to me. Everybody from the executive housekeeper to the vice president for nursing sees me about something almost every day. The range of problems they bring to me is something you wouldn't believe."

"There is sometimes a problem with having too many people reporting to one manager," the professor said as she nodded knowingly.

"It's just impossible for me to keep on top of things when so many people demand my time with so many different kinds of problems. Sometimes I think I've created a monster here—a monster I've lost control over."

"What do you mean?"

"Well, for example, we've got a million dollar lawsuit pending against us for a patient who died here—you may have known him—Luther Fillerey?"

"I knew of him but I didn't know him personally. I hear he was quite a businessman."

"Yes, he was, and I believe that his death is at least partly a result of the fact that I just can't keep on top of everything—we've grown so large that I have to rely on other people to see that things go the way they should— obviously, they don't always!"

"I think I understand your concern, and I can offer some advice on the way an organization such as Memorial Hospital should be structured," the professor replied.

They set up a series of meetings to discuss this matter. The professor left at 10:30 A.M., and as she walked through the outer office, she noticed three other people waiting to see the president.

INTRODUCTION

Once the objectives and the methods to achieve the objectives have been established through the planning function, the manager must develop an intentional pattern of relationships among people so that the methods to achieve the objectives can be utilized. The resulting structure is called the *organization,* and the developmental efforts are called the *organizing function* of management. A very important fact about organizations is that they are built in two ways. On the one hand, managers structure the set of relationships among people to a large extent. They decide who will have the responsibility for particular work and who will report to whom, and so on. This pattern of relationships, developed by management, is termed the *formal organization.* On the other hand, given the way people in groups behave, there will also be an informal pattern of relationships that emerges because the workers, but not necessarily the managers, want them. This arrangement is termed the *informal organization.* Thus, every organization will have two basic parts: a formal structure developed by management and an informal structure that reflects the wishes and preferences of the people who make up the organization. This chapter will concentrate on the formal organization. Chapter 6 will treat the very important topic of the informal organization. Both chapters must be considered together for a complete understanding of the organizing function.

There is no one "best" way to organize that can be generally applied to every situation. The manager must follow a contingency approach and let the variables in a particular situation dictate the choice of a particular organization design. Obviously, in any particular situation, a wide range of variables will have to be considered. Three of the most important have already been touched on: objectives, methods, and people. The objectives and the methods used to achieve them can be quite different from one situation to another. The manager of the admissions department of a hospital has one set of objectives and methods, and these will be different from those of other departments such as the pharmacy or the dietary department. Similarly, the objectives and methods developed for a major medical center will be different from those of a small group practice of physicians, and both will be different from those of a small hospice. The variation in the "people" variable is quite literally limitless. Some people need and want clearly defined work of a routine nature and may require careful and close supervision of their efforts to do their best work; others may prefer a high degree of freedom in choosing how they will work and will resist close supervision. In between these extremes lie an almost infinite variety of preferences in terms of how people would like to work and in what kind of structure they will work best. Thus, we can see that the manner in which a manager carries out the organizing function can be affected by many variables—primarily the objectives that are sought, the methods that are used, and the nature and preferences of the people who form the organization. The manager, in carrying out the organizing function, must take these variables into account in the design of an effective and efficient organization.

Poor organization lies at the root of many problems that managers face. For instance, a chief medical technologist faced a situation in which two technologists were constantly bickering and arguing. The chief had decided that there was a basic personality conflict between the two. To solve the problem, she was in the process of deciding how to terminate one of the technologists. Both were fairly productive workers, but their actions were disruptive and threatened to involve other workers. The chief technologist, in discussing the situation, realized that the arguments might be a symptom and not the problem. She discovered that the real problem was that the relationship between them had not been *organized* properly (by clearly delineating the work responsibility of each technologist). When this was done, most of the problem cleared itself up and she had two workers who did their work and got along reasonably well. This situation repeats itself many times over in the typical health services organization. While personality conflicts do exist, they are often caused by poor organization.

Essentially, the organizing function grows out of the human need for cooperation. When one considers the complexity of the typical health services organization with its varied activities and the diversity of the people who perform those activities, it is clear that the necessity for organization exists in these organizations to a greater degree than in almost any other type of organization in our society.

Even in a single unit of the health services organization, such as the nursing service or the radiology department, there is such a wide range of work performed by people of several skill levels that organization is a vitally important aspect of overall effectiveness and efficiency. These two concepts, *effectiveness* and *efficiency*, although different, must be considered together because they are both important. An organization structure is *effective* if it facilitates the contribution of individuals in the attainment of the objectives that have been set. It is *efficient* if it facilitates the accomplishment of objectives with a minimum of cost. Thus, it is possible to be effective but not efficient, or vice versa. The manager must keep both concepts in mind in the organizing function, especially in view of the growing and concurrent demands for high-quality services and containment of the costs of those services.

It is easy to see the need for organizing at the level of the institution, where so many people and functions are involved, but it is equally important to organize at each level down to and within the department level. To the manager at the departmental level, organization must therefore be viewed from two perspectives. The manager must be concerned about the organization as a whole and how he or she relates to it. The manager must also be concerned about the internal organization of the department. Fortunately, the same principles underlie the organizing function in both cases.

ORGANIZATION THEORY

Much as in medicine, modern management practices have evolved over time from refinement and improvement of earlier approaches. Present theory and knowledge about the organizing function owes a twofold debt to those early researchers and practitioners who sought the "best" approaches to the organizing function. On the one hand, some of the early developments of what has come to be called the *classical* approach are still applicable today, and on the other hand, much of the *modern* approach has emerged as a reaction to, or improvement over, the shortcomings of the classical approach. Thus, to really understand the organizing function, the manager must know about the work of the classical theorists *and* the modern theorists because the two approaches are intertwined. The classical theory, with its shortcomings, serves as a basis for understanding the modern approach to the organizing function.

CLASSICAL ORGANIZATION THEORY

Williams and Huber have summarized the importance of classical organization theory very well:[1]

> Most organizations are strongly influenced by classical theory. Some of its assumptions are questionable and many of its principles are deficient; its assertions are too sweeping, and its application has often led to undesirable results. It is, nevertheless, a brilliant expression of organization theory and a standard of reference which cannot be ignored or considered insignificant by theorist or practicing manager.

The literature base for the classical approach emerged largely during the first half of the twentieth century with the writing of such people as Fayol, Gulick, Urwick, Mooney, and Reiley.[2] One of the major developers of classical organization theory was Max Weber (1864–1920), a German sociologist, who is most often associated with the organization concept of bureaucracy. His work is a logical beginning point in the analysis of the organizing function because Weber thought that bureaucracy, in its pure form, represented an ideal or completely rational form of organization.[3]

The Bureaucratic Model

The term *bureaucracy* stimulates a negative image in the minds of many people. It has come to represent the undesirable characteristics of "red tape," duplication, delay, and general frustration found in many large organizations. The term as used by Weber meant something entirely different. He used it to describe an ideal organization structure based on the sociological concept of rationalization of collective activities. Weber's concept of bureaucracy was an "ideal" type because he abstracted the concept from observations of actual organizations; however, no real-world organization exactly follows the Weber model. Peter M. Blau has summarized Weber's conception of bureaucracy as follows:[4]

> Weber dealt with bureaucracy as what he termed an ideal type. This methodological concept does not represent an average of the attributes of all existing bureaucracies (or other social structures), but a pure type, derived by abstracting the most characteristic bureaucratic aspects of all known organizations.

Bureaucratic Characteristics

To achieve the maximum benefits of an ideal bureaucracy, Weber believed that an organization must be characterized by the following:[5]

1. A clear division of labor exists, so that each task to be performed by employees is systematically established and legitimatized by formal recognition as an official duty.
2. The functions within the organization are officially arranged in a hierarchical manner. That is, a chain of command from the top down is established.
3. The actions of employees are governed by rules and procedures which are formally prescribed and which are utilized in a uniform manner in every situation.
4. The officials of the bureaucracy apply the rules and procedures as impersonally as is humanly possible. The "people" element is given consideration after the entity itself.
5. Employment in the bureaucracy is based upon rigid selection criteria which apply uniformly and impersonally to each candidate applying or being considered for a position. The criteria for selection are based upon objective standards for the job which have been established by the officials of the organization.

Classical Principles of Organization

In much the same way that Weber's bureaucratic model of the organization was an attempt to describe the "ideal" organization, the classical theorists sought a set of universal principles that could be used in guiding the design of any organization. The main classical principles that will be described here include: specialization of labor, departmentalization, span of control, equal authority and responsibility, delegation, and unity of command.

Specialization of Labor

The classical theorists (and even before them, the economist Adam Smith) recognized the benefit of permitting each worker to specialize in the performance of a relatively few methods. The benefit is that each specialized worker can then become proficient and efficient in the performance of work. Health services organizations, as we noted in Chapter 1, utilize the talents of a tremendous array of workers—most of whom have developed particular specialties so that they can function in the complex health services organizations. The positive benefits of specialization (increased proficiency and efficiency) are, however, somewhat offset by certain problems. When work becomes excessively specialized, those who perform it often become bored. Sometimes specialists in one area cannot easily communicate with specialists in another area because they develop their own "languages." Finally, when a person becomes a specialist, he or she frequently feels that it is important to protect the boundaries of her or his specialty or profession from encroachment by others.

Departmentalization

A direct outgrowth of having organization participants who are highly specialized is the need to group them together on this basis (usually called the *functional* basis of departmentalization) so that all those performing similar functions are grouped together in a single unit or department. Thus in a hospital, nurses are in the nursing service, pharmacists are in the pharmacy department, and so on. Even within a department, the concept underlying the departmentalization principle can be followed to break the department down into smaller units. For example, a large clinical laboratory (which can be thought of as a functionally specialized department) may have even more functionally specialized and grouped units such as a blood bank, a chemistry section, and a hematology section, to name a few.

The single most important advantage of functional departmentalization is that it incorporates the benefits of specialization. Of course, it carries with it the possible dysfunction sometimes caused by the creation of departmental "empires" that conflict to the point of detracting from the organization's overall performance. Also, the problems of coordination become more complex as departments multiply. We will examine the function of coordination in depth in Chapter 8. The reader should note that this is another example of the interrelatedness of the functions of management: what is done in organizing affects what is done in coordinating.

Span of Control

Span of control may be defined simply as the number of subordinates reporting directly to a superior. The classicists were in general agreement that there should be a limited number of subordinates reporting to a superior. Some of them even went so far as to attach specific numbers to the optimum span. More recent thinking suggests that there is no predetermined number of people that a manager can effectively supervise. It should be noted that the number of relationships existing between a superior and each possible combination of subordinates goes up at a startling rate as the number of subordinates increases. For example, if there are only five subordinates, the number of possible relationships between the superior and some combination of subordinates is 31. If the number of subordinates is doubled to 10, the number of relationships that are possible jumps to 1,023! If follows from this that a manager should be more effective in dealing with a relatively small number of subordinates than with a large number. Several factors enter into the question of span of control. The level in the organization has a great deal to do with determining a suitable span. At the top level five or six immediate subordinates may be all that should exist. At a lower level, where work tends to be more standardized and routinized, fifteen may not be too many. Another factor is the nature of the work being performed. It is easier to supervise ten file clerks than five head nurses. The abilities and availability of managers should also be taken into account. Obviously, the training and personal qualities of some managers permit them to handle more subordinates than others, thus facilitating a broader span. Similarly, the greater the training, capacities, and self-direction of subordinates, the fewer relationships they will need with management and the more subordinates a given manager can handle.

As Massie and Douglas have pointed out, the classical view of span of control refers to concern over the number of people a manager can directly *supervise*. This is not the same thing as the *span of management*, "which refers to the number of people whom one superior can assist, teach, and help reach their objectives—that is, the number who *have access* to the superior."[6] In most cases, the span of management can be larger than the span of control.

Equal Authority and Responsibility

In the view of the classicists, the legitimization of authority at a central source ensures that the superior "has the *right* to command someone else and that the subordinate person has the *duty* to obey the command. This is implied in the notion of official legitimacy, legal in nature rather than social and informal."[7]

The classical principle states that there must be an equal relationship between the responsibilities of a manager and the authority that he or she exercises. Urwick has noted:

> To hold a group or individual accountable for activities of any kind without assigning to him or them the necessary authority to discharge that responsibility is manifestly both unsatisfactory and inequitable. It is of great importance to smooth working that at all levels authority and responsibility should be conterminous and coequal.[8]

The principle of equal authority and responsibility does not provide a formula by which one can equate them. In fact, no sure formula exists. Yet this fact does not negate the basic premise that if one is given a responsibility in the organization, that person must also be given the authority to fulfill it. As has been noted, however, "in many instances health care managers find that their responsibility is indeed greater than their authority. They are charged with the efficient operation of their unit or department but find their hands are tied when it comes to making decisions for straightening out the situation."[9]

Delegation

Another classical principle of organization is based upon the fact that no one person can accomplish or even be directly responsible for the establishment and achievement of all of the objectives of a complex organization. Thus, there must be delegation or assignment of authority and responsibility to others in the organization. If departments and units made up of functionally specialized workers have been created, then they should be delegated the responsibility for performing those functions; they should be delegated the authority (over use of resources for example) necessary to perform them; and, finally, they should be held accountable for performing them. Delegation serves several positive purposes. By delegating those things that can be, managers free up their own time for other matters that cannot be delegated. If delegation is made as far as—but no further than—it should be, then those people in the organization who are best qualified will be responsible for accomplishing the work involved. Finally, subordinates are given the opportunity to reach their maximum level of contribution to the organization when they are delegated responsibility and authority consistent with their abilities.

Unity of Command

This classical principle suggests that the organization is a series of relationships between superiors and subordinates in which each subordinate takes orders from one, and only one, superior. This principle is related to the authority-responsibility principle described above in that the grant of authority and the assignment of responsibility should flow to a subordinate through one immediate superior. If taken to their full limit, these concepts result in a chain of command that flows from the top of the organization to the bottom in a vertical fashion.

If one applies these principles in carrying out the organizing function of management, the result will be an organization designed very much like those reflected in the organization charts of the hospital or the nursing home given in Chapter 1. (Go back and review Figure 1–8 and Figure 1–9.) The organization charts depicting the design of the formal organization in both cases are tangible evidence that these principles are usually followed in designing health services organizations. If the principles are applied to the design of a single department in a health services organization, the results are equally predictable. For example, Figure 5–1 is a partial organization chart that would result from applying these principles to the design of a clinical laboratory department.

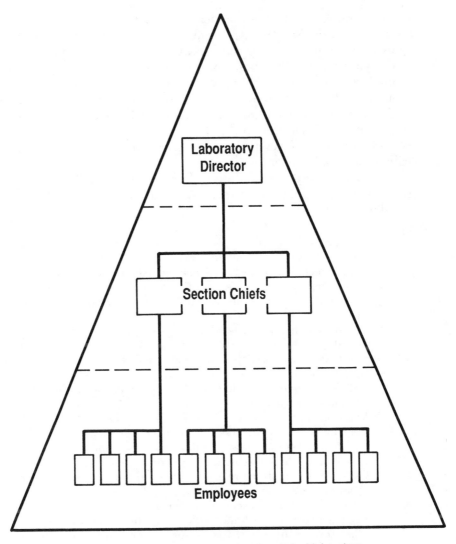

Figure 5–1. Organization chart of a clinical laboratory.

MODERN ORGANIZATION THEORY

The application of the classical principles of organization described above accounts for the structural design of almost all health services organizations—indeed, of almost all formal organizations in the Western world. This does not mean, however, that the organizing function is simply the application of these principles. The classical principles have been criticized on a number of bases. These criticisms have spawned modifications of and alternatives to the classical approach. Beginning in the 1940s and continuing into the 1950s, a number of writers and researchers began to question seriously the classical principles, primarily on the basis of the underlying assumptions held by the classicists about human beings in the workplace. To counter what they saw as an inappropriate view of the human element in the classical approach, these writers and researchers worked to build a better understanding of the role and behavior of people in formal organizations. Since they did not entirely reject the classical approach but sought to resolve what they saw as its main shortcoming, they have been called the *neoclassicists*.

The major criticisms of the classical approach—the ones which the neoclassicists sought to correct—have been summarized by Stoner and Wankel as follows[10]:

1. It neglects the human aspects of organization members, assuming they are motivated only by economic concerns. As educational levels, affluence, and work expectations have risen, this criticism has become more severe.
2. It does not suit rapidly changing and uncertain environments. Formalized bureaucratic organizations have difficulty in changing their established procedures.
3. It assumes that upper-level managers will be respected and obeyed by subordinates because of their superior knowledge and skills. Therefore, they can guide the work of subordinates effectively. But as the organization increases in size, top-level managers lose touch with lower levels. And in periods of rapid technological change, young newcomers frequently have relevant knowledge and skills not possessed by managers above them.
4. As organizational procedures become more formalized and individuals more specialized, means often become confused with ends. Specialists, for example, may concentrate on their own finely tuned goals and forget that their goals are a means for reaching the broader goals of the organization.
5. The bureaucratic structure has also been criticized for encouraging what Victor Thompson calls "bureaupathology."[11] Because managers compete for advancement, are held accountable for mistakes, and direct subordinates who may have superior technical knowledge, they may feel insecure. Thompson believes that bureaucratic structures permit counterproductive personal insecurities to flourish and that some managers try to protect their authority and position by aloof, ritualistic behavior. This is "pathological," according to Thompson, because it can prevent the organization from meeting its goals.

The most basic distinction between the classical and neoclassical approaches to the organizing function was in the assumptions made about the nature of human beings in the workplace. Douglas McGregor (a neoclassicist) has summarized these assumptions in developing what he called *Theory X* assumptions (those held by the classicists) and *Theory Y* assumptions (those held by the neoclassicists). These assumptions can be summarized as follows:[12]

Theory X:

1. The average person has an inherent dislike for work and will avoid it if he or she can.
2. Because of this human characteristic of dislike of work, most people must be coerced, controlled, directed, and threatened with punishment to get them to put forth adequate effort toward the achievement of organization objectives.
3. The average person prefers to be directed, wishes to avoid responsibility, has relatively little ambition, and wants security above all.

Theory Y:

1. The expenditure of physical and mental effort in work is as natural as play or rest.
2. People will exercise self-direction and self-control in an effort to achieve objectives to which they are committed.
3. Commitment to objectives is a function of the rewards associated with their achievement.
4. The average person learns, under proper conditions, not only to accept but to seek responsibility.
5. The capacity to exercise a relatively high degree of imagination, ingenuity, and creativity in the solution of organizational problems is widely, not narrowly, distributed in the population.

As the reader can see, these assumptions are quite different and organizations designed by managers who hold the Theory X assumptions are likely to be quite different from those designed by managers who hold the Theory Y assumptions about human behavior in an organizational setting. The Theory Y assumptions give a more realistic view of human behavior in organizations and, to a large extent, represent the major contribution to our understanding of the organizing function made by the neoclassicists. However, a word of caution about Theory Y is in order. McGregor described the "average" human being. The "average" person is a nonexistent, statistical concept. In the real world, some people fit the Theory X model. McGregor's argument is that the Theory Y assumptions describe a far larger proportion of people than was assumed to be the case by the classicists—but not everyone.

In addition to McGregor, other neoclassicists include Abraham Maslow, whose work is so basic to our understanding of human motivation that we will discuss it at length in Chapter 7, where motivation is one of the main topics. The work of the neoclassical theorists has led to *modern organization theory.* The reader is cautioned that the term *modern theory* does not mean that neoclassical theory is now out of date. As Williams and Huber have stated, modern and neoclassical organization theories "coexist, interact and in places are indistinguishable."[13] It is useful to view modern organization theory as an emerging, though incomplete, transition from the classical and neoclassical approaches. An excellent treatment of evolution and interrelatedness of these theories can be found in Weisbrod's *Productive Workplace: Organizing and Managing for Dignity, Meaning, and Community.*[14]

Distinguishing Features of Modern Theory

Two features distinguish modern organization theory. First is its concentration on the organization as an integrated system in which all of the parts are interrelated. Second, after years of searching by the classicists, and many of the neoclassicists, for the "one best way" to structure organizations, the modern view that the structure of an organization should be contingent upon the particular situation in which it finds itself has emerged. As we noted earlier in this chapter, the most important variables that the design must take into account are the objectives of the organization, the methods that will be used to accomplish them, and the people who will utilize the methods. The manager's job, in the modern contingency approach to organization design, is to develop an effective fit between the organization's structure and these variables.

The typical health services organization is organized along classical lines. There is a high level of division of work (as indicated by a high degree of specialization and subspecialization); there is departmentalization along functional lines, and limited span of control along with delegation of authority and responsibility result in the bureaucratic pyramid (although in hospitals there are the two pyramids of administration and medical staff).

Although the typical health services organization is still organized along classical lines, some are beginning to make changes in view of the criticisms outlined above. A problem of particular severity has been that of designing an organization structure that brings the health professionals more directly into the management and decision making of the organization. An approach that holds great potential in this area is matrix organization. We will describe the development of matrix organization and see how it might be applied in health services organizations.

MATRIX ORGANIZATION

Many types of organizations now utilize *project organization* when management decides to focus a great amount of attention and resources for a given period on a specific project goal. A project "team" of various specialists is put together under the direction of a project manager.

Health services organizations can utilize the project organization concept very easily by superimposing it over their existing functional organization. The result of the superimposition is called *matrix organization*. It provides a horizontal, lateral dimension to the traditional vertical orientation of the functional organization.

Duncan Neuhauser has suggested that hospitals can do this very easily and naturally by establishing patient care teams under the leadership of individual physicians for individual patients.[15] Figure 5–2 illustrates this. The design also shows where the term "matrix" organization comes from. Most hospitals have many characteristics of a matrix design, even if they do not formally call it by this name. Most health professionals, such as nurses, physical therapists, pharmacists, occupational therapists, and social workers, have a formal reporting relationship to their department, but are also accountable to physicians for the care provided to particular patients. Additional information on matrix organization can be found in Ryan's article, "Better Style for Change: Matrix Management."[16]

An important issue in regard to patient care teams is the matter of who really leads them. Johnson and Tingey argue that "although the physician is responsible for the initial formulation of a therapeutic plan (and in that sense,

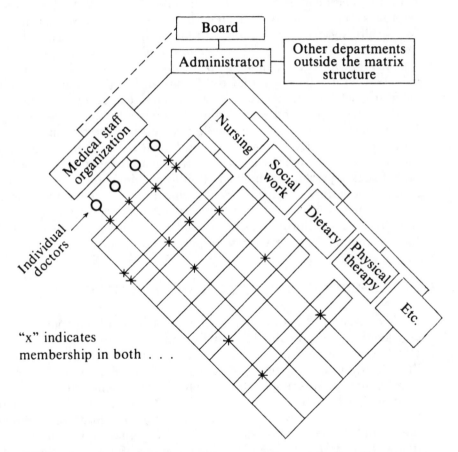

Figure 5–2. The hospital diagrammed as a matrix organization. *(From Neuhauser D: The hospital as a matrix organization, in Kovner AR, Neuhauser D (eds): Health Services Management: Readings and Commentary, ed 2. Ann Arbor, Mich, Health Administration Press, 1983, p 256. Reprinted with permission.)*

provides direction for the patient care team), bringing the plan to actuality is the function of the nurse. The physician simply is not physically present long enough to coordinate the implementation of patient care programs".[17] This point is an important one. It may well be that hospitals that wish to utilize the matrix approach will have to have co-team leaders, a physician and a nurse, for each patient care team. This is a good example of the contingency approach to organization design in that it fits the dictates of the particular situation at hand.

In addition to thinking of patient care teams as a form of matrix organization, in recent years many hospitals have adopted a product–line or program approach to organization. Figure 5–3 illustrates this for a psychiatric hospital.

It should be noted that the matrix organization concept does not do away with the classical organization structure—it simply builds upon it and improves on it. As we pointed out earlier in this chapter, there is no definitive way health services organizations (or any other type of organization) *should* be designed. The technical term, *equifinality*, is very applicable to the organization function. The concept means that similar final results may be achieved with different initial conditions and in different ways. This view suggests that the organization (or a part of it) can accomplish its objectives with varying inputs and with varying internal activities. It suggests also that the manager can use a varying bundle of inputs into the organization, can transform these in a variety of ways, and still achieve satisfactory output. Extending this view even further suggests that the management process is not necessarily one of seeking a rigid optimal solution to problems but rather one of having available a variety of satisfactory solutions to management problems.

The manager who is trying to organize an area of responsibility can draw upon the classical principles of organization, but should also be aware that these principles can, very often, be improved upon.

STAFFING ASPECTS OF THE ORGANIZING FUNCTION

An organization structure can easily be designed on paper. To make the organization come to life it must be staffed. To ensure the organization's effectiveness, it must be staffed with competent people. The process of filling the organization structure with competent people, through selection and development of personnel to fill the roles designed into the structure, is called "staffing." All managers have a responsibility for staffing. When a manager is given responsibility over a particular part of an organization, staffing is one of the central aspects of this responsibility. The organization chart, in conjunction with job descriptions and job specifications, will specify the numbers and types of workers needed to fill the various positions.

The manager will be aided substantially in the staffing process by the services of the personnel department. Usually the personnel department is

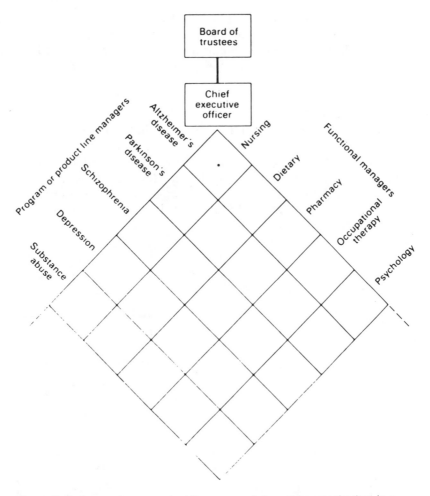

Figure 5–3. A program or product-line approach to matrix organization in a psychiatric hospital. *(From Leatt P, Shortell SM, Kimberly JR: Organization design, in Shortell SM, Kaluzny AD (eds):* Health Care Management: A Text in Organization Theory and Behavior, *ed 2. New York, Wiley, 1988, p 324. Reprinted with permission.)*

attached to the health services organization in a staff capacity. This means that its purpose is to counsel, advise, and provide services to the other departments and units in the organization. It is important to remember, however, that the responsibility for staffing rests with the line managers (i.e., those in charge of departments or units) of the organization. Sometimes, in its eagerness to be of service or as the result of a weak manager's abdication of some responsibility, the personnel department may assume too large a role in the staffing process. This should be guarded against; if the manager permits the personnel department to make staffing decisions for him or her, relationships between manager and employees will sooner or later be weakened.

This is not to say that the personnel department has no importance in the staffing process. Rather, staffing requires a coordinated and balanced effort on the part of the personnel department and the manager. If both realize their responsibilities and carry them out properly, staffing problems can be minimized.

The Staffing Process

Staffing activities result in the appointment of individuals to vacant or newly created organization positions, either by attracting them as candidates for employment from outside the organization or by moving them into the position by promoting or transferring them from within the organization. Successful staffing is a complicated process requiring proper performance of a number of specific steps. Figure 5–4 illustrates these steps and emphasizes their interdependence.

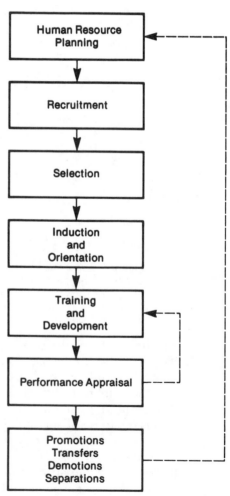

Figure 5–4. The staffing process.

A meaningful treatment of the steps in the staffing process is beyond the scope of this book. It will be useful, however, to describe briefly each step in the staffing process so that the health services manager understands both the importance and the complexity of the staffing process. This description is adapted from Stoner and Wankel.[18]

1. *Human Resource Planning.* Human resource planning is designed to ensure that the personnel needs of the organization will be constantly and appropriately met. Such planning is accomplished through analysis of current and expected skill needs, vacancies, and department expansions and reductions. As a result of this analysis, plans are developed for executing the other steps in the staffing process.
2. *Recruitment.* Recruitment is concerned with developing a pool of job candidates, in line with the human resource plan. The candidates are usually located through newspaper and professional journal advertisements, employment agencies, and visits to college and university campuses.
3. *Selection.* The selection process involves evaluating and choosing among job candidates. Application forms, résumés, interviews, and reference checks are commonly used selection techniques.
4. *Induction and Orientation.* This step is designed to help the selected individuals fit smoothly into the organization. Newcomers are introduced to their colleagues, acquainted with their responsibilities, and informed about the organization's objectives and methods.
5. *Training and Development.* The process of training and development aims at increasing the ability of individuals and groups to contribute to organizational effectiveness. *Training* is designed to improve job skills. For example, employees might be instructed in the proper use of a new piece of equipment or a new patient care procedure. *Development* programs are designed to educate employees beyond the requirements of their present position so that they will be prepared for promotion and able to take a broader view of their roles in the organization.
6. *Performance Appraisal.* This step compares an individual's job performance against standards or objectives developed for the individual's position. If performance is high, the individual is likely to be rewarded (by an increase in salary or a promotion, for example, or by more challenging work assignments). If performance is low, some corrective action (such as additional training) might be arranged to bring the performance back in line with desired standards.
7. *Transfers.* A *transfer* is a shift of a person from one job, organizational level, or location to another. Two common types of transfers are *promotion*—a shift to a higher position in the hierarchy, usually with added salary, status, authority, and opportunity—and *demotion*—a shift to a lower position in the hierarchy.

8. *Separations.* A *separation* may involve resignation, layoff, discharge, or retirement. The type and quantity of separations can provide insights into the effectiveness with which the organization is managed. For example, too many resignations might signify a noncompetitive pay scale; too many discharges might indicate poor selection or training procedures; and too many retirements might show poor management of the age mix among organization members.

SUMMARY

The management function of organizing can be defined as relating people and things to each other in such a way that they are all combined and interrelated into a unit capable of being directed toward organizational objectives. In the complex health services organization, this function grows out of the critically important need for cooperation among the various organizational participants.

There is no definitive theory about the way organizations should be designed. The manager is faced with both classical and modern theories. The main point of this chapter is that there are many components of both classical and modern theories of organizational design that are appropriate to the modern health services organization. Several concepts and principles, beginning with Weber's bureaucratic model and including division of work, unity of command, equal authority and responsibility, limited span of control, and delegation, are applicable to some extent in the modern health services organization. However, it is useful to view the application of these principles from a modern perspective. We have done this by emphasizing the concept of matrix organization, which does not ignore classical structure but builds upon it and improves on it.

An organization, no matter how carefully designed, cannot exist on paper. It must be brought to life by filling the various positions with competent men and women. The staffing process is an integral part of the total management function of organizing.

REFERENCES

1. Williams JC, Huber GP: *Human Behavior in Organizations*, ed. 3 Cincinnati, South-Western Publishing Company, 1986, p 270.
2. Fayol H: *General and Industrial Management*, Storrs, C (trans). London, Sir Isaac Pitman and Sons, Ltd, 1949; Gulick L, Urwick L (eds): *Papers on the Science of Administration*. New York, Institute of Public Administration, 1937; Urwick L: *The Elements of Administration*. New York, Harper & Row Publishers, Inc, 1943; Mooney JD, Reiley AC: *Onward, Industry!* New York, Harper and Brothers, 1931; Mooney JD: *The Principles of Organization*. New York, Harper and Brothers, 1947.

3. Weber M: *The Theory of Social and Economic Organization*, Henderson AM, Parsons T (trans). New York, Oxford University Press, 1947.
4. Blau PM: *Bureaucracy in Modern Society*. Chicago, University of Chicago Press, 1950, p 34.
5. Weber M: The essentials of bureaucratic organization: An ideal-type construction, in Merton RK et al (eds): *A Reader in Bureaucracy*. Glencoe, Ill., The Free Press, 1952, pp 18–27.
6. Massie JL, Douglas J: *Managing: A Contemporary Introduction*, ed 4. Englewood Cliffs, NJ, Prentice-Hall, 1985, p 138.
7. Pfiffner JM, Sherwood FP: *Administrative Organization*. Englewood Cliffs, NJ, Prentice-Hall, 1960, p 75.
8. Urwick: *The Elements of Administration*, p 46.
9. Hodgetts RM, Cascio DM: *Modern Health Care Administration*. New York, Academic Press, 1983, p 143.
10. Stoner JAF, Wankel C: *Management*, ed 3. Englewood Cliffs, NJ, Prentice-Hall, 1986, p 317.
11. Thompson VA: *Modern Organization*. New York, Knopf, 1961, p 152.
12. McGregor D: *The Human Side of Enterprise*. New York, McGraw-Hill, 1960, pp 33–34, 47–48.
13. Williams, Huber: *Human Behavior in Organizations*, p 286.
14. Weisbrod MR: *Productive Workplace: Organizing and Managing for Dignity, Meaning, and Community*. San Francisco, Jossey-Bass Publishers, 1987.
15. Neuhauser D: The hospital as a matrix organization, in Kovner AR, Neuhauser D (eds): *Health Services Management: Readings and Commentary*, ed 2. Ann Arbor, Mich, Health Administration Press, 1983.
16. Ryan JE: Better style for change: Matrix management. *Hospitals*, November 16, 1980, pp 105–108.
17. Johnson GV, Tingey S: Matrix organization: Blueprint of nursing care organization for the 80's. *Hospital and Health Services Administration*, Winter 1976, p 34.
18. Stoner, Wankel: *Management*, pp 319–321.

SIX

The Informal Aspects of Organization

April 30
11:12 A.M.

The medical records administrator at Memorial Hospital picked up the telephone receiver and dialed the secretary on the unit where Luther Fillerey had recently died. When the secretary answered, she heard, "Look, I know I'm supposed to go through the department heads with a request like this but I just don't have the time to wait for them. I've got to get the medical record for Luther J. Fillerey, patient number 3222–004, completed for the president—this lawsuit business, you know. Some of the nurses' notes are not signed, and there are some lab and radiology reports that haven't been placed in the record yet. Can you look after this for me? It's important, and I just don't have the time to go through all the channels."

The secretary replied, "Sure, I'll take care of it. Bring the record with you when we meet for lunch, and I'll get it taken care of this afternoon."

"Great! I'll see you in the cafeteria at noon."

It was 11:16 A.M. as the medical records administrator replaced the phone and thought to herself, "It's so easy to get things done when you are on friendly terms with people. That would have taken a week if I had gone through channels. Especially since those people in the lab can be so uncooperative sometimes. Well, on to other things!"

INTRODUCTION

Existing within the formal organization's pattern of authority-responsibility relationships is another equally important structure—the informal organization. As seen in the previous chapter, the formal organization is a planned structure. It represents the deliberate attempt to establish patterned relationships among participants in the organization. A great deal of management time and effort goes into the establishment and maintenance of the formal organization. These efforts include the development of an organization structure as depicted by the organization chart, job descriptions, formal rules, operating policies, work procedures, control procedures, compensation arrangements, and many other devices used to guide employee behavior. However, as people who have participated in an organization know, there are many interactions between and among members of an organization that are not prescribed by the formal structure. *The relationships and interactions that occur spontaneously out of the activities and interactions of members of the organization, but that are not set forth in the formal structure, make up the informal organization.*

One of the things that distinguish the classical organization theorists from the modern theorists (especially the behaviorists) is that the classical thinkers concentrated on the formal organization and the behaviorists have concentrated primarily on informal relationships. This has led to an artificial division of the two (something that is specifically *not* intended by having separate chapters on the two in this book). The formal and informal organizations coexist and are inseparable. They are totally intermeshed. As pointed out by Blau and Scott[1]:

> It is impossible to understand the nature of a formal organization without investigating the networks of informal relations and the unofficial norms as well as the formal hierarchy of authority and the official body of rules, since the formally instituted and the informally emerging patterns are inextricably intertwined. The distinction between the formal and the informal aspects of organization life is only an analytical one and should not be reified; there is only one actual organization.

NATURE OF THE INFORMAL ORGANIZATION

Real awareness and interest in the informal organization stemmed from the famous Hawthorne studies of the 1930s.[2] These studies showed that informal organization is an integral part of the total work situation. Since the informal organization arises from the *social interaction* of participants in an organization, it has come to be synonymous with small groups and their patterns of behavior. Most of what managers know about the informal organization has come from the work of sociologists and social psychologists. Many of their contributions will be described in this chapter.

The basic distinction between the formal and informal organizations is that the formal organization emphasizes *positions* in terms of authority and functions, whereas the emphasis in informal organization is on *people* and their relationships. It follows that informal organization is not subject to management control in the way that formal organization is.

There are three facts about informal organization that the manager should be keenly aware of from the outset:

1. The informal organization is inevitable. Management can eliminate any aspect of the formal organization because it is created by management. The informal organization is not created by management, and it cannot be cancelled by management. As long as there are people in an organization, there will be an informal organization.

2. Small groups are the central component of the informal organization, and group membership strongly influences the overall behavior and performance of members. Many sociologists now believe that the social unit (group), rather than the individual, is the basic component of the human organization.

3. Informal organization has both positive and negative consequences. We shall examine the advantages and the disadvantages in depth later. To capitalize on the advantages and to minimize the disadvantages, the manager must understand the informal organization, and to do this it is necessary to understand the groups within it.

Why People Form Groups

When one considers why another human being does anything, the obvious starting point is *motivation*. Motivation theory has taught us that humans are basically motivated by things that satisfy their needs. If the formal organization satisfied all the needs of all organizational participants, then there would be no informal organization. Informal groups come into being primarily in response to those needs of its members that cannot be fully met in the context of the formal organization alone. The interpersonal contacts within the small group provide some relief from the boredom, monotony, and pressures of the formal organization. The individual in a group is usually surrounded by others who share similar values, thus reinforcing the individual's own value system. A second reason that people join small groups is the fact that informal status (which may be nothing more than belonging to a distinct little unit that is more or less exclusive) can be accorded by the group. Third, group membership provides a degree of personal security; the group member feels acceptance by peers as an equal. Group membership permits the individual to express views before generally sympathetic listeners. The individual, in the context of the group, gains satisfaction of recognition, participation, and communication needs. The group member may even find an outlet for leadership drives. These important forms of satisfaction are available in the group—usually to a greater degree than the formal organization permits. Another very important reason for group membership is to secure information. The grapevine is a phenomenon familiar to all organizational participants. Technically, it is the informal communication channel of the organization. (Chapter 7 will treat this topic more completely.) Suffice it to say here that informal group membership provides the member an inside track on the flow of informal communication in the organization. The common denominator of all of these reasons for group membership is that they meet specific needs of members that cannot be fully met by the formal organization. Informal groups arise and persist in the organization because they perform desired functions for their members.

Characteristics of Informal Groups

Mondy and colleagues have shown that an informal group, or the entire informal organization, is likely to possess certain identifiable characteristics[3]:

First, its members are joined together to satisfy needs. They may, however, be seeking to satisfy completely different needs. One worker may want to make friends, and another may be seeking advancement. Second, the informal organization is continuously changing. Relationships that exist one day may be gone the next. Third, members of various organizational levels may be involved. The informal organization does not adhere to the boundaries established by the formal one. A manager in one area may have close ties to a worker in another. Fourth, the informal organization is affected by relationships outside the [organizational context]. A top-level manager and a supervisor may associate with each other because they are members of the same golf club. Finally, the informal organization has a pecking order: certain people are assigned greater importance than others by the informal group. Workers who adhere more closely to the group norms tend to be given greater respect.

The first of these reasons has already been touched on. We have seen that the motivation to form these groups is that they provide a mechanism for members to satisfy needs not satisfied by the formal organization structure.

A key element in the functioning of informal groups is leadership, even if it is unofficial. The role of small group leaders has been studied extensively.[4] Some of the general conclusions about them can be summarized as follows:

1. The leadership role is filled by an individual who possesses the attributes that the group members perceive as being critical for satisfying their needs.
2. The leader embodies the values of the group from which he or she emerges. The leader is able to perceive these values, organize them into an intelligible philosophy, and verbalize them to nonmembers.
3. The leader is able to receive and filter communication relevant to the group and effectively communicate the new information to the group. This role can be thought of as an information center.

The informal group leader emerges from within the group because he or she can serve several functions for it. The leader serves not only to initiate action and provide direction but to compromise differences of opinion that exist on group-related matters. Furthermore, the group leader serves to communicate values and feelings to nonmembers. Only as long as the leader is able to perform these functions can the leadership role be maintained.

Another important characteristic of small groups is their tendency to develop a highly complex structure of relationships. In the informal organization, structure is determined by the different status positions that people have. Essentially, there are four status positions:

1. Group leader
2. Member of the primary group
3. Fringe status
4. Out status

Suppose, for example, that we wanted to determine the structure of a group of nine people working in a physical therapy department. These people are located in a close general area much of the time, and there are no artificial barriers, such as walls, to prevent their frequent association with one another. Experience tells us that each person will not associate with each other person with equal frequency. Instead, they will be selective in their association, regularly including some and excluding others.

By sociometric techniques, which may be nothing more than observation, this phenomenon can be measured, and an accurate picture of the nature of the informal organization of these people can be obtained. See Figure 6–1. The solid square in the center represents the leader of the small group. Clustered around the leader are four other members of the primary group. Their association is close and is characterized by intense interaction and communication. The three people in the fringe area are most likely new-comers. They are, in effect, being evaluated by the primary group and may in time become full members. If they are not accepted, they will move to out status. In this case, one person is already in out status. Although a part of the informal organization, this person is not accepted by the members of the primary group. Such status can have profound behavioral effects if the person in the out status wants to belong to the primary group. In some cases, the rejection is mutual or may even be rejection of the group by the person in out status. In these cases, the person in out status may get along quite well without primary group membership.

The informal organization is not limited to group membership. It also exists as people in the formal organization deal with one another in the accomplishment of work within the context of the formal organization. Figure 6–2 indicates the actual contacts between particular people in an organization. Observe that not all contacts go through formal channels; in some cases

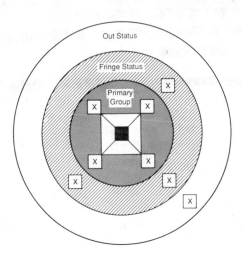

Figure 6–1. A model of informal organization.

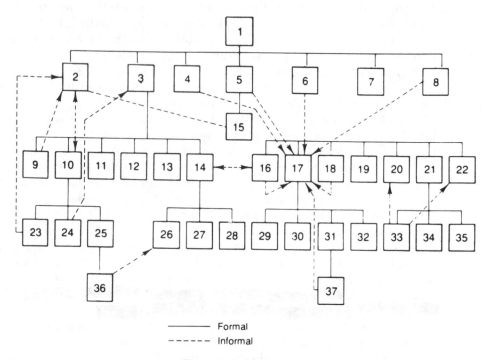

———— Formal

- - - - - Informal

Figure 6–2. A contact chart.

certain levels of the organization are bypassed, and in other cases cross-contact is seen from one chain of command to another. Such charts do not show the reason for the informal relationships, but they do serve the purpose of illustrating the complexity of the informal organization.

A final attribute of the informal group that we should examine is its tendency toward stability. To the manager it may appear that the informal organization resists all change. In truth, the informal organization resists only those changes that are interpreted as threats. It takes a great deal of time to establish the strong interpersonal ties that exist among people in the informal organization. Abrupt acts of management can break these ties instantaneously. For this reason, changes that are seen as a threat to established patterns in the informal organization will be resisted. For example, let us assume that the business office of a large group practice has been functioning for some time with a certain physical layout. The informal groups and relationships that have evolved over time are probably deeply entrenched. The manager may decide, however, to rearrange the layout of the business office in the interest of efficiency. The decision could cause the breakup of the patterns of social relations among the office staff and would quite likely be resisted. In many cases, changes of this type are countered by resistance in the form of complaints, work slowdown, reduction in quality, absenteeism, and so on. If management is to influence the acceptance of such change, it must be aware of and understand the dynamics of the informal organization.

POSITIVE ASPECTS OF THE INFORMAL ORGANIZATION

Complements the Formal Organization

The key benefit of the informal organization is that it blends with the formal organization to generate an operable system for the accomplishment of work. The formal plans and policies of the organization tend to be too inflexible to meet all the needs of a dynamic situation. Thus, the flexible and spontaneous characteristics of the informal organization can be of great advantage if they permit or even encourage deviations in the interest of material contributions toward the organization's objectives.

Dubin was among the first to recognize the necessary complementarity of the formal and informal organization when he stated, "Informal relations in the organization serve to preserve the organization from the self-destruction that would result from literal obedience to the formal policies, rules, regulations, and procedures."[5]

Provides Necessary Social Values and Stability to Work Groups

Turnover may be caused by a poor matching of person and job or by such pragmatic reasons as a better job or a necessary move. However, research has shown that some resignations occur because the new employee is unable to become a primary member of one or more informal groups. Group membership is a basic means by which employees achieve a sense of belonging and security. If an organization is so cold and impersonal that informal, interpersonal contacts are not encouraged or even, in some cases, permitted, then some new employees may seek employment elsewhere. Of course, informal group membership can be carried to such an extreme that the workplace becomes merely a social circle, which results in a detrimental effect on work output. Good management can avoid this extreme and provide an atmosphere where workers, through informal relationships, can meet their human needs of acceptance and gregariousness.

Simplifies the Manager's Job

In a very real sense, the informal organization can make things easier for the manager *if he or she remains in control of the situation.* It has been shown that when informal group support is available to the manager, supervision in a much more general way is possible than when such support is not available. The manager can delegate and decentralize when the informal group is cooperative. Obviously, the converse of this is true. The task of the manager is to understand the informal organization and use it to advantage. As has been stated, awareness of the nature and impact of informal organization often leads to better management decisions. The acceptance of the fact that formal relationships will not permit full accomplishment of organization tasks should stimulate management to seek other means of motivation. Management should seek to improve the knowledge of the nature of the people in general, and their subordinates in particular. They should realize that organization of performance can be affected by the worker's willingness to grant cooperation and enthusiasm. Means other than formal authority must be sought to develop attitudes that support effective performance.[6]

Provides an Additional Channel of Communication

A well-known benefit of the informal organization is that it provides an additional channel of communication for the organization. The grapevine can add to managers' effectiveness if they will study and use it. It can serve to get certain information to employees and can be used to determine employee feelings and attitudes on various issues. The grapevine can cause problems, however, if it is not understood by management. In a very real sense, all of the advantages of the informal organization carry the seeds of trouble. Some of the potential disadvantages are examined in the following section.

NEGATIVE ASPECTS OF THE INFORMAL ORGANIZATION

Anyone who has had to deal with an informal organization realizes that the advantages outlined above are not always realized—indeed, in many cases the disadvantages far outweigh the potential advantages. The formal organization deals with human behavior as we would like it to occur in the organization, while the informal organization deals with human behavior as it actually occurs.

The most clear-cut disadvantage is that in many situations the individuals and groups that comprise the informal organization can and on occasion do work at cross-purposes with the goals and objectives of the formal organization. It is a basic fact of organizational life that what is good for the employee is not always good for the employer, and vice versa. The employee may want to meet the requirements of both the group and the employer, but often these requirements are in conflict. What results is known as *role conflict*.

Suppose we take the situation of the head nurse as an example. On the one hand, management's expectations stress the head nurse's role in the managerial system and the need for decision making and planning and controlling activities in his or her area of responsibility. On the other hand, as a first-line supervisor, the head nurse often has close ties with the nursing personnel in the unit he or she heads. These people are former peers in many cases. Their expectations for the head nurse do not necessarily coincide with those coming down from higher levels of management. Furthermore, he or she has many inputs from other head nurses and his or her own perception of the role to be played. Obviously, it is not possible to satisfy simultaneously the expectations of two or more participants when compliance with one set of expectations precludes compliance with the others.

A good bit of this role conflict can be avoided by recognizing that the more compatible the interests, goals, methods, and evaluation systems of the formal and informal organizations can be made, the more productivity and satisfaction can be expected. However, as has been pointed out, there will always be differences between the formal and informal organizations' expectations of people.[7] It should be noted that even the potentially negative impact of conflict should be weighed against its constructive and positive function in fostering creativity and innovation. A relatively conflict-free organization tends to be static. Thus some conflict should exist as a condition for the generation of fresh ideas.

LIVING WITH THE INFORMAL ORGANIZATION

We have seen that the coexistence of the informal organization within the formal structure is a fact of organizational life. The formal and informal aspects of the organization must be balanced if optimum performance and objective attainment (both for individuals and for the organization) are to be achieved.

If management tries to suppress the informal organization, it creates a destructive situation. The informal organization, in order to protect its members and to make the work situation acceptable in their view, gains strength to counteract autocratic management. The opposing forces clash, and the result is reduced organizational effectiveness. On the other hand, if the formal organization is too weak to accomplish its objectives, the informal organization can grow in strength. This may lead to such undesirable abuses of power as work restriction, insubordination, disloyalty, and other manifestations of a generally anti-institution attitude.

The optimum situation is one in which the formal organization is strong enough to maintain a unified thrust toward attainment of its objectives but at the same time permits a well-developed informal organization to maintain group cohesiveness and teamwork; in other words, the ideal is when the informal organization is strong enough to be a positive force, but not so strong as to dominate the formal organization.

A relationship such as the one described above is, at best, difficult to achieve. There are, however, some steps that can be taken to move the organization in the direction of a properly balanced formal and informal relationship. Among them these two are especially important:

1. Management must understand the informal organization, and its actions must convince employees that it understands and accepts the informal organization. For any action taken by management, it is of

paramount importance to consider the impact on, and the resultant implications for, the informal organization.

2. Management must, to the maximum extent possible, integrate the interests of the informal organization with those of the formal organization. In doing this, management should attempt to keep actions taken through the formal organization from unnecessarily threatening the informal pattern of relationships.

The informal relationships that exist in any organization are very important. They deserve the attention of everyone concerned with the effectiveness of the organization. Recognition of the informal organization reflects the manager's recognition that people in organizations are not mechanistic—they are instead changing, complex, and social beings.

SUMMARY

This chapter addresses the informal aspects of organization and should be viewed as an extension of the previous chapter on the formal aspects of organization. In truth, the formal and informal aspects of the organization do not exist as separate areas of concern for the manager because they are so entwined as to be inseparable.

We have defined the informal organization as those relationships and interactions that occur spontaneously out of the activities of members of the organization, but that are not set forth in the formal structure. The astute manager will recognize three key facts about the informal organization:

1. It is inevitable.
2. Small groups are the heart of the informal organization.
3. The informal organization has both positive and negative consequences.

To understand fully the informal organization, the manager must understand small groups and their behavior patterns. Small groups form in the work setting for several reasons, among them needs of the group members that are not satisfied by the formal organization such as informal status and security, and a means of securing information.

Although the existence of the informal organization presents some problems for the manager, such as the fact that often the informal organization may work at cross-purposes with the formal organization, it does have certain advantages. It can complement the formal organization, especially where too much inflexibility is built into the formal structure. It may provide very important social values and stability to work groups. In fact, it can simplify the managers job *if he or she remains in control of the situation*. The effective manager recognizes the existence of *both* formal and informal aspects of the organization and uses both to advantage.

REFERENCES

1. Blau PM, Scott WR: *Formal Organizations.* San Francisco, Chandler Publishing Co, 1962, p 6.
2. Roethlisberger FJ, Dickson WJ: *Management and the Worker.* Cambridge, Mass: Harvard University Press, 1939.
3. Mondy RW, Sharplin A, Flippo EB: *Management: Concepts and Practices,* ed 4. Boston, Allyn & Bacon, 1988, pp 281–282.
4. Scott WG, Mitchell TR: *Organization Theory.* Homewood, Ill, Richard D Irwin, Inc, 1976, pp 175–182.
5. Dubin R: *Human Relations in Administration.* Englewood Cliffs, NJ: Prentice-Hall, 1951, p 68.
6. Mondy, Sharplin, Flippo: *Management: Concepts and Practices,* pp 286–287.
7. Davis K, Newstrom JW: *Human Behavior at Work: Organizational Behavior,* ed 7. New York, McGraw-Hill, 1985, p 313.

SEVEN
Directing: The Interpersonal Aspect of Management

May 1
3:40 P.M.

The surgeon who had operated on Luther Fillerey caught up with the vice-president for nursing just as she was leaving the hospital to go to a meeting of other local nursing service managers.

"Listen," she said, a little breathless from her long run down the corridor, "I've been meaning to talk to you for some time now about the way your people handled this situation with Luther Fillerey!"

The vice-president for nursing looked at the surgeon, a woman whom she thought was highly skilled as a surgeon but entirely too abrasive in her relationships with other people at Memorial Hospital, and responded, "What do you mean?"

"I mean the Fillereys have been my friends for years, and I left strict orders that if there was *any* change in his condition I was to be called—no matter when!"

The vice-president looked at the surgeon sternly and replied, "Doctor, you know very well that the usual policy is to call the chief resident when a problem occurs after 9 P.M."

"I know that," she retorted, "but I left specific instructions with your head nurse that I was to be called in this case."

The vice-president folded her arms and replied, "I don't know who is at fault here. My nurses always try to carry out doctors' orders for their patients—even when they lie outside the usual hospital policy. I'll look into the matter and get back to you."

"I just want you to know that I'm very disturbed by this incident. If you can't get your nurses to follow directions, you should find some who can!" With that, the surgeon wheeled around and went on to make her afternoon rounds in the hospital.

The vice-president for nursing got into her car and left for the meeting. As she drove she thought, "Somebody should have called her, I suppose. The day shift probably forgot to pass the word along to the night shift people—anyway, it isn't the usual policy to call anyone but the chief resident at that time of night. That delay is going to make me late for my meeting. It's already four o'clock."

INTRODUCTION

At some point in the management process there has to be a means for the manager to indicate to the managed what he or she wants done. Once plans have been made and an organizational structure has been created to put them into effect, a necessary function of management is to stimulate the effort needed to perform the required work. When viewed as parts of the whole management process, planning and organizing can be considered as preparatory managerial functions. As we shall see, the purpose of controlling is to find out whether or not objectives are being met. Thus, directing and coordinating (as we will see in Chapter 8) are the connecting and actuating links between these other functions. The importance of directing is contained in one thought—it is the managerial function that initiates action.

In general, directing means the issuance of orders, assignments, and instructions by the manager that permit subordinates to understand what is expected of them, and the guidance and overseeing of subordinates so that they can contribute effectively and efficiently to the attainment of organization objectives.

In many ways, directing is the most complex of the management functions. This is so mainly because the directing function is the interpersonal aspect of managing. Managers must deal with people as individuals and as group members. They soon learn that people do not automatically take as their own the objectives of the organization.

THE HUMAN FACTOR

Managers have been skilled in using the material factors of production for a long time. A great deal of information and knowledge about how best to utilize material factors has been generated by economists, engineers, and financiers. In contrast, the human factor has been far less well understood and far less effectively utilized as a factor of production. Although much is *not* known, contemporary theory and research have a great deal to say about why people behave the way they do in organizations.

If one analyzes what has been discovered about the nature of human beings, a number of important facts present themselves. Among them are these:

1. *There is no such thing as the average human being.* People differ in terms of basic mental abilities, personality, interests, level of aspiration, energy, education, experience, and so on. From the day of birth, each person is unique. For the rest of a person's life, the people, things, and events with which he or she comes in contact make each

person even more different because they constitute a part of life experience. Attempts to take some kind of arithmetical average of people will fail, and attempts to deal with individuals as if they represented some hypothetical average will fail. Many managers are unsuccessful because they take a standard, across-the-board way of relating to other people in almost every situation. This tendency is exhibited by many managers because it greatly simplifies their job, at least as they view it.

2. *Human beings work to satisfy their own needs.* All normal human behavior is caused by a person's need structure. Workers have a perception of their needs that often differs from what management thinks they have. Furthermore, not all workers perceive their needs in the same way. An even more complex factor is that as people grow older, their perception of their own needs changes. These facts make it very difficult for a manager, especially one who supervises a large number of people, to create an environment in which workers can satisfy their needs. After all, the manager only thinks he or she knows what subordinates' needs are. This is made even more complex by the fact that needs are so different from one worker to another and by the fact that the needs of an individual are constantly changing. Yet the manager must keep in mind that getting a worker to carry out a directive is caused behavior. Since this behavior is caused by the employee's attempt to satisfy some need, the manager has but two ways to get the employee to carry out a directive. He or she can make the employee see that a desired action will increase need fulfillment, or the manager can convince the employee that he or she must carry out the directive to avoid a decrease in need fulfillment.

What this means is that management's ability to direct successfully depends almost entirely on the fact that, from the employee's point of view, management controls some of the means by which employees can meet many of their needs.

We shall return to this matter of need fulfillment in a later section when the topic is motivation, because need satisfaction is at the heart of motivation.

3. *Human beings respond to leadership.* There is a great deal of evidence that this is true. Yet the reasons why it is true are not well understood. It is clear that a leader is followed if she or he can help the followers meet their needs as they see them. It is important for the manager to take advantage of this part of human nature in the workplace. Leadership is not something that can be learned in its entirety. However, certain techniques and procedures have been developed that can assist the manager in the leadership role. Leadership as a part of the directing function of management will be dealt with at length in a later section.

KEYS TO SUCCESSFUL DIRECTING

If one generalization about the directing function can be made, it is this: Success in directing others depends more on the *attitude* of the manager toward the subordinate than on any other single factor. This is true because the manager's attitude toward subordinates dictates the approach taken to directing their activities.

For example, one manager may be convinced that most human beings have an inherent dislike of work and seek to avoid it. Another may believe that they do not inherently dislike work and that they in fact want to work as a part of their basic nature. These opposing attitudes will result in one manager using coercion to get work done while another relies to a larger extent on the workers' own initiative. Most managers probably lie somewhere in between these two attitudes, but the point is that what the manager believes about subordinates affects the methods used in directing them; this in turn determines success in the effort.

Another dichotomous attitude is that some managers feel very strongly that most human beings prefer to be directed; others believe that subordinates want to exercise their own initiative and imagination in seeking creative solutions to work problems. Clearly, these opposing attitudes will yield different styles of management and, in most cases, different results.

Management authorities, in observing such opposing attitudes in managers, have labeled them "traditional" and "modern." The evidence is all around us that most people, given the chance for meaningful work, relish it and seek to exercise initiative, seek responsibility, and seek to display ingenuity and creativity in their approach to work. These concepts have come to be called the modern, or the human-relations, approach to management. Successful directing, based on modern attitudes, depends largely on the maturity of the manager and the subordinates. Often managers are inclined not to relinquish tight control over the activities of their subordinates because they believe that workers lack the maturity for self-control. This position defines maturity in mutually exclusive terms as a state of existence that an employee either does or does not possess. In reality, maturity is more accurately defined as a goal rather than as something static. Maturity is developed, and the rate at which it develops depends on environmental factors that allow and encourage it to grow in the individual.

In applying the modern approach to directing subordinates, the manager's central task is to demonstrate that the subordinate's objectives and the objectives of the health services organization are essentially compatible. While organizational objectives are not identical to those of the individual, the similarity is often greater than some managers assume. Even when the worker's objectives are not identical to those of the health services organization, this does not mean that they must be mutually exclusive.

THE CENTRAL TASK IN DIRECTING: ISSUING ORDERS

No matter what approach managers take to directing subordinates, at some point they have to indicate what they want done. The order is the technical means through which a subordinate understands what is to be done. In health services organizations, as in other organizations, the right to give orders, from a purely legal perspective, stems from a contract involving the services of subordinates. The organization employs the individual to perform certain duties, undertakes to explain what is needed through its managers, and pays the employee for his or her services. The employee undertakes the specified activities and receives remuneration for doing so. This legalistic explanation, however, does not tell the whole story.

Ideally, there should be understanding and acceptance of the order by the subordinate. To facilitate this there are certain characteristics of good orders which managers should be aware of:

1. The order should be clear, concise, and consistent. The purpose is to give sufficient information to ensure understanding.
2. Orders should be based on obvious demands of particular situations. If the order conforms to the requirements of a particular situation, it seems logical to the subordinate and not just an arbitrary whim of the manager.
3. The tone of the order is important. If subordinates are to accept orders fully, they must feel that the manager is doing his or her job by pointing out something that needs to be done and not merely exercising power over the subordinate. The manner in which the manager delivers the order has a great deal to do with its acceptance by the subordinate.
4. Whenever possible, the reason for the order should be given. Subordinates will accept an order more readily if they understand the need for it. There are occasions when lack of information on the part of the manager or scarcity of time prohibits this; however, this should be the exception and not the rule.

DELEGATION AS A MEANS OF DIRECTING

Delegation of authority is a more general form of directing than issuance of orders. In *delegation*, the manager usually gives a subordinate authority to act in a certain area of activity by means of a general statement. Delegation is less exact than an order, since it often merely states that the subordinate is authorized to carry out assigned duties. The degree of detail in a grant of authority is usually determined by how detailed the work assignment is. Delegation is more often the means by which one manager directs the activities of a subordinate manager than the means by which a manager directs a worker. However, in situations involving professionals or highly trained technical people, the manager may use delegation as a means of avoiding too many specific orders.

MOTIVATIONAL ASPECTS OF THE DIRECTING FUNCTION

Picture for a moment a manager and two employees. The manager issues an order to both employees. One employee receives the order and carries it out. He performs the assignment to the best of his ability as soon as his schedule permits. He does not complain that he has been assigned the task unfairly; he questions the assignment only to the point necessary for him to completely understand it, and he uses whatever abilities and skills he has to make certain the assignment is properly carried out. The other employee receives the same order. He complains that the assignment should not be his. He tells the manager that he won't have time to carry out the task anytime soon. After considerable "pushing" by the manager, the employee finally carries out the assignment, but only in a very halfhearted and minimal way. The differences between the two situations, both in the way the assignment is performed and the feelings of the manager as well as the employees, are the differences motivation makes and account for its importance. All other things being equal, we can assume that the first employee is more highly motivated than the second. Perhaps the most difficult task managers in an organization face is that of motivating employees—managerial and nonmanagerial alike—to perform the work assigned to them in a manner that meets or exceeds expected standards.

Many methods have been used to encourage employees to put forth their best efforts. The existence of so many approaches to motivation, along with the fact that they have not been entirely successful, illustrates the complexity of the problem of motivation.

Motivation Defined

Motivation is not a simple concept. The central thread that runs through the current thinking on motivation is that motivated behavior is *goal-directed* behavior. Figure 7–1 illustrates this. The diagram shows that the process begins with a need that must be satisfied by the individual who feels it. This results in activity or behavior that is intended to satisfy the need (goal-directed behavior). It may be blocked, which results in frustration for the individual. The cyclical nature of the motivational process is shown in the diagram by the fact that when a need is satisfied (a goal is achieved), individuals redefine their needs in light of what they have learned; this, added to previously unsatisfied needs, initiates another round of the process. Managers are concerned with motivating workers to achieve higher levels of productivity or quality, but human behavior in general is motivated by this need-satisfying process. Needing power, one person runs for political office;

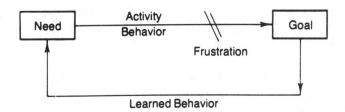

Figure 7–1. The process of motivation.

wanting status, another buys into a certain country club; fearing threats to self-esteem, another person avoids situations in which her or his intellectual competence might be compromised. And so it goes through life and work—a need is felt, goal-directed behavior alleviates the need, and new or redefined needs take its place. Thus *motivation* refers to the way in which needs (urges, aspirations, desires) control, direct, or explain the behavior of human beings.

Motivation Theories

The complexity of motivating human behavior is perhaps best illustrated in the diversity of theoretical underpinnings that have been developed to explain it. Several of the most important theories are described in this section. These theories can be divided into two broad categories: (1) content theories and (2) process theories.[1]

The content theories attempt to identify specifically what it is within the individual or within the individual's environment that initiates, sustains, and eventually terminates behavior. The process theories are intended to explain how behavior is initiated, sustained, or terminated. The process theories define the variables that explain motivated behavior and then try to show how the variables interact with and influence one another to produce certain behavioral patterns within people. The theoretical development of both types of motivation theories is described below.

Content Theories

Classical Theory. The most basic example of a content theory can be traced back to the work of Frederick W. Taylor in the early 1900s.[2] His reasoning was straightforward: Make it possible for people to earn more by producing more and they will. Taylor was able to increase the average number of tons of iron ingots handled by each person per day at Bethlehem Steel from 12½ to 47½. The average cost of handling a ton was reduced from 9.2¢ to 3.9¢, and at the same time, the workers' average daily earnings went from $1.15 to $1.85. These are impressive statistics, and comparable improvements in productivity would be welcomed in any health services organization today. Unfortunately, the straightforward power of money as a motivator is not so great today. In fact, it never fully explained motivation for all people. To believe it did, or does, would mean ignoring all those who have forsaken financial security for the betterment of the human condition. Money can motivate some people to some extent, but it is not the whole answer to motivation—it is not the only need that people work to satisfy.

Hierarchy of Needs. Abraham H. Maslow is the author of one of the most widely known content theories of motivation. Maslow, a psychologist, stressed two fundamental premises in his theory of motivation:

1. People are wanting creatures whose needs depend on what they already have. Only needs not yet satisfied can influence behavior; an adequately fulfilled need is not a motivator.
2. People's needs are arranged in a hierarchy of importance. Once a particular need is fulfilled, another emerges and demands fulfillment.

Maslow's need theory, first publicized in the early 1940s, stressed a hierarchy with certain "higher" needs becoming dominant after other "lower" needs were satisfied.[3] Figure 7–2 illustrates the hierarchy. Each need category is briefly described below:

1. *Physiological needs.* This category consists of the basic survival needs for food, water, sex, and so on.
2. *Safety and security needs.* Once the survival needs are met, attention can be turned to ensuring continued survival by protecting oneself against physical harm and deprivation.

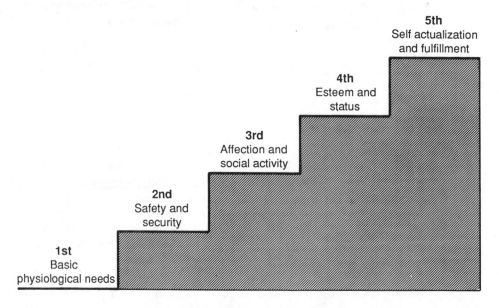

Figure 7–2. Hierarchy of human needs.

3. *Affection and social activity needs.* This third level of needs is related to the social and gregarious nature of humans. This is something of a breaking point in the hierarchy in that it begins to get away from the physical or quasiphysical needs of the first two levels. These needs exhibit themselves in people's need for association or companionship with others, for belonging to groups, and for giving and receiving friendship and affection.

4. *Esteem and status needs.* These are the needs for self-respect or self-esteem, which come from an awareness of one's importance to others. One's status, or level of importance relating to others, is an important need in this category.

5. *Self-actualization needs.* This highest level of human needs includes the need to achieve the fullest development of one's potential. It exhibits itself in the need to be creative and to have the opportunity for self-expression.

These categories of needs can be separated for purposes of analysis or discussion, but in truth they are interacting together within the individual. The lower-level needs are never completely satisfied—they recur from time to time. The needs for esteem and self-actualization are such that once they become important to a person he or she seeks indefinitely for more satisfaction of them. In fact, people can never fully satisfy all of their needs. Even if all those an individual has today could somehow be satisfied, the person would generate new ones.

The need hierarchy model essentially says that satisfied needs are no longer strongly motivating. People are motivated by what they are seeking much more than by what they already have.

Figure 7–3 shows the relative mix of needs for an individual as the person develops over time. It shows progressive changes and the relative importance, number, and variety of needs. The diagram shows that the peak of a "lower"-level need must be passed before a "higher"-level need becomes dominant.

The application of this theory in the workplace necessitates a realization that human beings have a variety of needs that will motivate them. The management task becomes one of developing situations in the workplace that permit employees to satisfy their needs. People, however, are not always able to satisfy their needs, and the manager should know what kinds of behavior this elicits. In general, frustration occurs when people are blocked from meeting one or more of their needs. It is important for the manager to recognize and understand frustration as it affects subordinates as well as the manager. Frustration may occur when an employee has a strong need for esteem but the job situation is such that this need cannot be satisfied. In this instance, it is up to management to restructure the job so that such needs can be met. There is no job in the health services organization that is not in some way related to patient care. The employee who is scrubbing floors may not

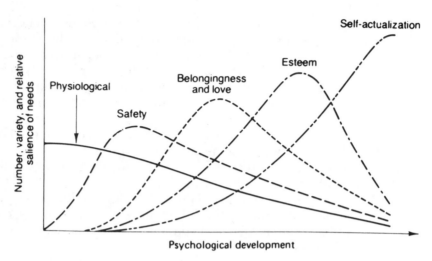

Figure 7–3. Relative importance of needs as motivators. *(From Krech D, Crutchfeld RS, Ballachey EL:* Individual in Society, *New York, McGraw Hill, 1962, p 77. Reprinted with permission.)*

realize this because the relationship has not been explained. When such an employee realizes, however, that the job is not merely scrubbing floors but, rather, helping to provide the sanitary environment so necessary for good patient care, then the chance that needs for feeling self-respect and esteem in work can be fulfilled in the context of this work is greatly improved.

Frustration is a *feeling* rather than a *fact.* It is a feeling that arises when one encounters certain kinds of blocks to fulfilling needs. These feelings arise when the blocks seem insurmountable and when failure to surmount them threatens one's personal well-being. When frustration occurs for an individual, the person gets aggressive. If people are optimistic about their ability to reach a goal (or satisfy a particular need by reaching the goal), they get aggressive outwardly. The obstacle is attacked. If people are pessimistic about their own ability, the aggression is focused inwardly. Self-attack results. This is a key concept because it allows perceptive managers to better understand both themselves and their frustrations and those of their subordinates.

For example, suppose a nurse needs a feeling of accomplishment in his work. For some reason (usually to satisfy some need of her own), a physician constantly belittles the nurse and his work. The result is a block put in the path to his satisfaction of the need for esteem, and frustration follows. The nurse may react by being aggressive to the physician—by sharp words to her or to other people about her. On the other hand, he may attack himself and his own abilities and end up feeling less valuable and capable than he really is.

The manner in which the frustrated person reacts can range from a scowl to an overt physical attack. This reaction is influenced by the personality of the frustrated individual. The reaction may not be chosen consciously but may be the product of unconscious learning. Many of these unconscious reactions to the tensions created by frustrations are called *defense mechanisms*. Some of the most common defense mechanisms seen in the workplace are:

1. *Withdrawal*. One way to avoid frustration is to withdraw or avoid frustrating situations. This may result in physically leaving the scene, but more likely will result in apathy.
2. *Displacement*. Often it is not possible to be aggressive toward the person who is causing the frustration (a superior, for example), so the aggression is directed toward another person—a spouse, a child, or a peer.
3. *Compensation*. Sometimes a person goes overboard in one area of activity to make up for deficiencies in another area.
4. *Repression*. Sometimes a person can repress a frustrating situation by losing awareness of it since it would cause discomfort if allowed to remain at the conscious level of the mind.
5. *Regression*. Some people revert to childlike behavior in their attempt to avoid an unpleasant reality. This often exhibits itself as horseplay in the workplace.
6. *Rationalization*. People are often able to convince themselves that a reason for not being able to satisfy a need lies outside themselves. This is often less ego-deflating than the real reason. For example, a medical technologist may explain poor lab work by blaming obsolete equipment rather than some deficiency of his own.

Two-Factor Theory. Years ago, Herzberg, Mausner, and Snyderman reported research findings suggesting that people have two sets of needs: their need as animals to avoid pain and their needs as humans to grow psychologically. These findings led them to advance a "dual-factor" theory of motivation.[4]

Whereas previous theories of motivation were based on causal inferences of the theories and deduction from their own insights and experience, the dual-factor theory of motivation was inferred from a study of need satisfactions and the reported motivational effects of these satisfactions on 200 engineers and accountants. The subjects were first requested to recall a time when they had felt exceptionally good about their jobs. The investigators sought, by further questioning, to determine the reasons for their feelings of satisfaction and whether these feelings had affected their performance, their personal relationships, and their well-being. Finally, the sequence of events that served to return the workers' attitudes to "normal" was elicited.

In a second set of interviews, the same subjects were asked to describe incidents in which their feelings about their jobs were exceptionally negative—cases in which their negative feelings were related to some event on the job. Herzberg and his associates concluded from their interview findings that job satisfaction consisted of two separate independent dimensions.[5]

1. There are some conditions of the job that, when absent, operate primarily to dissatisfy employees. However, the presence of these conditions does not build strong motivation to contribute more effort. Herzberg called these factors *maintenance* factors, since they are necessary to maintain a reasonable level of satisfaction. He also noted that many of these factors have often been perceived by managers as motivators, but that they are, in fact, more potent as dissatisfiers when they are absent. He concluded that there were 10 maintenance factors, namely:
   (a) organization policy and administration
   (b) technical supervision
   (c) interpersonal relations with supervisor
   (d) interpersonal relations with peers
   (e) interpersonal relations with subordinates
   (f) salary
   (g) job security
   (h) personal life
   (i) work conditions
   (j) status
2. There are other job conditions that, if present, operate to build high levels of motivation and job satisfaction. However, if these conditions are not present, they do not prove highly dissatisfying. Herzberg described 6 of these factors as *motivational* factors or satisfiers:
   (a) achievement
   (b) recognition
   (c) advancement
   (d) the work itself
   (e) the possibility of growth
   (f) responsibility

When the Herzberg and Maslow models are compared, it can be seen that they both emphasize the same set of relationships. Both are content theories in that they look at *what* motivates human behavior. Maslow looked at the human needs of the individual, while Herzberg focused on how the job conditions affect the individual's basic needs. Figure 7–4 illustrates their interrelatedness. The basic advance of Herzberg's theory of motivation over the Maslow model of need-priority is that it shows the distinction between maintenance and motivational factors. Of importance for the application of motivation theory in the workplace, Herzberg's theory also showed that motivation derives mostly from the work itself.

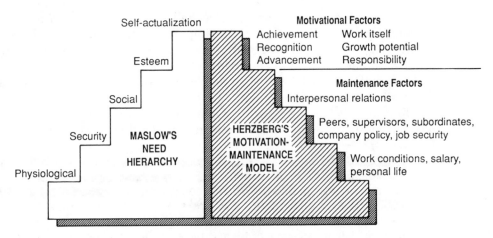

Figure 7–4. A comparison of the Maslow and Herzberg models. *(From Donnelly JH Jr, Gibson JL, Ivancevich JM: Fundamentals of Management, ed 6. Plano, Tex, Business Publications, Inc 1987, p 302. © 1987 by Business Publications, Inc. Reprinted with permission.)*

Process Theory — how

Preference-Expectation Theory. We have looked at three content theories. There are some others such as McClelland's three-needs theory (need for achievement, need for power, and need for affiliation)[6], and B. F. Skinner's reinforcement theory, which holds that human behavior can be explained in terms of previous positive or negative experience with certain behaviors.[7] But they do not add significantly to the basic content theories we have examined.

In recent years, the popular view of motivation theory has been to explain behavior in terms of individuals' preferences and their expectations of achieving their preferences. Victor H. Vroom has developed a motivational model, which enlarges the concepts of Maslow, Herzberg, and others, and which can be considered a process theory.[8] His preference-expectation theory is more an explanation of the motivation phenomenon than it is a description of what motivates (the content theories we have looked at). Vroom's theory explains how two variables (preference and expectation) work to determine motivation. Preference, in Vroom's model, refers to the possible outcomes that an individual might experience as the result of any activity. If, for example, a clerk in the business office files more documents than other clerks, she or he may receive higher pay, get a promotion, impress the supervisor, or make co-workers jealous. Many other outcomes are possible—including the possibility that nothing will happen. The clerk clearly has a preference.

The other part of the Vroom model is expectancy. This is the individual's expectation that a desired outcome will actually happen. An individual with a preference for an outcome must also feel that he or she can achieve the outcome by doing certain things. The importance of the Vroom model is that it emphasizes the fact that motivation as a process is an individual thing. It depends upon the individual having a specific, preferred outcome coupled with a belief or expectation that certain activities or behavior will bring about the desired outcome.

Keith Davis has suggested that managers, by utilizing expectancy theory wisely, can increase employee motivation in a rather straightforward way:[9]

> First, we can increase the positive value of outcomes through such means as better communication about their values and actually increasing them (i.e., increasing rewards). Second, we may increase the expectancy that the work really will lead to the desired outcome, that is, we can strengthen the connection between the work and the outcome. We may do this through improved communication, or we may increase the actual probabilities of the outcome. Since expectancy depends entirely on the employee's view of the connection between work and outcome, often a simple, straightforward incentive is more motivating than a complex one. The complex one may provide so much uncertainty that the employee does not sufficiently connect effort with outcome. The simple incentive, on the other hand, provides a workable path that employees can see and understand; therefore, its expectancy is higher.

Porter and Lawler's Equity Model. A second important process theory based on expectancy theory has been developed by Porter and Lawler.[10] According to their theory, people are motivated by future expectations that are based on previously learned experiences. Figure 7–5 illustrates the Porter-Lawler theory. This model is more comprehensive than Vroom's because it includes the relationship between rewards and performance.

Although the model is straightforward, the reader should be aware that the wavy line between performance and extrinsic rewards denotes that the two are not always directly related and the semi-wavy line between performance and intrinsic rewards indicates that a direct relationship exists only if the job has been designed to allow a person who performs well to actually feel a sense of accomplishment.

Furthermore, the model suggests that performance causes satisfaction. This contrasts with the view held by many authorities that satisfaction causes performance. No one really knows, at this point, which comes first. Obviously, the complexity of human motivation is not fully understood. In addition, this model does not consider whether the cost of high job satisfaction (higher pay, better working conditions, sense of accomplishment from one's job) is offset by higher levels of job performance. As a rule, however, managers in health services organizations must elicit cooperation, performance, and high quality of work effort from their employees. In this setting, the concept of job satisfaction and its linkage to performance is worthy of careful consideration by managers.

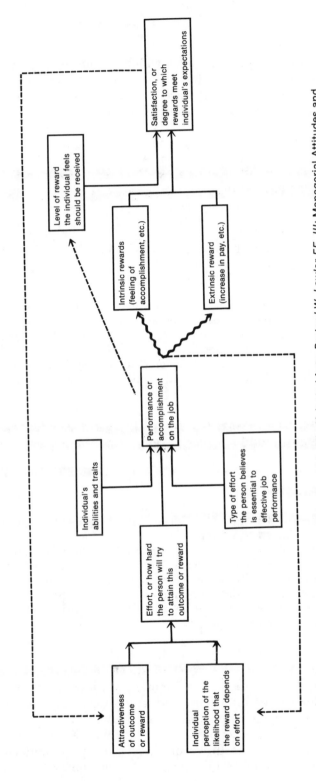

Figure 7–5. Porter and Lawler's Motivational Model. *(Adapted from Porter LW, Lawler EE, III: Managerial Attitudes and Performance. Homewood: Ill, Richard D. Irwin Co, 1968, p 165, in Hodgett RM: Management Theory: Process and Practice. Philadelphia, Saunders, 1975, p 331. Reprinted with permission.)*

The Porter and Lawler model, which is more complex than other theories and models we have examined, is a more complete portrayal of the way motivation occurs in the workplace. It suggests that motivated behavior, while goal-directed, is not a simple cause-and-effect matter.

Equity Theory. A final important contribution to our understanding of motivation comes from the work of J. Stacy Adams in the area of equity theory. This work extends that of Porter and Lawler and addresses the very important issue of whether people in an organization perceive the reward structure as being fair.[11] The essence of equity theory may be expressed as:

$$DØ \frac{\text{Outcomes by a person}}{\text{Inputs by a person}} = \frac{\text{Outcomes by another person}}{\text{Inputs by another person}} ?$$

As Robbins[12] has noted:

> Equity theory recognizes that individuals are concerned not only with the absolute rewards they receive for their efforts, but also with the relationship of these rewards to what others receive. They make judgments concerning the relationship between their inputs and outcomes and the inputs and outcomes of others. Based on one's inputs, such as effort, experience, education, and competence, one compares outcomes such as salary levels, raises, recognition, and other factors.

The implication for managers is that there should be an essential balance between the outcomes/inputs ratio for one person in comparison with another person.

As Koontz and Weihrich point out, some inequity, or perceived inequity, may be tolerated,

> but prolonged feelings of inequity may result in strong reactions to an apparently minor occurrence. For example, an employee being reprimanded for being a few minutes late may get angry and decide to quit the job, not so much because of the reprimand but because of long-standing feelings that the rewards for this person's contributions are inequitable in comparison with others. In another illustration, a person may be very satisfied with a weekly salary of $500 until he or she finds out that another person doing similar work gets $10 more.[13]

We have looked at several motivational theories. All are different, yet all are related. The common thread is that motivated behavior is goal-directed. For Taylor the goal was simple—money. Maslow suggested a range of needs that all human beings share and that exist in a hierarchy. Herzberg's two-factor theory develops a distinction between maintenance factors (necessary to avoid dissatisfaction) and motivational factors (the needs by which workers can be motivated). Vroom suggests a way to understand the motivational process: people's preference as to outcomes for their activities and behavior coupled with their expectation that desired outcomes can be achieved, drive the motivation of human beings. The work of Porter and Lawler and later, Adams, extends the understanding of this basic relationship.

The Application of Motivation Theory

The present state of the art of motivation theory does not permit us to say with unassailable conviction *what* motivates people or *how* the phenomenon takes place. Theories are constantly challenged, expanded, and sometimes discarded. Yet the manager in the health services organization is faced with the day-to-day operational necessity to motivate employees.

There is a growing body of sound empirical evidence that the best motivator is a *challenging job* that allows a feeling of achievement, responsibility, growth, advancement, enjoyment of the work itself, and earned recognition. This is especially true with professional and high-skill-level workers.

A question that concerns many managers is why employees seem so preoccupied with concerns about money and factors that are peripheral to the job (including such things as rules, titles, and their physical surroundings) if these are not the things that really motivate them. The answer is that these are tangible things that easily occur to all of us. The higher-order psychological and sociological needs that people have are not as readily understood by managers or their subordinates. Workers focus on those things that are obvious, when in truth there are more subtle needs that they are often unable to understand or verbalize. One of the great challenges in motivation is developing in managers the ability to help their subordinates really understand their needs and to help satisfy them within the organization. This is a tremendously complex task for the manager in view of the fact that each employee has a different set of needs and that the needs of each individual are constantly changing.

Even in view of the difficulties associated with motivation, there are some things managers can do to facilitate motivation of their subordinates:

1. *Determine clearly the objectives and purposes of the work to be done.* To motivate, one must first know what he or she is trying to motivate someone to do. This sounds simple, but it is a step that is often overlooked by managers.

2. *The manager must empathize with subordinates.* The manager must see a situation as the employee sees it and feel about it as the employee feels about it. Unless the manager does this, motivation efforts are going to remain chance affairs probably based on money, since that is the traditional motivator. A significant part of following through this step is to try to help employees fully understand their needs and wants.

3. *The manager must communicate with employees.* The manager may have determined the best motivators to use with a particular employee

or group of employees, but unless an understanding of what is being done can be communicated to the employee, the employee will not be motivated. Too often, bright managers who develop excellent ideas are unable to get them across. Managers who are certain that they are communicating full understanding to employees should reconsider, because communicating effectively is among the most difficult of all management tasks.

4. *The manager must integrate the needs and wants of the employee with the interests of the health services organization.* The organization, as an enterprise, has certain goals and objectives. Employees have their own objectives as determined by their needs. These objectives are not the same. The degree of success of the manager will be largely determined by how well he or she can integrate the objectives of the employee with those of the organization.

5. *The manager must remove obstructions between the employee and the work to be done.* Effective motivation cannot occur until such obstructions as lack of training, poor equipment and facilities, and working conditions that make it difficult for employees to do their work have been removed.

6. *The manager must develop teamwork among subordinates.* This is done by integrating each employee's need satisfaction with that of the other employees so that there is a coordinated group effort. This means that it may not be possible to do things that the manager has decided will motivate a certain employee if the effect on several other employees will be negative. Managers must think of their employees as a group and do what is best for the entire group. However, through careful thought and planning, the manager can do a great deal of individual employee motivation, which will make the group as a whole more effective.

A final point about motivation of health professionals pertains to the role of the intrinsic rewards inherent in working in a helping profession. It is often argued that professionals who are involved in helping sick people get better obtain such intrinsic rewards from this that they are inherently motivated to perform high-quality work. Often, this is true for many health professionals. Managers in health services organizations, however, should not be naively seduced into thinking that these considerations alone will keep health professionals highly motivated. As has been pointed out[14]:

> Social comparisons, for example, will be made. And if a group of health care employees feels that another institution can pay them at a rate closer to what they feel they deserve, turnover to the new setting may occur. Twenty years ago the words "unionization" and the "health care employee" would never be uttered in the same context. Today, nurses participate in collective bargaining, health care workers go on strike over pay, and medical residents engage in work slowdowns over working conditions. Equity considerations

and extrinsic rewards can make a difference in influencing the motivational levels of professionals as well as nonprofessionals. Effective health care managers need to consider these rewards in addition to the inherently motivating ideals and values professionals and nonprofessionals hold.

LEADERSHIP AS A PART OF THE DIRECTING FUNCTION

Leadership is a basic and integral part of management. Yet it is an ephemeral and elusive concept. It can be defined, at least in the context of the way it functions in health services organizations, as *the accomplishment of organizational objectives as the result of interpersonal relationships between the leader and those he or she leads.* In some ways this definition is similar to the definition of management itself. The two concepts, however, are not really the same. A manager must plan and organize, but a leader must simply get others to follow. The fact that a leader can get others to follow is no guarantee that the leader will be a good manager. Strong leaders who are weak in planning or some other managerial activity may be able to get people going, but they may not take them in directions that serve the organization's objectives. So good leadership ability does not mean the same thing as good managerial ability. It is true, however, that leadership ability is of great value to a manager and that usually a good manager possesses leadership ability. The point is that they are not the same thing.

The Nature of Leadership

Leadership is the ability to inspire and influence others to contribute to the attainment of objectives. This is obviously necessary for getting work done through and by others—which is the manager's task. Traditionally, success in leadership was thought to be dependent on personal traits of the leader. More recently, it has been shown that successful leadership is the result of the interaction between leaders and their subordinates in a particular organizational situation. The different concepts of leadership that have been developed focus around these two broad theoretical approaches: (1) the trait theory and (2) the situational theory.

Until the middle 1940s, most theories of leadership centered around traits possessed by successful leaders. The traits thought to be necessary included such things as objectivity, judgment, initiative, dependability, decisiveness, honesty, drive, and so on. For several reasons, it is not possible to explain leadership fully in terms of personal traits. The chief reason is that the search of social scientists for universal traits in leaders has been unsuccessful. It has not been possible so far to isolate and identify specific traits that are common to all leaders. Furthermore, the trait theory fails to consider the influence of situational factors in leadership. Personal traits are only one part of the whole environment of leadership. Though a certain trait exists, it will not become active until a certain group in a certain situation calls for it. This means that there is no sure connection between traits and leadership acts.

For these reasons, as well as others, the more modern theories of leadership take the situationist approach and emphasize the existence of leadership roles and skills that are evoked by situations or contexts. Of course, a purely situational view of leadership fails to take into account that leadership is a complex process in which the traits of the leader do play a part.

What these considerations mean is that both the trait and the situational theories have added to our understanding of leadership, although neither has fully explained it. It is clear that leadership ability is influenced by personal traits of the leader, but successful leadership also depends upon the followers, the goals and objectives of all concerned, and the environment in which leadership is practiced. The conclusion to be drawn from this is that a single pattern of leadership behavior used without discretion is not likely to be successful in a wide variety of managerial situations. Thus the successful leader is not a blind follower of particular leadership methods; the effective leader chooses the method considered most appropriate for a given situation. The choice of method is made by considering the overall situation, especially the people to be led and the effect the leader's actions will have on them. While it is true that no single pattern of leadership behavior will work in every situation, managers should develop a style that provides them an overall framework in which to practice leadership.

Leadership Style

A number of styles of leadership have been identified. As usual, those that occupy extreme positions have received the most attention. For example, most authorities dichotomize leadership styles as either autocratic or democratic. They may use different terms such as "participative leadership" or the "human-relations approach to leadership" to describe democratic leadership and the "scientific-management approach to leadership" to describe autocratic leadership, but the idea is the same. The danger in dichotomizing leadership styles in this way is that we build up stereotypes of each style. These stereotypes mainly involve the attitude of the leader to the subordinates. But as we have seen, leadership involves much more than the kind of interpersonal relationship existing between leader and subordinate. With so many factors involved, it seems highly unlikely that leadership styles can be realistically classified into one of two classifications: autocratic or democratic. Instead, the relationship between leader and subordinate follows a continuum of leadership behavior, as seen in Figure 7–6. Let's consider each of these seven gradations of leadership behavior[15]:

1. *Manager makes decision and announces it.* This form of leadership represents the most autocratic form (i.e., there is no chance for subordinates to express their thoughts either in the formulation or the solution of the problem.) The superior formulates the problem, solves it, and announces his or her decision. Coercion, to ensure the execution of the decision, is not necessarily implied, since subordinates may be willing to follow such directions.

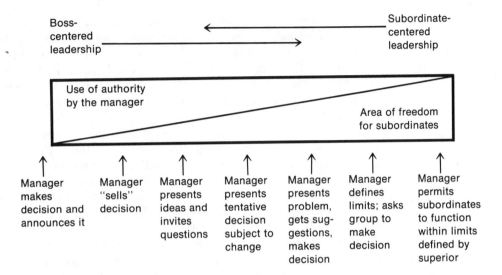

Figure 7–6. Continuum of leadership behavior. *(From Tannenbaum R, Schmidt WH: How to choose a leadership pattern.* Harvard Business Review *34(March-April 1958), p 96. Copyright © 1958 by the president and Fellows of Harvard College; reprinted with permission.)*

2. *Manager "sells" decision.* At this stage the manager recognizes the feelings of subordinates and the possibility that there might be resistance to his or her decision. Consequently, the manager/leader attempts to persuade subordinates to recognize the merits of the decision. However, the manager is still in control of all phases of the decision-making process.

3. *Manager presents ideas and invites questions.* The third form of leadership behavior marks the beginning of a degree of participation on the part of subordinates—at least they are being asked to express their ideas. However, the manager has already made the decision. Nonetheless, the presentation of the manager's ideas to subordinates with the opportunity to express themselves opens up the possibility that the decision may be modified.

4. *Manager presents a tentative decision subject to change.* Here, at the midpoint of the range of leadership styles, there is definite participation on the part of subordinates in shaping a final decision. Although the manager's decision is tentative, he or she still defines the problem and works out the initial solution.

5. *Manager presents problem, gets suggestions, makes decision.* This is the first time the manager comes to the group without having at least a tentative solution to the problem; however, the manager still defines the problem in general terms. Consultation with the group prior to making a tentative decision increases the number of possible solutions.

6. *Manager defines limits, asks group to make decision.* Up to this point the decision is made by the manager with varying degrees of participation on the part of subordinates in influencing the decision; this is the first time that the group makes the decision. However, the manager still states the problem and the limits within which the decision must be made. Usually these limits are expressed in terms of either cost or time, or both.

7. *Manager permits subordinates to function within limits defined by superior.* The last stage of managerial behavior on the scale represents the maximum degree of subordinate participation within formal organizations. Managers, who are also usually subordinates, are limited in the extent to which they may permit participation by the limits of authority granted to them. The greatest degree of subordinate participation is possible within the framework of a functional-teamwork or task-force type of operation. Even here, the objectives of the organization are stated by higher authority, but subordinates may define and solve problems consistent with the attainment of the objectives of the health services organization.

Selecting An Appropriate Leadership Style

The continuum of leadership styles, therefore, ranges from the completely authoritarian situation with no subordinate participation to a maximum degree of democratic leadership, enabling the subordinate to participate in all phases of the decision-making process. This concept is a realistic view of the leadership styles available to the manager. The problem then becomes one of selecting the style that is most appropriate.

A number of considerations must be taken into account when selecting one's own style. The following discussion will examine three of the most important considerations and should serve to illustrate that the best leadership style depends on a number of factors, and the style that is best in one situation may not be best in another.

The Organizational Environment. Generally, as an organization becomes larger and more complex, leadership styles become more authoritarian in nature. There is a positive relationship, evidenced by the presence of organizational charts, job descriptions, and other means of formal control, between the size of organizations and the formalization of organization structure and relationships. Larger organizations also tend to rely more heavily upon written rather than oral communications, a condition that tends to restrict leadership to more formal, authoritarian styles. Obviously, the structure of an organization provides the technical apparatus through which leadership is made effective or ineffective and thereby has a great deal to do with leadership style.

In organizations such as those delivering complex health services, a great many departments and work units must work cooperatively in meeting their objective of providing high-quality care. This requires a high degree of interaction among members of the organization (both among various departments and within individual departments). Managers in these organizations should, therefore, use leadership styles of a more participative, informal nature whenever possible.

The Personalities of Organization Members. It has been shown in a number of studies that leadership styles are directly affected by the personalities and expectations of subordinates. Subordinates who do not expect participation and who are dependent upon others for motivation react best to authoritarian styles of leadership; those who expect participation and are motivated largely from within react best to participative or democratic leadership styles. Clearly, subordinates like nurses and technologists or other highly trained and professionalized health workers generally fit in the latter category.

The Congruence of Objectives. When the objectives of the organization and those of its members are congruent, participative leadership practiced in a less formal structure is appropriate; but when organizational objectives and members' objectives are divergent, greater reliance must be placed upon authoritative leadership and a more formal organization structure. In highly professionalized organizations such as those providing health services there is much more congruence of objectives than in a manufacturing enterprise or a bank, for example. This means that, once again, the less formal participative style of leadership will usually be best.

These three considerations emphasize that there is no single successful style of leadership. Many factors contribute to its effectiveness. Personalities and expectations are important as are the situational or environmental factors. Of greatest importance, however, is the *attitude* of the leader, for he or she brings to the position a definite concept of the role of the leader. If a manager's leadership style is going to be effective, the manager must be able to assess accurately the potentials of the situation and the capabilities and needs of the subordinates and choose a style accordingly.

Cultivating Leadership Attitudes

Since it is clear that attitudes of the leader are very important to successful leadership, the interpersonal relationships between leader and followers can be improved if the leader cultivates certain attitudes. Successful leaders realize that they get their job done through people and therefore try to develop social understanding and skills. They develop a healthy respect for people, if for no other reason than that their success as leaders depends on the cooperation of people. They approach problems in terms of the people involved even more than in terms of the technical aspects involved. There are two especially important attitudinal areas that the manager should try to cultivate: empathy and objectivity.

Empathy, in this context, means the ability to place oneself in the position of another, simulating that person's feelings, prejudices, and values. The manager without empathy for subordinates assumes that the subordinates have the same objectives, ambitions, values, and so on as the manager. Almost invariably this assumption is wrong. As managers contemplate their subordinates in an attempt to understand their feelings and attitudes, they may be severely handicapped. Outside of their work, managers know very little about their subordinates—their personal relationships, economic and health conditions, ambitions, loyalties, and so on. Placing oneself in the position of subordinates is indeed difficult. Yet a real and conscientious effort to understand a subordinate is much better than no effort at all. The simple act of managers asking themselves how they would react if they were the subordinate is an attempt to learn; with practice it will become a valuable skill.

Objectivity is an equally important attitude for the manager. Managers should try to observe and evaluate the causes of events unemotionally. This is difficult because managers must depend heavily on subordinates, which often leads them to become emotional about them. It is very important, however, to evaluate from a distance, to be able to determine the real causes of events, and then to take intelligent steps to correct or to encourage, as the case demands.

Obviously, the manager must walk a tightrope between empathy and objectivity. Empathy requires an attitude opposite to the remoteness and unemotional analysis necessary for objectivity. A workable balance between empathy and objectivity is difficult to achieve, but such a balance is essential to effective leadership.

COMMUNICATIONS ASPECTS OF THE DIRECTING FUNCTION

We have seen that the exercise of leadership in the directing function *and* a thorough understanding of the way human motivation is intertwined with directing are both important. Yet no amount of expertise in these areas will suffice unless the manager is effective at communicating. In a very real sense, communicating is the key to directing. Unless what is to be done, how it is to be done, by whom it is to be done, and why it is to be done can all be effectively communicated, the chances of adequately carrying out the directing function are greatly reduced. Communicating depends upon formally establishing channels up and down the organization and then seeing that they work. This is a very complex and very important task.

Communication in highly complex health services organizations is a multidirectional process requiring movement downward, upward, and in all directions. It is a process of people relating to one another. As people relate to one another in doing work and in solving problems, they communicate facts, ideas, feelings, and attitudes. If this communication is adequate, the work gets done more effectively, and the problems are solved more efficiently. In an organized effort of any kind, communication is essential for people to work together because it permits them to influence and to react to one another.

Communication is vital to the directing function of management. But because of the relationship of directing to the other management functions, communication is important to them as well. One way to visualize this importance is to view the manager on one side of a barrier and the work group on the other. Communication is the means the manager has of breaking through the barrier to attain work group productivity. Figure 7–7 illustrates this.

If managers can communicate, then their efforts to perform the functions of management can be successful. If they cannot penetrate the barrier between manager and work group, then the functions cannot be effectively performed.

For a function so vital to managerial success, communication receives all too little attention by managers. As part of a larger study conducted by the author, the communication between superiors and subordinates in 17 large general hospitals was measured. The measurement was based on the degree of agreement on five basic aspects of the subordinate's function. The assumption was that if there was successful communication about these factors, then there should be a high level of agreement about them. Table 7–1 contains the results of this study. As can be seen, there is poor agreement on such things as future changes in the subordinates' jobs and the obstacles in the way of the subordinates' performance of their jobs. This is empirical evidence of the extent of communication problems that exist in hospitals. It is reasonable to assume that similar results would be found in other types of health services organizations.

Communication Defined

By definition, *communication is the passing of information and understanding from a sender to a receiver.* Clearly, this definition does not restrict the concept to words alone, either written or spoken. It includes all methods by which meaning is conveyed from one person to another. Even silence can convey meaning and must be considered part of communicating.

A key point in this definition is that conveyed by the term "understanding." A sender will want the receiver to understand what was sent, which means that the sender wants the receiver to interpret the message exactly as the sender intended. Unfortunately, communication seldom results in complete understanding. This is true because there are so many factors that can prevent understanding. Many of these will be discussed as we continue. It is

Figure 7–7. Relationship of communication to management.

TABLE 7–1. PERCENTAGE DISTRIBUTIONS OF RATINGS ASSIGNED TO SUPERIOR-SUBORDINATE PAIRS ON FIVE BASIC AREAS OF THE SUBORDINATE'S JOB

	0 Almost no agreement on topics	1 Agreement on less than half the topics	2 Agreement on about half the topics	3 Agreement on more than half the topics	4 Agreement on all or almost all the topics
Methods of upward communication	12.5	0	6.3	12.5	68.7
Job duties	0	0	0	31.3	68.7
Job requirements (Subordinate's qualifications)	6.3	0	6.3	31.3	56.1
Future changes in Subordinate's job	75.0	0	18.7	0	6.3
Obstacles in way of subordinate's performance	43.7	18.7	12.5	12.5	12.5

important for managers to realize that they can make others hear them, but they cannot *make* them understand.

The communication process can be diagrammed as seen in Figure 7–8. When communication is two-way (i.e., when there is an effective feedback), the chances that understanding will be transmitted are greatly enhanced. This is true because there is opportunity for the receiver to ask questions, seek additional information, and generally be assured that he or she understands the message. It also provides the sender a means of judging whether the message has been received and understood or not.

A number of barriers to communication exist in health services organizations. These barriers or filters to communication can be broken down into (1) environmental barriers and (2) personal barriers. The environmental barriers are those things that minimize the opportunities for communication to occur. These include, among other things, poor means of communication and time constraints that prevent the opportunity to communicate. They are relatively easy to remove once it is known that they exist.

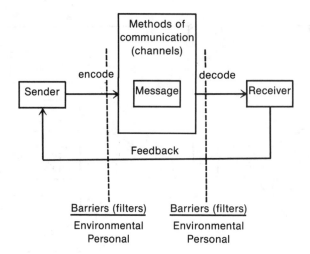

Figure 7–8. The communication process. *(From Rakich JS, Longest BB Jr, Darr K:* Managing Health Services Organizations, *ed 2. Philadelphia, Saunders, 1985, p 376. Reprinted with permission.)*

A more difficult set of barriers are the personal barriers. These usually arise from perceptual differences of persons in communicating relationships. Many of the problems are the result of attitudes and beliefs held by the sender or receiver. For example, senders determine what will be communicated and how it will be phrased according to their perceptions of themselves (their self-image), the image of the receiver, their concept of their own roles in the organization, and the expected feedback and reactions to the communication.

Figure 7–9 points out some of the personal barriers that exist in a situation where communication is taking place. Obviously, severe distortions of the message are possible as a result of personal, often psychological, barriers.

The Importance of Two-Way Communication

When a sender sends a message to a receiver who listens and then sends meaningful feedback to the sender, who also listens carefully, there is effective two-way communication. This is important for the manager because good two-way communication is an absolute necessity for good human relations and effectively carrying out the directing function of management. Furthermore, it greatly enhances the likelihood that directives from the manager will be completely understood. There have been a number of studies that have demonstrated that the accuracy of work and, almost as importantly, the confidence in the accuracy of their work by employees are improved where effective two-way communication is practiced between managers and workers. Listening is crucial to effective two-way communication. Unfortunately, many managers are not good listeners. Figure 7–10 contains helpful suggestions for improving listening skills.

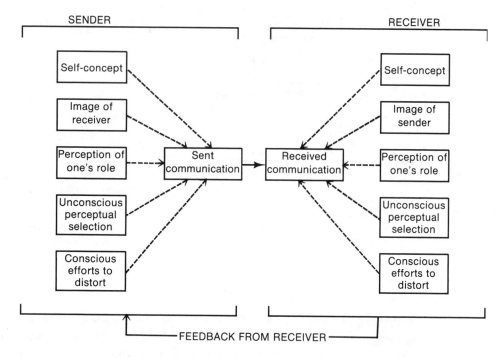

Figure 7–9. Personal barriers to effective communication.

Oral Versus Written Communication

Communication flows in any direction via oral or written mechanisms. There are advantages and disadvantages to both. The directness of oral communications is unsurpassed. It is often face-to-face, which gives the communicators a chance to appraise the degree of understanding achieved, to ask questions, and to clarify meanings. Of course, oral communication is limited to those situations where time and the nature of the message permit direct contact. A further disadvantage is that perception of the spoken word is usually less accurate than perception of the written word.

There are some communications that must be made relatively permanent. These include reports, research information, policies, rules, and agreements. Written communications usually have the advantage of being more carefully thought through than oral communications, and the message can be checked for accuracy before it is sent. With written communications, the sender and receiver do not have to have time to communicate simultaneously. This is important in a busy health services organization. On the other hand, there is the problem of keeping written communications up to date and the impossibility of always clarifying and elaborating meaning at the time the message is sent. There is also the problem of making certain that the receiver has read the written message.

1. **Stop talking!**
   You cannot listen if you are talking.
   Polonius *(Hamlet):* "Give every man thine ear, but few thy voice."

2. **Put the talker at ease.**
   Help a person feel free to talk.
   This is often called a permissive environment.

3. **Show a talker that you want to listen.**
   Look and act interested. Do not read your mail while someone talks.
   Listen to understand rather than to oppose.

4. **Remove distractions.**
   Don't doodle, tap, or shuffle papers.
   Will it be quieter if you shut the door?

5. **Empathize with talkers.**
   Try to help yourself see the other person's point of view.

6. **Be patient.**
   Allow plenty of time. Do not interrupt a talker.
   Don't start for the door or walk away.

7. **Hold your temper.**
   An angry person takes the wrong meaning from words.

8. **Go easy on argument and criticism.**
   These put people on the defensive, and they may "clam up" or become angry.
   Do not argue: Even if you win, you lose.

9. **Ask questions.**
   This encourages a talker and shows that you are listening.
   It helps to develop points further.

10. **Stop talking!**
    This is first and last, because all other guides depend on it.
    You cannot do an effective listening job while you are talking.

- Nature gave people two ears but only one tongue, which is a gentle hint that they should listen more than they talk.

- Listening requires two ears, one for meaning and one for feeling.

- Decision makers who do not listen have less information for making sound decisions.

Figure 7–10. Suggestions for effective listening. *(From Davis K, Newstrom JW: Human Behavior at Work: Organizational Behavior, ed 7. New York, McGraw-Hill, 1985, p 438. Reprinted with permission.)*

One of the keys to good communication is the ability of the manager to exercise judgment in seeking a relative balance between the use of written and oral communications. Selection of which method to use should be based on the relative success of the two methods in a given situation.

A great deal of written communication is in the form of reports that contain historical, current, or forecast information. Figure 7–11 illustrates the important role of written reports in health services organizations.

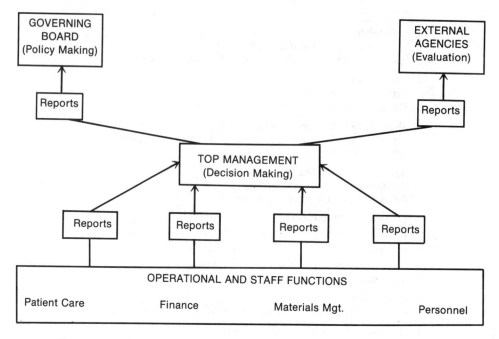

Figure 7–11. Functions of reports in the modern health services organization.

Informal Communication

Coexisting with the communication flows of formal organization is an informal communication flow commonly known as the grapevine. This term, by the way, arose during the Civil War when telegraph lines were strung between trees much like a grapevine. The messages transmitted over these flimsy lines were often garbled. As a result, any rumor was said to come from the grapevine.[16]

The informal communication flows in an organization are as natural as the patterns of social interaction that develop. Like the informal organization, the informal communication flows coexist with the formal patterns established by management. The manager must realize that, good or bad, the grapevine is a fact of organizational life. Regardless of the grapevine's net effects, it cannot be done away with, so the organization needs to adjust to it. As has been noted[17]:

> The development of grapevines is inevitable. Although grapevines are neither good nor bad in themselves, the messages they carry are subject to distortion as messages transmitted from one human link to another become progressively more garbled. Their content is misinterpreted, abbreviated, embellished, and selectively transmitted in terms of what the sender believes the receiver wants or needs to know. Since the original message may be only partially true, it is not surprising that the grapevine is sometimes referred to as a rumor mill.

The grapevine is an undependable means of communication. In a given instance, many employees may be bypassed altogether. The grapevine commonly reinforces messages which are transmitted through formal announcements, bulletins, memos, newsletters, and other formal channels. Since the truth of its messages is highly correlated with the willingness of management to communicate openly and effectively through other means, the best way to guarantee the relative accuracy of the grapevine is to provide reliable information sources against which its messages can easily be checked.

Opinions about the grapevine vary. Miner, for example, has said "there is very little that can be done to utilize the grapevine purposefully as a means of goal attainment. As a result, rumors probably do at least as much to subvert organizational goals as to foster them. They may well stir up dissension. They are contrary to fact."[18]

However, other authorities suggest that the informal communication flows are useful to the organization if properly managed. For downward flows, they tend to be much faster than the formal system; for upward and horizontal flows, they are essential. In health services organizations, much of the coordination that occurs between units in the organization comes about through the informal give and take of information exchange. For upward flow, informal communication can be a rich source of information about the performance, ideas, feelings, and attitudes of people in the organization. Because of its potential usefulness, and because of its pervasive existence, managers should try to understand the informal communication flow and use it to advantage.

As Davis and Newstrom have suggested[19]:

Managers occasionally get the impression that the grapevine operates like a long chain in which A tells B, who tells C, who then tells D, and so on, until twenty persons later, Y gets the information—very late and very incorrect. Sometimes the grapevine may operate this way, but it generally follows a different pattern, A tells three or four others [Employee B, R, and F, as shown in Fig. 7–12]. Only one or two of these receivers will then pass on the information, and they will usually tell more than one person. Then as the information becomes older and the proportion of those knowing it gets larger, it gradually dies out because those who receive it do not repeat it. This network is a "cluster chain," because each link in the chain tends to inform a cluster of other people instead of only one person.

In essence, the informal communication flow is present in every organization, it has good and bad potential for organizational effectiveness, and part of the manager's job is to use it to advantage in achieving organization objectives.

Suggestions for Improving Organizational Communications

Although they were posited many years ago, the following are ten suggestions that can help any manager improve his or her communication skills[20]:

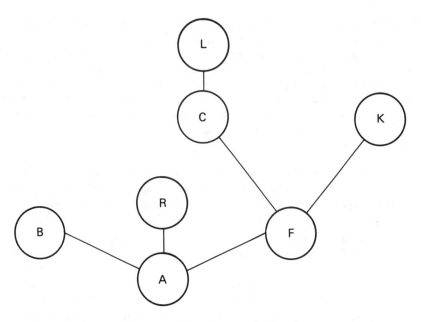

Figure 7–12. Cluster chain, the normal grapevine pattern.

1. *Seek to clarify your ideas before communicating.* The more systematically we analyze the problem or idea to be communicated, the clearer it becomes. This is the first step toward effective communication. Many communications fail because of inadequate planning. Good planning must consider the goals and attitudes of those who will receive the communications and those who will be affected by it.

2. *Examine the true purpose of each communication.* Before you communicate, ask yourself what you really want to accomplish with your message—obtain information, initiate action, change another person's attitude? Identify your most important goal and then adapt your language, tone, and total approach to serve that specific objective. Don't try to accomplish too much with each communication. The sharper the focus of your message, the greater its chances of success.

3. *Consider the total physical and human setting whenever you communicate.* Meaning and intent are conveyed by more than words alone. Many other factors influence the overall impact of a communication, and the manager must be sensitive to the total setting in which he or she communicates. Consider, for example, your sense of timing—i.e., the circumstances under which you make an announcement or render a decision; the physical setting—whether you communicate in private, for example, or otherwise; the social climate that pervades work relationships within the [organization] or a department and sets the tone of its communications; custom and past practice—the degree to which your communication conforms to, or departs from, the expectations of your audience. Be constantly aware of the total setting in which you communicate. Like all living things, communication must be capable of adapting to its environment.

4. *Consult with others, where appropriate, in planning communications.* Frequently it is desirable or necessary to seek the participation of others in planning a communication or developing the facts on which to base it. Such consultation often helps to lend additional insight and objectivity to your message. Moreover, those who have helped you plan your communication will give it their support.

5. *Be mindful, while you communicate, of the overtones as well as the basic content of your message.* Your tone of voice, your expression, your apparent receptiveness to the responses of others—all have tremendous impact on those you wish to reach. Frequently overlooked, these subtleties of communication often affect a listener's reaction to a message even more than its basic content. Similarly, your choice of language—particularly your awareness of the fine shades of meaning and emotion in the words you use—predetermines in large part the reactions of your listeners.

6. *Take the opportunity, when it arises, to convey something of help or value to the receiver.* Consideration of the other person's interests and needs—the habit of trying to look at things from his or her point of view—will frequently point up opportunities to convey something of immediate benefit or long-range value to the other person. People on the job are most responsive to the manager whose messages take their own interests into account.

7. *Follow up your communication.* Our best efforts at communication may be wasted, and we may never know whether we have succeeded in expressing our true meaning and intent, if we do not follow up to see how well we have put our message across. This you can do by asking questions, by encouraging the receiver to express his or her reactions, by follow-up contacts, by subsequent review of performance. Make certain that every important communication has a feedback so that complete understanding and appropriate action result.

8. *Communicate for tomorrow as well as today.* While communications may be aimed primarily at meeting the demands of an immediate situation, they must be planned with the past in mind if they are to maintain consistency in the receiver's view; but, most important of all, they must be consistent with long-range interests and goals. For example, it is not easy to communicate frankly on such matters as poor performance or the shortcomings of a loyal subordinate—but postponing disagreeable communications makes them more difficult in the long run and is actually unfair to your subordinates and your [health services organization].

9. *Be sure your actions support your communications.* In the final analysis, the most persuasive kind of communication is not what you say but what you do. When people's actions or attitudes contradict their words, we tend to discount what has been said. For every manager this means that good supervisory practices—such as clear assignment of responsibility–authority, fair rewards for effort, and sound policy enforcement—serve to communicate more than all the gifts of oratory.

10. *Last, but by no means least: Seek not only to be understood but to understand—be a good listener.* When we start talking we often cease to listen—in that larger sense of being attuned to the other person's unspoken reactions and attitudes. Even more serious is the fact that we are all guilty, at times, of inattentiveness when others are attempting to communicate to us.

Listening is one of the most important, most difficult—and most neglected—skills in communication. It demands that we concentrate not only on the explicit meanings another person is expressing, but on the implicit meanings, unspoken words, and undertones that may be far more significant. Thus we must learn to listen with the inner ear if we are to know the inner person.

SUMMARY

Directing is the management function that initiates action in the organization. Specifically, it means the issuance of orders, assignments, and instructions that permit subordinates to understand what is expected of them and the guidance and overseeing of the subordinates so that they can contribute effectively and efficiently to the attainment of the objectives of the health services organization.

Since the management function of directing is the interpersonal aspect of managing, it is quite complex. Success at directing will be largely determined by managers' understanding of human nature and by their attitudes toward subordinates. Issuing orders and delegation are the two techniques managers have at their disposal in directing subordinates.

We have seen that leadership is the accomplishment of organizational objectives through interpersonal relationships between the leader and those he or she leads. A leader's personal traits help determine the quality of leadership, but so do those of the followers, their objectives, and the situation in which leadership is practiced. Leadership styles can take many forms along a continuum ranging from the completely authoritarian style with no subordinate participation to the maximum degree of democratic leadership which enables the subordinate to participate in all phases of the decision-making process. The appropriate leadership style is largely determined by the organizational environment, the personalities of those involved, and the congruence of the objectives of the organization and those who work in it. Finally, it is important that leaders cultivate attitudes that permit them to balance empathy with objectivity as they lead subordinates.

Effective communication is essential to the directing function of management. It is the passing of information and understanding from a sender to a receiver. The process itself is simple, but the environmental and personal barriers to good communication often make it a demanding management activity.

The manager must be aware of the advantages and disadvantages of written and oral communications in various situations and select the appropriate method. The manager's communications are usually enhanced by a two-way flow of information between the sender and receiver.

There are a number of steps that can be taken to improve communications. Among the most important are:

1. Clarify what is to be communicated. This includes being certain of what the communication is to accomplish.
2. Use all reasonable means to convey not only information but understanding.
3. Follow up communications and be certain that actions support communications.
4. Remember that often it is equally, if not more, important to be a good listener than speaker. Feedback is crucial to effective communication.

REFERENCES

1. Fulmer RM: *The New Management*, ed 4. New York, Macmillan, 1988, pp 280–291.
2. Taylor FW: *Scientific Management*. New York, Harper & Row, Pub., 1919.
3. Maslow AH: A theory of human motivation, in *Motivation and Personality*, ed 2. New York, Harper & Row, Pub., 1970.
4. Herzberg F, Mausner B, Snyderman B: *The Motivation to Work*, ed 2. New York, Wiley, 1959.
5. Donnelly JH Jr, Gibson JL, Ivancevich JM: *Fundamentals of Management*, ed 6. Plano, Tex, Business Publications, Inc, 1987, pp 298–299.
6. McClelland DC: *The Achieving Society*. New York, Van Nostrand Reinhold, 1961.
7. Skinner BF: *Science and Human Behavior*. New York, Free Press, 1953; *Beyond Freedom and Dignity*. New York, Knopf, 1972.
8. Vroom VH: *Work and Motivation*. New York, Wiley, 1964.
9. Davis K: *Human Behavior at Work*, ed 5. New York, McGraw-Hill, 1977, p 61.
10. Porter LW, Lawler EE III: *Managerial Attitudes and Performance*. Homewood, Ill: Richard D. Irwin, Inc, 1968.
11. Adams JS: Inequity in social exchange, in Berkowitz L (ed): *Advances in Experimental Social Psychology*. New York, Academic Press, 1965, pp 267–299.
12. Robbins SP: *Management: Concepts and Applications*, ed. 2. Englewood Cliffs, NJ: Prentice-Hall, 1988, p 349.
13. Koontz H, Weihrich H: *Management*, ed 9. New York, McGraw-Hill, 1988, p 422.
14. Greenberger D, Strasser S, Lewicki RJ, Bateman TS: Perception, motivation, and negotiation, in Shortell SM, Kaluzny AD (eds): *Health Care Management: A Text in Organization Theory and Behavior*, ed 2. New York, Wiley, 1988, p 123.
15. Tannenbaum R, Schmidt WH: How to choose a leadership pattern. *Harvard Business Review*, March–April 1958. Copyright 1958 by the President and Fellows of Harvard College; all rights reserved.
16. Davis K, Newstrom JW; *Human Relations at Work*, ed 7. New York, McGraw-Hill, 1985, pp 314–315.
17. Williams JC, Huber GP: *Human Behavior in Organizations*, ed 3. Cincinnati, South-Western Publishing Co, 1986, pp 360–361.
18. Miner JB: *Personnel Psychology*. New York, Macmillan, 1969, p 259.
19. Davis, Newstrom: *Human Relations at Work*, p 317.
20. *Ten Commandments of Good Communication*. New York, American Management Association, 1955.

EIGHT
Coordinating: The Essence of Management

May 2
9:30 A.M.

The head nurses filed into the conference room for their weekly meeting with the vice-president for nursing. After giving status reports on several issues that confronted the nursing service, the vice-president turned her attention to a topic that had not been on the agenda—coordination.

"I want to tell you about an incident that occurred yesterday afternoon," she said. "Luther Fillerey's surgeon stopped me as I was leaving for a meeting to complain about the fact that she was not called by the night shift nurses the night Mr. Fillerey died. We've got to do a better job of coordinating between shifts than that."

The head nurse for Fillerey's unit said, "I don't remember passing the word about that along. Of course, we have to get so much information to the other shifts that I could have forgotten. Anyway, our usual policy is to call the chief resident and that's what the night shift nurse did—we get so busy sometimes that not everything can be perfectly coordinated."

The vice-president quickly added, "I'm not trying to place the blame on anybody. I'm simply using this to illustrate how important it is for us to coordinate things between the shifts."

Another head nurse raised a related point. "Coordination between us and the other departments seems to be a more serious problem than coordination between shifts of nurses. Last week we had a patient who had to be rescheduled for a barium enema because somebody forgot to tell food service that he wasn't supposed to get lunch until after the radiology people were through with him."

The head nurse on the pediatric unit also voiced her concern. "The lab people always come around to draw blood just at the time we start morning baths for our patients. It's hectic enough at that time without having them around drawing blood."

The vice-president for nursing responded, "I've talked to the laboratory director about that problem before. He always tells me that if they don't draw the blood early in the morning, then they can't get the tests done in time for the afternoon rounds by the doctors. It's a problem we'll just have to live with."

The meeting continued for almost an hour, with every head nurse revealing at least one coordination problem on his or her unit. The meeting adjourned at 10:30 A.M., with the vice-president agreeing to bring up the topic of coordination at the next department heads' meeting.

INTRODUCTION

In the typical health services organization—which is made up of diverse participants and activities—a central management function is that of coordinating the various participants and activities so that they are all channeled in mutually supportive directions. *Coordination is the management function of synchronizing differentiated activities and diverse participants so that they function smoothly in the attainment of the organization's objectives.*

As Fayol[1] described it years ago, the act of coordinating pulls together all the activities of the enterprise to make possible both its working and its success. Ordway Tead[2] said that coordination is "the effort to assure a smooth interplay of the functions and forces of all the different component parts of an organization to the end that its purposes will be realized with a minimum of friction and a maximum of collaborative effectiveness." Since coordination pertains to the synchronization of the actions of people within an organization, one of the important functions of every manager is to achieve this synchronization or coordination. Charns and Schaefer[3] note that "in health care organizations, coordination among different groups of providers and between providers and support services encompass critical interconnections in the delivery of care." How well these are addressed contributes directly to organizational performance. Some authorities use the term *integration* for this concept. Lawrence and Lorsch define *integration* as "the process of achieving unity of effort among the various subsystems in the accomplishment of the organization's tasks."[4] Obviously, the two terms have similar meaning.

Coordination is not easily attained. Each special departmental interest in an organization stresses its own opinion of how the organization's purposes should be accomplished, and each tends to favor one approach or another, depending upon its function and viewpoint. Haimann and Scott say[5]:

> The problem of the different viewpoints applies both in and among the several levels in a managerial hierarchy. It takes real thoughtfulness, listening power, and good will to see and understand a problem of work relationships with the group above or below. In spite of cooperative attitudes and self-coordination or self-adjustment by each member of a group, there will be duplication of action and conflicts of efforts unless management synchronizes all of them. Through coordination, management can bring about a total accomplishment far in excess of the sum of the individual parts. Each part has significance, but the result can be of much greater significance if management achieves success at coordination.

More recently, these authors have pointed out that coordination becomes more difficult as organizations grow. "Obviously the more activities there are, the more difficult it is to coordinate them. But the number isn't the only problem. As the organization grows more complex, so do its activities and communication channels."[6] Because health services organizations have grown so complex, they can become fragmented, fractionated, and split into isolated units if management does not carry out the coordinating function effectively. In short, the parts of health services organizations must be linked together, and this is especially important in these organizations because the component parts are so *interdependent*.

INTERDEPENDENCE[7]*

Interdependence among the individuals and units within an organization or among organizations, while always present, varies with the structural complexity and goals of organizations. Thompson, for example, has identified three forms of interdependence: pooled, sequential, and reciprocal.[8]

Pooled interdependence occurs when individuals and units are related but do not bear a close connection; they simply contribute separately in some way to the larger whole. For example, a group of geographically dispersed nursing homes owned by a single corporation may be viewed as linked in the sense that each contributes to the overall success of the corporation, but they have very little direct interdependence. Their activities are *pooled* to make the corporation more effective.

Sequential interdependence occurs when individuals and units bear a close, but sequential, connection. For example, patients admitted to acute-care hospitals become the focal point for an extended chain of sequentially interdependent activities. The admitting office checks the patient in, schedules the patient for the operating room, notifies the dietary department of special needs, notifies the laboratory of the need for tests, and so on. Most of what is done until the patient is discharged occurs in a *sequential* manner.

Reciprocal interdependence occurs when individuals and units bear a close relationship and the interdependence goes in both directions. For example, a vertically integrated health care system with acute-care and long-term-care units exhibits reciprocal interdependence. The long-term-care beds are occupied by patients referred from the acute-care beds; the acute-care unit depends upon the long-term-care unit as a place to which to discharge certain patients. The acute-care unit suffers if the long-term-care unit cannot accept a patient. Conversely, the long-term-care unit suffers if

---

* This section draws heavily upon the author's collaborative treatment of this subject in Longest BB and Klingensmith JM: Coordination and communication, in Shortell SM and Kaluzny AD: *Health Care Management: A Text in Organization Theory and Behavior*, ed 2. New York, Wiley, 1988, pp. 234–264.

patients are not discharged to it from the acute unit. The interdependence between these units is *reciprocal*.

Bolman and Deal have pointed out that the level of interdependence intensifies as its form moves from pooled to sequential to reciprocal.[9] The higher the level of interdependence, the greater the need for managerial attention to effective linkages. Health services organizations generally exhibit very high levels of interdependence among their component parts, usually of the sequential or reciprocal forms. Thus the need for effective coordination is usually very great in these organizations. In any organized effort, coordination is essential for people to work together; in highly interdependent health services organizations, coordination is a critical task for managers.

TYPES OF COORDINATION

It is important to note that coordinative activity varies within and among organizations according to the objectives toward which it is directed and the motivations that underlie it. For example, one can initiate coordinative activity in response to an existing problem or to prevent an anticipated problem. It may be initiated without any reference to a particular problem. Therefore, it is possible to group coordinative activities into various types. Georgopoulos and Mann[10] have developed a classification of four types of coordination. They are: corrective, preventive, regulatory, and promotive coordination.

Corrective coordination is defined as those coordinative activities that rectify an error or correct a dysfunction in the organization after it has occurred. In contrast, *preventive coordination* is defined as those coordinative activities that are aimed at preventing the occurrence of anticipated problems of coordination or, at least, minimizing the impact of these problems. *Regulatory coordination* is defined as those coordinative activities that are aimed at the maintenance of existing structural and functional arrangements in the organization. It does not require cognizance of any particular malfunctions or problems, whether in retrospect or anticipation. The fourth type of coordination, *promotive coordination,* is defined as those coordinative activities that attempt to improve the articulation of the parts of the organization, or to improve the existing organizational arrangements without regard for specific problems. Such coordinative activity does not stem from an awareness of particular problems in the organization. Rather, it stems from the simple assumption that the organization is imperfectly coordinated at any given time and that there is always room for improvement. In one research study that examined the relationships of these four types of coordination to efficiency and quality, it was found that organizations that use preventive and promotive coordination provide higher quality of care and provide it more efficiently than those relying more on corrective coordination.[11]

MECHANISMS OF COORDINATION[12]

The mechanisms of coordination (i.e., the activities managers use to achieve coordination[13]*) are diverse; these mechanisms have different levels of success, depending upon the characteristics of specific situations. This contingency view of coordination is very important for the reader to keep in mind; clearly, no single coordinating mechanism is best for all situations.

The need for a contingency approach to coordination is even greater in health services organizations because of the predominance of professionals within these organizations. Scott points out that because the activities of health professionals are seen as being complex, uncertain, and of great social importance, distinctive structural arrangements have evolved to support the autonomy of the professions. Scott identifies three types of such structural arrangements. The *autonomous arrangement* is present when an organization delegates to a professional group goal setting, implementation, and evaluation of performance, and management controls the support staff. Most health services organizations historically have had such an arrangement with their medical staffs. The *heteronomous arrangement* alternatively occurs when professionals are subordinated to the management structure with specific responsibilities delegated to various professional groups. Nursing and social service, for instance, traditionally have had such a relationship with hospitals. A third relationship, *the conjoint arrangement*, occurs when the professionals and management are equal in power. Although few examples of this form of structural arrangement currently exist, Scott notes that physician groups increasingly are moving toward the heteronomous and conjoint forms in response to various external pressures. Clearly, the type of structural arrangement affects the coordinating mechanisms employed.

In the same way that the manager's choice of coordination mechanism(s) is dependent on the structural arrangement with professionals, there are different levels of need for coordination within organizations. The activities required for organizational performance are separated through vertical and horizontal differentiation. *Differentiation*, in this context, is defined as "the state of segmentation of the organizational system into subsystems, each of which tends to develop particular attributes in relation to the requirements posed by its relevant environment."[14] *Vertical differentiation* establishes the hierarchy and number of levels in the organization. *Horizontal differentiation* comes about to separate activities so that they may be performed more effectively and efficiently.[15] This usually results in the formation of departments within the organization. For instance, in a hospital, horizontal differen-

---

* It should be noted that coordination is most usefully discussed in conjunction with control. Because control has traditionally received a great deal of attention in research on health care organizations, it is treated as a separate topic in Chapter 9. Coordination mechanisms that are not backed up by control mechanisms, however, quickly lose their effectiveness. Control provides the muscle that makes coordination mechanisms effective.

tiation accounts for radiology, pharmacy, and pathology. Vertical differentiation accounts for a president, a second level composed of vice-presidents, a third level composed of department heads, and continuing on down. Once the organization's activities have been differentiated, they must be coordinated. Of course, the requirements of the environment and technical system involved very often determine the degree of coordination needed. In some organizations, it is possible to separate activities in such a way as to minimize the degree of coordination needed. In others, particularly those functionally departmentalized, such as most health services organizations, a high degree of coordination is essential. It is necessary to recognize the interaction between the need to specialize activities and requirements for coordination. The more differentiation of activities and specialization of labor, the greater the need for coordination.

As Rakich et al, have noted, organizations establish several mechanisms to achieve coordination.[16] Litterer suggests three primary means: through the hierarchy, the administrative system, and voluntary activities.[17] In *hierarchical coordination*, the various activities are linked by placing them under a central authority. In a simple organization, this form of coordination might be sufficient. However, in complex health services organizations that have many levels and many specialized departments, hierarchical coordination becomes more difficult. Although the president is a focal point of authority, it would be impossible for one person to cope with all the coordinating problems that might arise in the hierarchy. Therefore, coordination through the hierarchical structure must be supplemented.

The *administrative system* provides a second mechanism for coordinating activities in Litterer's typology. "A great deal of coordinative effort in organizations is concerned with a horizontal flow of work of a routine nature. Administrative systems are formal procedures designed to carry out much of this routine coordinative work automatically."[18] Many work procedures, such as memoranda with routing slips, help coordinate efforts of different operating units. To the extent that these procedures can be programmed or routinized, it is not necessary to establish specific means for coordination. For nonroutine and nonprogrammable events, means such as committees may be required to provide integration.

A third type of coordination, according to Litterer, is through *voluntary action*, when individuals or groups see a need for coordination, develop a method, and implement it.[19] Much of the coordination may depend upon the willingness and ability of individuals or groups to voluntarily find ways to integrate their activities with other organizational participants.

Achieving voluntary coordination is one of the most important yet difficult problems for the manager. Voluntary coordination requires that individuals have sufficient knowledge of organizational objectives, adequate information concerning specific problems of coordination, and the motivation to do something. Fortunately, in health services organizations, voluntary coordination is often facilitated by the high degree of professionalism extant in many participants. Writing about hospitals (although their comments are equally applicable to all kinds of health services organizations), Georgopoulos and Mann[20] have said, "The hospital is dependent very greatly upon the motivations and voluntary, informal adjustments of its members for the attainment and maintenance of good coordination. Formal organizational plans, rules, regulations, and controls may ensure some minimum coordination, but of themselves are incapable of producing adequate coordination, for only a fraction of all the coordinative activities required in this organization can be programmed in advance." One of the primary forces ensuring voluntary coordination is the overall value system supportive of the patient's welfare. This fabric of shared values is developed through the training and professionalization of many participants in health services organizations.

Mintzberg identifies five coordinating mechanisms. They are mutual adjustment, direct supervision, standardization of work processes, standardization of work outputs, and standardization of worker skills.[21] Figure 8–1 illustrates these coordinating mechanisms. They can be summarized as:

- *Mutual adjustment,* which primarily provides coordination by informal communications. Similar to voluntary actions, the work is controlled and coordinated by those who perform the work (Figure 8–1a).
- Like hierarchical coordination, *direct supervision* occurs when one person takes responsibility for the work of others, including issuing them instructions and monitoring their actions (Figure 8–1b).
- *Standardization of work process* is an alternative coordinating mechanism that specifies or programs the contents of the work. Hospitals, for instance, attempt to standardize work processes whenever possible, such as inpatient admission and discharge procedures (Figure 8–1c).
- *Standardization of output* specifies the product or the expected performance, with the process to get there left to the doer.
- *Standardization of worker input skills* occurs when neither the work nor its output can be specified and the resultant standardization occurs through the training of the doer. This form of standardization is that most frequently found in health services organizations, where the complexity of the work often does not allow for the standardization of work processes or outputs.

The coordination mechanisms described above are not the only such mechanisms. Hage, for instance, describes four kinds of coordination mechanisms for health services organizations: programming, plans, customs, and feedback.[22] In general, this framework builds on the early work of March and Simon,[23] as modified by both Thompson[24] and Perrow.[25] Each of the four mechanisms is unique, although, in a sense, they can be viewed as overlapping. These mechanisms are, with the exception of customs, similar to those of Van de Ven et al.[26]

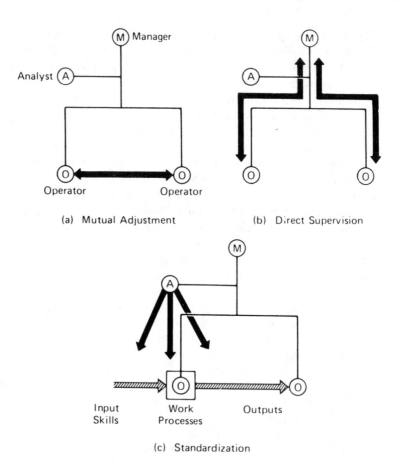

Figure 8–1. Mintzberg's five coordinating mechanisms. *(From Mintzberg H: Structure in Fives: Designing Effective Organizations. NJ, Prentice-Hall, 1983, p 5. Reprinted with permission.)*

An important mechanism in Hage's typology is *programming*. Organizations develop explicit rules and prescriptions, called *programs*, that define the job of each person in the organization, and the sequence of activities for all of the jobs within a department and for the organization as a whole. With programs, everyone can learn his or her job and execute it. The purpose of programming is to reduce the need for communication, except for questions about interpretation of a particular rule. The programming of an organization is accomplished with rules, manuals, job descriptions, personnel procedures, promotion policies, and so on. (This category is quite similar to Litterer's administrative system described above.) Health services organizations often rely very heavily on programming as a means of coordination.

Planning differs from programming in that a plan usually delineates a set of objectives that the organization hopes to achieve and the methods by which it expects to achieve them. Planning and programming can, of course, be combined. Programs are the specific enactments of the means used to achieve the organization's planned objective(s). The usefulness of planning as an intraorganizational coordination mechanism can be seen in the need to think of planning in one unit of a health services organization as part of a larger whole. For example, the expansion plans of a health services organization must be taken into account in its nursing services' human resources planning. No departmental plan should be made that does not contribute to the objectives set out in the plans of the organization. It is the responsibility of senior management to ensure that all managers understand the objectives of the organization. It is the joint duty of all managers to determine whether their plans are compatible with all other plans in the organization. If this is done initially, coordination will be facilitated.

Customs also are a coordination mechanism. Many organizations rely upon the history and customs of the organization as coordination mechanisms. While programming is a rational attempt to spell out specific norms of human behavior in organizations, customs are norms developed over time that specify behavior of different participants in the social system. In this sense, customs may be more rational than programming rules because customs, based on a history of trial and error, represent a distillation of good practice, whereas programming can result from a manager's ideal sense rather than from lessons learned from reality. Customs can be an important coordinating mechanism; but in complex health services organizations they are not, in and of themselves, sufficient to achieve effective coordination.

Feedback, the fourth in Hage's typology of coordination mechanisms, occurs in both verbal and nonverbal forms. Indeed, machines are often designed with feedback mechanisms to improve performance. In coordination, verbal communications feedback indicates when the organization is not functioning well or when problems of conflict or inefficiency arise. Not all forms of communication represent feedback, but some, particularly those involving committees and horizontal communication, are likely to represent attempts on the part of the organization to coordinate through feedback.

Another approach to coordinating activities is through *committees*. Frequently, committees are made up of members from a number of departments or functional areas and are concerned with problems requiring coordination. Using committees for purposes of coordination is a well-established approach in health services organizations. Committees serve other purposes besides coordination; they may act in a service, advisory, informational, educational, or decision-making capacity. However, their chief purpose is coordination. (We will discuss committees in more depth in a later section of this Chapter.)

Additional means of coordination have developed in many organizations. Lawrence and Lorsch[27] studied six organizations operating in the chemical processing industry to determine how they achieve integration or coordination. These organizations use a technology that requires not only differentiated and specialized activities, but also a major degree of integration. The study analyzed how organizations achieve both substantial differentiation and tight integration when these forces seem contradictory. Results showed that successful organizations use *task forces, teams,* and *project offices* to achieve coordination. In the most successful organizations, Lawrence and Lorsch found the influence of *integrators* (people who seem to hold the key to successful integration) stems from professional competence rather than from formal position. These people are successful integrators because of specialized knowledge and because they represent a central source of information in the organization. Although examples of effective integrators can be found among all health professionals, in most hospitals individual nurses, regardless of their formal position, often function as integrators, linking practicing physicians with the organization's formal administrative structure. These same individuals also often provide significant coordination among the hospital's various administrative units, particularly as they relate to the patient.

Project management [28] and its more advanced form, called *matrix organization* (see Chapter 5 for further discussion), are structural forms that can facilitate coordination within an organization. Project management is a structural means for coordinating a large amount of talent and resources for a given period on a specific project. The project team of various specialists is assembled under direction of the project manager, who is responsible for coordinating their efforts. A project team in a regional home health care program, for instance, could be utilized to plan for the organization's new automated telephone system.

Other structural forms have been recommended to help with problems of coordination. Likert believes that one mechanism for achieving integration could be to have people serve as *"linking pins"* between various units in the organization. Horizontally, there are certain organizational participants who are members of two separate groups and who serve as coordinating agents between them. On the vertical axis, individuals serve as linking pins between their level and those above and below. Thus, through this system of linking pins, the coordination necessary to make the dynamic system operate effectively is achieved. This forms a multiple overlapping group structure in the organization. Likert says [29]:

> To perform the intended coordination well, a fundamental requirement must be met. The entire organization must consist of a multiple, overlapping group structure with every work group using group decision-making processes skillfully. The requirement applies to the functional, product, and service departments. An organization meeting this requirement will have an effective interaction–influence system through which the relevant communications flow readily, the required influence is exerted laterally, upward, and downward, and the motivational forces needed for coordination are created.

A relatively new mechanism for improved coordination within organizations is the *quality circle*. Originally developed in the United States, but brought to a high art in Japan, this mechanism is gaining considerable acceptance as a means of coordination, especially at the operational level. This mechanism features small-group, problem-oriented meetings in which employees focus on changes needed to improve morale, productivity, or quality.[30] It is reported that quality circles enhance the quality of patient care and services, reduce errors, build an attitude of problem prevention, improve communications, and inspire more effective teamwork in health services organizations.[31] This technique involves processes such as the nominal group process, multicriteria decision making, and critical-incident examination. According to Wolff[32]:

> A quality circle is a voluntary employee group meeting regularly during working hours with the goal of identifying and solving task-related problems. Solutions are communicated directly to management at a formal presentation session. Management accepts, rejects, or modifies the group-developed solution. Members and their leader receive training in the areas of cause/effect problem solving, statistics, data collection/display, brainstorming, and group dynamics. Group size usually is less than 20. Leaders may or may not be the members' supervisor. Members generally are from a common work site or task area. Personnel area problems normally are not addressed. Practice varies as to problem origins, i.e., whether problems are assigned by management or selected by members. Extrinsic rewards such as money generally are not given to members for solutions effected.

Figure 8–2 illustrates the quality-circle approach to solving a problem. As we can see, the final decision on implementing the decision rests with management. To be successful, quality circles require support from management in providing (1) approval for meetings during work hours, (2) training for circle leaders, (3) a responsive attitude toward proposals for improvement developed by circle members, and (4) incentives for achieving improvements.

To summarize, there are a number of coordination mechanisms available to the manager, including: administrative system, committees, customs, feedback, hierarchy, integrators, linking pins, matrix organization, plans, programming, project management through task forces or teams, standardization, quality circles, or voluntary action. Managers in health services organizations use various combinations of these mechanisms to achieve coordination; usually a number of them are used concurrently. Two basic dimensions help categorize the different types of health services organizations and explain the circumstances under which various coordination mechanisms might be used: scale of operations (small to large) and interdependence (pooled to sequential/reciprocal). Using this typology, Figure 8–3 illustrates clusters of coordination mechanisms that might be most effective in various health services organizations.

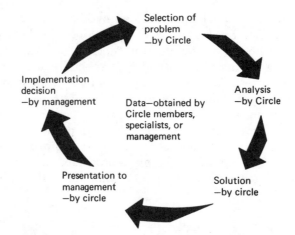

Figure 8–2. Problem solving in quality circles. *(From Sasaki N, Hutchins D:* The Japanese Approach to Product Quality: Its Applicability to the West. *Oxford, England, Pergamon, 1984, p 68. Reprinted with permission.)*

CONFLICT IN HEALTH SERVICES ORGANIZATIONS

When coordination fails, or is ineffective, conflict results. *Conflict* may be defined, in broad terms, as all kinds of opposition or antagonistic interaction. Most health services organizations, because of the tremendously complex organizational structure and the diversity of participants, experience a rather

Interdependence	Scale of Operations	
	Small	**Large**
Pooled	Customs	Administrative system
	Feedback	Direct supervision
	Mutual adjustments	Hierarchy
	Programming	Programming
	Voluntary activities	Matrix organization
Sequential/reciprocal	Administrative system	Integrators
	Feedback	Linking pins
	Programming	Plans
	Quality circles	Project management
		Standardization

Figure 8–3. A typology of coordination mechanisms. *(From Longest BB Jr, Klingensmith JM: Coordination and communication in Shortell SM, Kaluzny AD (eds):* Health Care Management: A Text in Organizational Theory and Behavior, *ed 2. New York, Wiley, 1988, pp 244. Reprinted with permission.)*

high level of conflict. Schultz and Johnson, writing about hospitals, for example, have stated[33]:

> Evidence of conflict in hospitals is readily apparent. Nurse and nonprofessional hospital employee strikes receive wide publicity. Periodically, administrator-medical staff conflicts break into public view. Furthermore, hospital-client conflicts seem to be increasing as consumers of hospital services level charges of inefficiency and inattention to consumer expectations.

The same can be said about most modern health services organizations.

Attitudes about the role of conflict in organizations are diverse and are undergoing a transition with the passage of time. The early management theorists had a straightforward attitude. During the period prior to the mid-1940s, almost all management thinkers saw all conflict as destructive and viewed management's role as one of ridding the organization of conflict.

The traditional approach was followed by the human-relations view, which is still a prevalent view about managing conflict in modern organizations. Essentially, this approach reflects an acceptance of conflict as a fact of organizational life. It is unquestionably a fact in the complex health services organization. Disagreements over objectives for the organization can be found among administrators, trustees, physicians, nurses, and other participants. Departments and individuals compete for recognition, prestige, and power. Empires are built, often at the expense of some other part of the organization.

Managers who take a human-relations approach to conflict resolution seek to rationalize conflict. For example, Katz has said, ". . . it should be added that we are not assuming that all conflict is bad and that the only objective toward which we should work is the resolution of conflict. Group conflict has positive social functions . . ."[34]

The current theoretical perspective on conflict, one which is taken by an increasing number of managers, is a more positive approach called the "interactionist view" by Robbins. He suggests that the interactionist approach differs from the behavioral viewpoint in that it[35]:

1. Recognizes the absolute necessity of conflict,
2. Explicitly encourages a minimum level of conflict,
3. Defines conflict management to include stimulation as well as resolution methods, and
4. Considers the management of conflict as a major responsibility of all managers.

The interactionists accept and sometimes encourage conflict by recognizing that just as the level of conflict may be too high and require reduction, it may also be too low and in need of increased intensity. The interactionists believe organizations that do not have conflict increase the probability of stagnant thinking, inadequate decisions and, in extreme cases, organizational demise.

The problem with conflict in hospitals and other types of health services organizations is that it can affect the quality of patient care. Georgopoulos and Mann, for instance, have found higher quality in hospitals where physicians and nurses have a greater understanding of each other's work, problems, and needs.[36] Studies in mental hospitals report that patients are affected adversely by staff conflict.[37] The task for the manager is to balance the level of conflict so that the positive benefits (chiefly innovative organizational changes as described in Chapter 10) can be achieved without disrupting the quality of patient care. As one might expect, this is an extremely difficult task.

THE COMMITTEE AS A MEANS OF COORDINATION

Health services organizations make considerable use of committees to achieve coordination. The governing board of the typical health services organization, as well as the medical staff, is organized on the basis of committees. In addition, the organization has many standing and *ad hoc* committees, and the various departments and subunits of the organization rely heavily on committees. Committees serve other purposes besides coordination; they may act in a service, advisory, informational, or decision-making capacity. However, their chief purpose is coordination. The committee is a formally designated group; therefore, the reader may wish to review the material in Chapter 6 on small groups. It should be pointed out that although the material in Chapter 6 pertains directly to the formation of small *informal* groups, committees (which are formally designated groups) take on many of the characteristics of small informal groups. Committees, and their work, are often criticized as being ineffective. For example, it has been said that the best committee is a five-person committee with four members absent. The classical theorist, Luther Gulick, wanted to limit the use of committees to abnormal situations because he thought they were too dilatory, irresponsible, and time-consuming for normal administration.[38] Urwick was an even harsher critic. He listed no fewer than fourteen faults of committees, the main ones being that committees are often irresponsible and are costly.[39] Thus the classicists tended to emphasize the negative, but the more modern view recognizes that committees have both positive and negative attributes.

Committees are time-consuming and expensive. The next time you are in a committee meeting, calculate the person-hours and the cost in salaries alone of the meeting (some of you may see this as an unnecessary, time-consuming, and expensive exercise—but just this sort of thing goes on in meetings!).

From an organizational standpoint, there are some potential problems inherent in committees. The most obvious is divided responsibility. This is to say that often in a committee, there is group responsibility or accountability but not individual responsibility. Thus, critics argue, the committee in reality turns out to have no responsibility or accountability. In fact, individuals may use the committee as a shield to avoid personal responsibility for bad decisions or mistakes. One solution to this problem is to make all committee members responsible, and another is to hold the chairperson responsible. Both approaches have many obvious difficulties. For example, if the entire committee is held responsible for a wrong decision, what about the individual members who voted against the majority? Holding them accountable for the committee's decision could have disastrous effects on their morale, but holding only those who voted for a particular decision responsible would create an inhibiting effect that would destroy the value of committee action.

Besides being time-consuming, costly, and having divided responsibility, committees may reach decisions that are products of excessive compromise, logrolling, and one-person or minority domination. This represents the reverse of the advantages of integrated group judgment and pooling of specialized knowledge. Where unanimity is either formally required or an informal group norm, the difficulties are compounded. A final decision may be so extremely watered down or "compromised to death" that it is ineffective. The strength of committee action comes through a synthesis and integration of divergent viewpoints, not through a compromise of the least common denominator. One way to avoid the problem is to limit the committee to serving as a forum for the exchange of information and ideas. Another possibility is to let the chairperson have the final decision-making perogative. Yet these solutions are not always satisfactory because, when the committee is charged with making a decision, considerable social skill and a willingness to cooperate fully must exist if good, effective decisions are to evolve.

Given these problems with committees, why do health services organizations make such wide use of them? The obvious answer is that there are some benefits that outweigh the problems. In many cases, committee action has a number of advantages over individual action. One of its most important attributes is the combined and integrated judgment that committee action makes possible. Members can bring a wide range of experience, knowledge, ability, and personality characteristics to bear on problems that the committee is faced with solving. There is evidence that brainstorming (which a committee structure facilitates) yields more creative solutions to problems than individuals working alone.

From a human standpoint, the primary advantage of committees may be the increased motivation and commitment derived from participation. By being involved in the analysis and solution of committee problems, individual members will more readily accept and try to implement what has been decided. A committee can also be instrumental in human development and growth. Group members, especially the young and inexperienced, can take advantage of observing and learning from other members with more experience or with different viewpoints and knowledge. A committee provides the opportunity for personal development that individuals would never receive on their own.

The most important attribute of committees in health services organizations is the promotion of coordination between departments and subunits of the organization. In effect, committees foster communication. Through committee discussion, each member has an opportunity to better understand the purposes and problems faced by others in the organization and to see the interrelatedness of various participants and activities in the organization.

Committee functioning and the contribution of individuals to committee work can be enhanced by a better understanding of the way committees work. Research has shown that they are most effective when the chairperson exerts considerable influence and does not attempt to share this role with others.[40] A certain amount of "take-charge" attitude seems required, along with a focusing on task considerations. Generally, chairpeople perceived as fulfilling role expectations, structuring activities, and exercising control are viewed as more skillful.

Since managers in health services organizations spend so much time in committee meetings, the following guidelines to the successful operation of committees may be useful[41]:

1. Authority

   The committee's authority should be spelled out so that members know whether their responsibility is to make decisions, to make recommendations, or merely to deliberate and to give the chairperson some insights into the issue under discussion.

2. Size

   The size of the committee is very important. . . . If the group is too large, there may not be enough opportunities for adequate communication among its members. On the other hand, if the group consists of only three persons, there is the possibility that two may form a coalition against the third member. No precise conclusions can be drawn here about the appropriate size. As a general rule, a committee should be large enough to promote deliberation and include the breadth or expertise required for the job, but not so large as to waste time or foster indecision. The optimum committee size is thought by some to be at least five or six, but not more than fifteen or sixteen. An analysis of small-group research indicates that the ideal committee size may be five when the five members possess adequate skills and knowledge to deal with problems facing the committee. It is obvious that the larger the group, the greater the difficulty in obtaining a "meeting of the minds," and the more time necessary to allow everyone to contribute.

3. Membership

   The members of the committee must be selected carefully. If a committee is to be successful, the members must be representative of the interests they are intended to serve. They must also possess the required authority, and be able to perform well in a group. Finally, the members should have the capacity for communicating well and reaching group decisions by integrating group thinking rather than by inappropriate compromise.

4. Subject Matter

   The subject must be carefully selected. Committee work should be limited to subject matter that can be handled in group discussion. Certain kinds of subjects lend themselves to committee action, while others do not. Jurisdictional disputes and strategy formulation, for example, may be suitable for group deliberation, while certain isolated, technical problems may be better solved by an expert in the specialized field. To make committees effective, an agenda and relevant information should be circulated well in advance so that the members can study the subject matter before the meeting.

5. Chairperson

   The selection of the chairperson is crucial for an effective committee meeting. Such a person can avoid the wastes and drawbacks of committees by planning the meeting, preparing the agenda, seeing that the results of research are available to the members ahead of time, formulating definite proposals for discussion or action, and conducting the meeting efficiently. The chairperson sets the tone of the meeting, integrates the ideas, and keeps the discussion from wandering.

6. Minutes

   Effective communication in committees usually requires circulating minutes and checking conclusions. At times, individuals leave the meeting with varying interpretations as to what was agreed. To avoid this, it is good to take careful minutes of the meeting and circulate them in draft form for correction or modification before the final copy is approved by the committee.

7. Cost Effectiveness

   The committee must be worth its cost. It may be difficult to count the benefits, especially such intangible factors as morale, enhanced status of committee members, and the committee's value as a training device to enhance teamwork. But the committee can be justified only if the costs are offset by tangible and intangible benefits.

PROFESSIONALISM AND COORDINATION

The means of achieving coordination (and thereby controlling conflict) outlined above are useful techniques. However, given the degree of complexity of health services organizations, they are not enough. In order to deal with unusual and nonroutine events, it is necessary to have a high level of voluntary coordination and a willingness to work effectively with others. Writing about hospitals (although their comments are equally applicable to all kinds of health services organizations), Georgopoulos and Mann noted many years ago that

> The hospital is dependent very greatly upon the motivations and voluntary, informal adjustments of its members for the attainment and maintenance of good coordination. Formal organizational plans, rules, regulations, and controls may ensure some minimum coordination, but of themselves are incapable of producing adequate coordination, for only a fraction of all the coordinative activities required in this organization can be programmed in advance.[42]

This view is still salient today. One of the primary forces ensuring voluntary coordination is the overall value system supportive of the patient's welfare, which is developed through the training and professionalization of health professionals.

SUMMARY

In a complex health services organization, with a diversity of participants and activities, coordination is a critically important concern for the manager. We have defined coordination as the management function of synchronizing differentiated activities and diverse participants so that they function smoothly in the attainment of the organization's objectives. There are several basic approaches to coordination: corrective, preventive, regulatory, and promotive.

The end result of inadequate coordination is conflict, which is defined as all kinds of opposition or antagonistic interaction. The manager must realize that conflict can be harmful *but* that it also has some positive benefits to the organization. The chief benefit of conflict is the stimulation of innovative organizational change.

There are several mechanisms through which the organization can achieve coordinated effort. The most basic way is through the hierarchy of the organization (someone is given authority over a set of people and activities). In complex organizations this usually has to be supported by other mechanisms, such as through the administrative system, which automatically carries out a good deal of the necessary coordinative activity. Also, in health services organizations, the high degree of professionalism leads to a significant amount of voluntary coordination, especially where the patient care activity is involved. The committee is used in health services organizations to achieve coordination, among other things. The committee approach fosters communication among the participants and thus can improve coordination.

REFERENCES

1. Fayol H: *General and Industrial Management*. Storrs C (trans). London, Sir Isaac Pitman and Sons, Ltd, 1949, p 104.
2. Tead O: *Administration: Its Purpose and Performance*. New York, Harper and Brothers, 1959, p 36.
3. Charns MP, Schaefer MJ: *Health Care Organizations: A Model for Management*. Englewood Cliffs, NJ, Prentice-Hall, 1983, p 144.
4. Lawrence PR, Lorsch JW: Differentiation and integration in complex organizations. *Administrative Science Quarterly*, 1967; 11:1.
5. Haimann T, Scott WG: *Management in the Modern Organization*. Boston, Houghton Mifflin Co, 1970, p 167.
6. Haimann T, Scott WG, Connor PE: *Management*, ed 5. Boston, Houghton Mifflin Co, 1985, p 244.
7. Longest BB Jr, Klingensmith JM: Coordination and communication, in Shortell

SM, Kaluzny AD (eds): *Health Care Management: A Text in Organization Theory and Behavior,* ed 2. New York, Wiley, 1988, pp 234–264.

8. Thompson JD: *Organizations in Action.* New York, McGraw-Hill, 1967.
9. Bolman LG, Deal TE: *Modern Approaches to Understanding and Managing Organizations.* San Francisco, Jossey-Bass Publishers, 1984.
10. Georgopoulos BS, Mann FC: *The Community General Hospital.* New York, Macmillan, 1962, pp 277–278.
11. Longest BB Jr: Relationships between coordination, efficiency, and quality of care in general hospitals. *Hospital Administration,* Fall 1974, pp 65–86.
12. Longest BB Jr, Klingensmith JM: Coordination and communication, pp 234–264.
13. Scott WR: Managing professional work: Three models of control for health organizations. *Health Services Research* 1982; 17:213.
14. Scott: Managing professional work, p 213.
15. Kast FE, Rosenzweig JE: *Organization and Management: A Systems and Contingency Approach,* ed 4. New York, McGraw-Hill, 1985, pp 244–246.
16. Rakich JS, Longest BB Jr, Darr K: *Managing Health Services Organizations,* ed 2. Philadelphia, Saunders, 1985, pp. 146–149.
17. Litterer JA: *The Analysis of Organizations,* ed 2. New York, John Wiley & Sons, 1973, pp 447–474.
18. Litterer: *The Analysis of Organizations,* p 466.
19. Litterer: *The Analysis of Organizations,* p 459.
20. Georgopoulos BW, Mann FC: The hospital as an organization. *Hospital Administration* (now *Hospital and Health Services Administration*), Fall 1962, pp 57–58.
21. Mintzberg H: *Structure in Fives: Designing Effective Organizations.* Englewood Cliffs, NJ, Prentice-Hall, 1983.
22. Hage J: *Theories of Organizations: Forms, Processes, and Transformations.* New York, Wiley-Interscience, 1980. Adapted from Shortell SM, Kaluzny AD: *Health Care Management: A Text in Organization Theory and Behavior.* New York, Wiley, 1983, pp 241–243.
23. March JG, Simon HH: *Organizations.* New York, Wiley, 1958.
24. Thompson: *Organizations in Action.*
25. Perrow C: A framework for the comparative analysis of organization. *American Sociological Review* 1967; 32:194.
26. Van de Ven AH, Delbecq AL, Koenig R Jr: Determinants of coordination modes within organizations. *American Sociological Review* 1976;41:322.
27. Lawrence, Lorsch: Differentiation and integration in complex organizations.
28. Cleland DI, King WR: *Systems Analysis and Project Management,* ed 3. New York, McGraw-Hill, 1983.
29. Likert R: *The Human Organization.* New York, McGraw-Hill, 1967, pp 156–157.
30. Ingle S, Ingle N: *Quality Circles in Service Industries.* Englewood Cliffs, NJ: Prentice-Hall, 1983.
31. American Hospital Association: *Hospitals,* 1982; 50:72.
32. Wolff PJ: Quality circle intervention: structure, process, results. Read before the College of Business and Management, University of Maryland, 1983, p 1.
33. Schultz R, Johnson AC: Conflict in hospitals. *Hospital Administration,* Summer 1971, p 36.
34. Katz D: Approaches to managing conflict, in Kahn RL, Boulding E (eds): *Power and Conflict in Organizations.* New York, Foundation on Human Behavior, Basic Books, Inc, 1964.

35. Robbins SP: *Management,* ed 2. Englewood Cliffs, NJ, Prentice-Hall, 1988, pp 446–449.
36. Georgopoulos, Mann: *The Community General Hospital,* p 400.
37. Stanton AH, Schwartz MS: *The Mental Hospital.* New York, Basic Books, Inc, 1954, pp 342–365.
38. Gulick L: Notes on the theory of organization, in Gulick L, Urwick L (eds): *Papers on the Science of Administration.* New York, Institute of Public Administration, 1937, p 36.
39. Urwick LF: Committees in organization. Reprinted from the *British Management Review* by Management Journals, Ltd, 1933, p 14; and *The Elements of Administration.* New York, Harper & Row, Pub. Inc, 1943, pp 71–72.
40. Prince GM: How to be a better chairman. *Harvard Business Review,* January–February 1969, pp 98–108.
41. Koontz H, Weihrich H: *Management,* ed 9. New York, McGraw-Hill, 1988, pp 256–258.
42. Georgopoulos, Mann: The hospital as an organization, pp 57–58.

NINE

Controlling: The Straight and Narrow Path

June 1
4:30 P.M.

The medical audit committee chairperson, opening the meeting, said, "Today the president has asked us to review the Fillerey case and to develop recommendations on how to preclude such serious lapses in our quality control program." He then turned to the president and asked for a status report on the case.

The president stood up and said, "As you know, we have settled this case out of court. This was done on the advice of our insurance company and our attorney. The surgeon's insurance company has also settled with the Fillerey family, so that both suits have been dropped. The thing for us to do now is to try to look at the situation, determine where our quality control system went wrong, and develop recommendations that would prevent such a thing from happening again."

One of the committee members spoke at that point. "It concerns me that we are always looking at cases as past history. This one is no exception. It seems to me that good quality control would prevent such things as what happened to Luther Fillerey."

Another member agreed. "You're exactly right! I've reviewed this case, as everyone in this room has, and I think we all know what went wrong. Central supply fouled up by not properly sterilizing the instrument; the surgeon fouled up by failing to diagnose the infection that resulted; and the nurses fouled up by not keeping a close enough watch on Fillerey to see that he was going sour that night before it was too late for anybody to do anything about it!"

"You're saying," asked the chairperson, "that even if we find out what happened in this case and take steps to prevent it from happening again, that isn't enough to prevent other equally disastrous foul-ups?"

"Yes!"

"I agree with you," said the chairperson, "there is only so much that can be controlled."

"And control costs money," said the president. "I guess the ideal situation would be to have one person do something and another check on that person all along the way."

"That's not very practical!" rejoined one member.

"I know it isn't," retorted the president. "I'm just saying that control is not very easy to pull off. We don't have the money, the people, or the time to do it in a comprehensive way."

At that point the chairperson said, "Let's cool down here and remember the job at hand."

The committee reviewed every piece of written information they had on the Luther J. Fillerey case and discussed it at great length. By 6:30 P.M., they had agreed on the series of events that led to the death of Luther J. Fillerey, but as they adjourned, the only recommendation for the president was that it would be very important to keep everyone on their toes about quality control.

INTRODUCTION

If the plans made to meet organizational objectives were always conceived and executed flawlessly by an ideally structured organization where perfect coordination was achieved under the direction of an omnipotent leader, there would be no need for control. So far, no organization has achieved this utopian state. Until one does, all organizations will require the management function of controlling. In organizations involved with the delivery of health services, the control function takes on an even greater importance. This results from the ever-present necessity to control the quality of care provided so that the highest standards of care can be achieved on a routine basis. Furthermore, as we discussed in Chapter 1, the limited resources available to meet the health care needs of our society make it absolutely necessary that close control be maintained over the costs of providing health services in the organizational setting. Quality of care and cost of care are not the only factors that managers must control. They are, however, the most important factors in organizations set up to deliver health services. Thus, they will be described at length in this chapter as examples of how the controlling function of the management process takes place. Before these two applications are described, we should develop some basic concepts of controlling as a management function.

Controlling can be defined as the regulation of activities in accordance with the requirements of plans. By definition, controlling is directly linked to the planning function. This can be seen diagrammatically in Figure 9–1. The managerial function of control consists of measuring and correcting the activities of people and things in the organization to make certain that objectives and the plans made to attain them are accomplished. It is a function of all managers on all levels, and its basic purpose is to ensure that what is intended to be done is what is done.

The word *control* often carries a negative connotation. People frequently think of it as a somewhat sinister activity involving surveillance, correction, or even reproach. In truth, it need not be viewed in this way at all. Newman has described the real nature of control as a management function in the following way[1]:

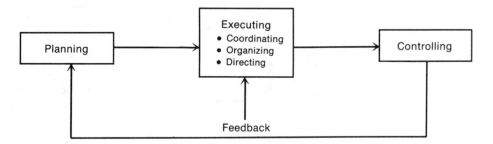

Figure 9–1. The relationship of controlling to planning.

1. *Control is a normal, pervasive, and positive force.* Evaluation of results accomplished and feedback of this information to those who can influence future results is a natural phenomenon. The cook watches the pie in the oven, the orchestra conductor listens to his orchestra—and its recordings; the doctor checks his patient; the oil refiner tests the quality of his end-product; the farmer counts his chickens; the football coach keeps an eye on the scoreboard . . .
2. *Managerial control is effective only when it guides someone's behavior.* Behavior, not measurements and reports, is the essence of control. We often become so involved with the mechanics of control that we lose sight of its purpose. Unless one or more persons act differently than they otherwise would, the control reports have no impact. Consequently, when we think about designing and implementing control, we must always ask ourselves, "Who is going to behave differently, and what will be the nature of his response?". . .
3. *Successful control is future-oriented and dynamic.* Long before the Apollo spacecraft reached the moon, control adjustments had been made. . . . We use early measurements to predict where our present course is leading, and modify inputs to keep us on target. . . .
4. *Control relates to all sorts of human endeavors.* The need for evaluation and feedback is just as pressing in charitable organizations as in profit-seeking corporations. Each is concerned with attaining its goals and each has limited resources. Moreover, control should not be confined to easy-to-measure results. The quality of service in a hospital or bank, the training and promotion of minority workers, and the resourcefulness of a purchasing agent in developing alternative sources for important supplies—all need to be controlled.

STEPS IN THE CONTROL FUNCTION

The control function, whether it is applied to cash, medical care, employee morale, or anything else, involves four steps: (1) establishing standards, (2) measuring performance, (3) comparing actual results with standards, and (4) correcting deviations from standards. Figure 9–2 illustrates these steps.

Standards can be defined as established criteria against which actual results can be compared. They are, in essence, the expression of objectives in

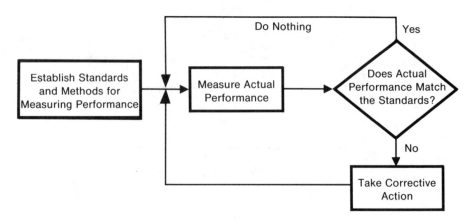

Figure 9–2. Basic steps in control function.

terms that actual performance can be measured against. Such standards can be quantity, cost, time, or quality measures. They are usually expressed in specific units, but this need not always be the case. For example, a manager may have the objective of a high level of employee morale. Standards can be set for such objectives, although probably not in numerical terms. Furthermore, means of determining whether action is toward or away from such objectives can be devised. These kinds of standards are much more difficult to quantify and measure than some others, but the managerial benefits make it worth the effort.

If standards are realistically developed and if means are available for determining exactly what subordinates are doing, measuring performance and comparing actual results with standards is fairly easy. In many situations, however, the nature of the activity is such that establishing standards and measuring performance are difficult.

Ideally, comparison will discover no significant deviations. If they are found, then corrective action must be taken. The purpose of such action is to either correct deviations from planned performance or alter the plan to allow for obstacles that cannot be removed. The point at which corrective action is taken is where control blends with the other management functions. The manager may correct by altering plans or modifying the objective from which the plan derived. The manager may correct through the organizing function—through reassignment of duties, additional staffing, or better training of employees. Correction can also be achieved through more careful coordination. Finally, the manager may correct through better direction such as a more complete explanation of the job or more effective leadership. This overlap of the control function with the other management functions illustrates the unity of the manager's job. Having taken a broad overview of the controlling function, perhaps we should look at each of its four steps in some detail.

Establishing Standards

Standards are criteria against which to judge results. They are "established levels of quality or quantity used to guide performance."[2] In carrying out the planning function, management sets the objectives that it hopes to meet. The most important idea in control is to determine to some extent what should result, or at least what is expected from a given action or activity.

There are a great many different types of standards. Sometimes they may be general qualitative standards in areas such as attitudes, morale, or interdepartmental relationships. These types of standards have the obvious problem of a lack of precision, which makes them difficult to establish and utilize. Nevertheless, managers must not overlook the importance of intangible standards in achieving a balanced control over their responsibilities.

In many situations it is possible to set standards that are quantitative. This means that they can be stated in specific units, such as a certain number of procedures per hour or a certain cost per procedure. Obviously, if enough thought is given, standards can be developed for virtually any activity, and, whether they are quantitative or qualitative, they can be useful in the control function.

There is such a large variety of possible standards that it is necessary for the manager to be selective. It is literally impossible to check the performance of each activity against all of the possible standards that might be applied to it. The technical term for those chosen for control purposes is *strategic control standards*. This means simply that the manager should select those standards that best reflect the objectives he or she is trying to meet and that best show whether or not they are being met. The standards selected should be timely, economical, and permit comprehensive and balanced control.

Timeliness is necessary so that adjustments can be made before serious damage is done. Another important reason for timeliness is that controlling should be a learning experience. When deviations are quickly detected, corrective action can be prompt. Everyone can learn from the experience, which would not be as likely if controlling occurred at a later time when the situation was not still familiar to the participants.

In view of the limited resources with which most managers are faced, economy is important in selecting standards, as it is in performing all management functions. One of the reasons for controlling is to keep costs at an acceptable level; therefore, it makes no sense to overspend on controlling.

Finally, it is necessary to select a range of strategic standards that will permit comprehensive and balanced control. Managers can be guided in part by their experience and knowledge of jobs to be performed within the departments. Most managers have a general idea as to how much time it takes to perform certain jobs, how much material is required, and what constitutes good quality of performance. Thus, job knowledge and experience are major sources for establishing the standards by which managers judge performance within their departments. They might also use previous budgets and departmental records to help them arrive at standards of performance.

There are other more scientific and systematic ways of establishing standards. *Job analysis* is the process of gathering information on all aspects of a specific job. One of the purposes of job analysis and measurement is to set standards for specific jobs. They represent the amount and quality of work expected of an employee. Essentially, standards aid in planning the work of a department and determining the number of employees needed. Only work that meets the following criteria should be measured and standardized:

1. The work is repetitive.
2. The content is uniform and consistent.
3. The work can be measured (i.e., it is discernible in quantitative terms).
4. Finally, the volume of work must be large enough to warrant the expense of measuring and standardizing.

Measuring Work and Setting Standards

There are a number of methods of measuring work and setting standards. Among them are: (1) analysis of past production records, (2) time analysis method, (3) work sampling method, (4) time study, and (5) motion study. A complete description of these and other methods is beyond the scope of this book. Application of these techniques usually requires the skills of the industrial engineer. Health services organizations that are too small to employ such people can utilize the services of consultants in this area. Even so, in order that the manager in the health care setting has some understanding of these techniques and can discuss them on an informed and intelligent basis with the industrial engineer, a brief discussion follows.

Analysis of Past Production Records. Perhaps this is the simplest method of measuring work and setting standards. Production records on the activities of the department can be maintained and analyzed. The manager can select the best past performance and use it as a standard on the assumption that if it was done before, the workers should be able to do it again. The advantages of this method are that it is easily used and at a relatively low cost with no need for highly trained personnel to administer it. The disadvantage is, of course, that existing inefficiencies are not corrected; they are merely recorded and analyzed.

The Time Analysis Method. This is a fairly simple method of establishing work standards. Various work activities done by an individual during the day are identified and placed on a form, then *the worker* records the actual time spent and units produced. The determination of a standard time from such information involves a great deal of subjectivity at best.

The Work Sampling Method. This method is an improvement over the time analysis method in that a trained analyst makes random observations (based on statistical methods) of the various work activities done by individuals. The data thus obtained are more reliable than those from the time analysis method. However, they do require the services of a trained analyst.

Time Study. This method measures job performance to establish the time required for performing each operation at an average pace. The purpose is to measure the output of a worker of average skill who is performing his or her work with average effort under standardized conditions so that standard times can be determined. A job is divided into work elements or groupings of basic movements. Element times are taken directly at the workplace by clock readings or remotely by motion picture analysis.

Motion Study. Its purpose is to make work performance easier and more productive by improving manual motions. The detailed motion study was originated at the end of the nineteenth century as a scientific method of eliminating wasted effort in work. Motion study consists of dividing work into the most fundamental elements possible, studying these elements separately and in relation to one another, and from these studies building methods of least waste.

It has been argued that in situations where the quality of patient care is involved, these industrial engineering concepts should not be applied. It is much easier to accept them as part of the assembly-line approach we have taken in manufacturing such things as automobiles and washing machines. Clearly, development of and adherence to standards are *more* applicable in the manufacturing environment. Yet we should not discount them entirely as valuable tools in the health service organization. There are many situations where they are applicable. Broad-minded managers should be willing to try whatever tools and techniques they can to provide high-quality care at the most reasonable cost.

A second important caution about setting standards involves the question of worker cooperation. The main purpose for setting any performance standard is to create effective goals for employees to work toward. This means that the standards are such that they can be achieved, and they should be considered fair by both managers and their subordinates. Standards are more likely to be effective if they are set with the active participation of both manager and subordinates. Workers are more likely to accept them as reasonable and fair if they have had a part in their formulation.

Measuring Performance and Comparing to Standards

Once suitable standards have been set, the next steps in the control process can be taken. These consist of measuring actual performance and comparing it to standards that have been established. Managers do this by personally observing work and checking on their employees, and by analyzing summaries of data and reports submitted to them. Comparing information obtained in these ways with existing standards is a continuous daily function of managers as they control their areas of responsibility.

There is no substitute for direct observation and personal contact by a manager in checking on employee performance. It is time-consuming, but in addition to providing information for control purposes, it also permits managers to make a continuous effort to improve the training and development of their employees. There is no better time to learn to do something correctly than just after it has been done incorrectly.

Whenever the manager observes employees at work, he or she should assume a questioning attitude, but not necessarily a fault-finding one. Managers should not ignore mistakes, but the manner in which they question is significant. They should ask whether or not there is any way in which they can help their employees do their jobs more easily, safely, or efficiently. Many standards are stated in general terms, but observations for control should look for specific instances such as inadequate output, sloppy work, or improperly performed jobs. At times, it may be difficult to convince an employee that his or her work is generally unsatisfactory. But if reference can be made to specific cases, it is easier for the employee to recognize the deficiencies that may exist.

Another method available to the manager for checking on performance is the written report, which is especially important if the department is large or if it operates in several different locations. Reports should be clear, complete, concise, and correct. If a department or unit operates around the clock, as they so often do in health services organizations, the manager will have to depend, to a large extent, on written reports to appraise the performance of those shifts during which he or she is not usually present.

As managers check reports, they will find that many activities have been performed according to standard and can pass over these sections. The manager must concentrate on the exceptions—those activities where performance deviates from established standards. In many cases, the manager can practice what has been called the *exception principle*. This means that he or she will request employees *not* to prepare reports on those activities that have attained preestablished standards, but merely to report on those items that are not up to the standard. After reviewing the reports, the manager can then take immediate action wherever it is needed. This approach often works very well where employees are highly trained and professionalized.

Taking Corrective Action

The final step in the controlling function is taking corrective action. If there are no deviations from standard in the performance that has been taking place, then the controlling function is fulfilled by the first three steps. If, on the other hand, there are deviations, then the controlling function is not fulfilled until the final step of corrective action is accomplished. This means curbing undesirable results and bringing performance back into line. As we stated earlier, correction of deviations in performance is the point at which control coalesces with the other managerial functions of planning, organizing, directing, and coordinating.

Where deviations have occurred, the manager should first carefully check and analyze the facts in order to determine causes and reasons. Here managers should bear in mind that the standards were based on certain prerequisites, forecasts, and assumptions, which may not have materialized. A check may determine that the deviation was not caused by the employee in whose work it showed up. The corrective action must be directed toward the real source of the discrepancy. There can be many reasons for deviations. Perhaps the employee was not qualified. Additional training and supervision might help. There might be a situation where directions have not been given properly, and the employee was not well enough informed to do what was expected. Here the manager should again explain the standards that the employee is expected to maintain. These are only some of the reasons that may account for deviations from standards.

Only after a thorough analysis of the reasons for a deviation will the manager be in a position to take corrective action. He or she must decide what remedial action is necessary and what modifications will secure improved results in the future. Corrective action may consist of a revision of standards, a simple discussion, a verbal reprimand, or numerous other means of rectifying the situation. It may even consist of replacing certain employees. At times, serious forms of disciplinary action may have to be taken, particularly if major infractions of rules or policies are involved. Figure 9–3 illustrates a progressive approach to disciplinary action.

The manager, of course, must follow up and study the effect that each corrective action has on performance in the future. With further study and analysis, the manager may find that additional or different action may be required to produce the desired results.

HUMAN REACTIONS TO CONTROLS

Ultimately, the success of managers' attempts to control is determined by the effectiveness in getting people to make necessary modifications in their own performance. Although many managers assume that people will automatically act to correct their own behavior when directed to do so, this does not necessarily happen. Individuals may resist attempts to control them for a variety of reasons. Among them are the following:

1. Controls tend to disrupt a person's self-image.
2. The person fails to accept the organization's objectives.
3. The person believes that the expected standard of performance is too high.
4. The person believes that standards are irrelevant to or, at least, an incomplete measurement of the organization's objectives.
5. The person may not object to the controls themselves, but to the assignment of control authority to particular people in the health services organization.

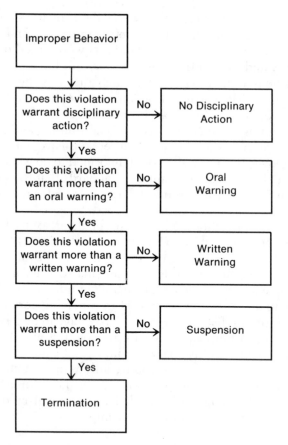

Figure 9–3. The progressive discipline approach. *(From Mondy RW, Noe RM, III: Personnel: The Management of Human Resources, ed 3. Boston: Allyn & Bacon, 1987, p 630. Reprinted with permission.)*

6. When informal group norms are consistent with control objectives, there will be a higher degree of acceptance of the control devices than when group norms are not consistent with control objectives.

Each of the reasons for resisting controls has its counterpart in a line of action that a manager might take to reduce the source of resistance. In addition to this, however, there is a general point of view which, when applied, enhances the likelihood that people will work toward the objectives of the control effort. It is this: in terms of personal acceptance of control procedures, it is generally the case that the more intimately people are involved in the establishment of control standards, the more likely it is that they will accept them and try to measure up to them.

THE BUDGET AS A CONTROL DEVICE

The budget is a plan in that it expresses the projected activities of the health services organization or a unit of it in numerical terms covering a specified period of time. The use of the budget is a controlling function. Perhaps no better example than budgets could be found to illustrate the interrelatedness of planning and controlling as management functions. For this reason, we should devote some attention to them as control devices for the manager in the health care setting.

Budgets are the most general control devices the manager has to work with. Therefore, it is essential for a manager to be familiar with the general aspects of budget making and budget control. *Budgets* can be defined as preestablished standards to which operations are compared and adjusted through the exercise of control. A budget is a means of control insofar as it reflects the plan against which actual performance is measured. It provides information that enables the manager to take action, if necessary, to bring results into conformity with the plan.

The term *budgeting* usually refers to making a plan to cover operations for a definite period in the future. A budget states anticipated results in specific numerical terms. Although the terms usually are of a monetary nature, not all budgets are expressed in dollars and cents. There are also personnel budgets, which indicate the number of workers needed for each skill level and the number of person-hours allocated for certain activities.[3]

The making of a budget, whether it is financial or otherwise, contributes to improved planning, since budget plans must be quantified and stated specifically. Considerable effort is involved in budgeting, since it means that managers must quantify their estimates about the future by attaching numerical values to specific plans. Figures placed in the final budget become the desired standard for achievement, thus becoming of vital concern and interest to the manager.

It is natural that people resent arbitrary standards; therefore, budgets should be established with the cooperation of those who are responsible for adhering to them. Managers should have an opportunity to participate in making the budget under which they are to work for the coming period. At the departmental level, the budget usually is established for one year, although it may be for a shorter period of time. Higher management may have other budgets that extend for some years in advance.

The most effective approach to budgeting in health services organizations is "bottom-up." Budgets should be initially prepared by those people who will implement them. The budgets are then sent up to higher-level managers for approval (sometimes with adjustments). This approach has five distinct advantages[4]:

1. Supervisors and lower-level department heads have a more intimate view of their needs than do managers at the top.

2. Lower-level managers can provide more realistic breakdowns to support their proposals.
3. They are less likely to overlook some vital ingredient or hidden flaw that might subsequently impede implementation efforts.
4. These managers will also be more strongly motivated to accept and meet budgets that they have had a hand in shaping.
5. Finally, morale and satisfaction are usually higher when individuals participate actively in making decisions that affect them.

Budgets are merely guides for management and not substitutes for good judgment. They should not be so detailed that they become cumbersome. Further, budgets should allow managers some freedom to accomplish the objectives of their departments with a reasonable degree of latitude and flexibility. To avoid having it become a straitjacket, enlightened management will assure flexibility of the budget by means of regular reviews so that actual performance can be checked and compared against it. If operating conditions have appreciably changed, and if there are valid indications that the budget cannot be followed in the future, a revision of the budget is in order.

Budgets do represent restrictions, and for this reason, some managers do not like them. They may have a defensive approach to budgets, an approach that has sometimes been acquired through painful experience. Budgets represent a barrier to spending; they may prohibit a raise in salary. Thus, in the minds of some managers and employees, a budget becomes associated with "top management's miserly behavior," rather than with planning and controlling vital activities. The manager should try to understand that budgeting is an orderly and disciplined approach to problems and that there is enough flexibility built into a budget system to permit commonsense departures in order to serve the best interests of the health services organization. Whatever can be done without a budget can usually be done better with one. The budgeting process is fairly complex, and its details are beyond the scope of this book. However, the reader will find *Budgeting Procedures for Hospitals*, a publication of the American Hospital Association, an easy-to-read and valuable resource on the budgeting process in health services organizations.[5]

PERFORMANCE APPRAISAL AS A CONTROL DEVICE

As we noted earlier in this chapter, control is effective only when it guides someone's behavior. A very direct method of control over an individual employee's behavior, and one of the most important control mechanisms available to the manager, is the formal *performance appraisal* procedure. Performance appraisal is simply the feeding back to employees of information about how well they are performing their work for the health services organization. While a great deal of this feedback occurs in the day-to-day interactions between managers and subordinates, we shall concentrate on the more formal annual or semiannual appraisals.

In many health services organizations, these formal performance appraisals are based on personal characteristics (such as intelligence, creativity, punctuality, or ability to get along with peers) of the person being appraised. The actual appraisals usually consist of superiors rating their subordinates or sometimes a group of superiors (a committee) rating subordinates or even, on occasion, a group of peers rating a colleague. The common denominator in these traditional approaches is that the basis of the rating is the personal characteristics or traits of the person being appraised.

This traditional approach to performance appraisal often fails to improve the performance of employees. There is a growing concensus that a better method of appraisal can grow out of the Management By Objectives (MBO) approach we discussed in Chapter 3. Recall that a central feature of MBO is periodic agreement between superior-subordinate pairs throughout the organization on the subordinate's objectives for a particular period. As was stated earlier in this chapter, the control function is intended to make certain that objectives are accomplished. This is true for the objectives at the level of the entire organization and for the departments and units that comprise it; but it is also true for each individual who works in the organization. Thus, a performance appraisal that uses the accomplishment of objectives by each individual as the criterion of performance can be very useful to the manager as a control device. In essence, the MBO approach is a *performance-based* performance appraisal instead of a personal characteristic- or trait-based method. The MBO approach to performance appraisal is increasingly being seen as a useful approach to the appraisal of individual workers and as an effective device for controlling their contribution to the organizations in which they work. There is a growing literature base that supports this view.[6]

However, there are difficulties with the MBO approach. For example, Kaluzny et al have noted that the approach requires[7]:

> a great deal of meeting time between superiors and subordinates, who already have extensive demands for actual service delivery activities. Usually, the process of defining goals and action plans is viewed as an appendage to existing work loads as opposed to an integrated part of activities. An exacerbating factor is that many of the objectives and activities associated with health service organizations are difficult to define, thus compounding the problems of establishing goals and specific activities.

Even so, the periodic reviews of performance based upon mutually established objectives in an MBO framework is a very positive method of performance appraisal. It has the further advantage of forcing the managers to clarify their own thinking and expectations and communicate them to their subordinates.

The budget and performance appraisal program are not the only control mechanisms available to the manager, but they are two of the most important ones.

With this background on the control function of management, we can now turn our attention to *what* has to be controlled in health services organizations. As we noted earlier, everything that falls under the manager's responsibility is subject to control. However, we will limit our discussion to the two most pervasive and important areas of control: cost and quality of health services.

CONTROLLING COSTS

As we said at the outset of this chapter, in view of the limited resources our society allocates for the purpose of providing health services, those responsible for such services must make the most efficient use of resources. This translates directly into a concern for the cost of providing health services. Thus, controlling costs is one of the important aspects of the manager's role.

At the departmental or unit level, costs can be broken down as follows: (1) payroll costs for departmental personnel, (2) the cost of supplies and services that must be purchased in order for the department to do its work, (3) capital investment in equipment, machines, and furniture, and (4) the more or less fixed costs of rent, utilities, taxes, insurance, and similar items where they apply. The first two elements of departmental costs suggested above are amenable to some managerial control. The last two lie largely outside of the departmental or unit manager's direct influence, although certain steps can be taken to control capital investment costs to a limited extent. Thus, departmental managers who are interested in controlling costs in their departments must realize that they can have an effective impact on only *some* of the things that influence cost in their departments.

We have stated that the control function consists of four steps: (1) establishing standards, (2) measuring performance, (3) comparing actual results with standards, and (4) correcting deviations from standards. In order to control personnel costs, standards must be set in the areas of number of personnel in the department, number of hours of overtime permitted, and amount of work to be done by each employee. As the work of the department progresses, actual performance can be checked against these standards. If deviations occur, then corrective action must be taken. In the area of personnel costs, deviations will either be in the number of personnel required or the amount of work done by employees. Controlling the numbers of personnel or of overtime worked is relatively easy compared to controlling the amount of work. Nevertheless, if the manager finds that employees are not producing at the level established as a standard, then something must be done. The first thing is, of course, to reevaluate the standard. It may very well be too high. If it is not, then the corrective action involves changing the manner in which employees perform their work. This is accomplished in a number of ways: (1) improving the manner in which the work is done through job analysis and work simplification, (2) training employees in the best way to perform the work, and (3) motivating employees to perform at maximum levels. These three things are synergistic in that their sum is greater than the sum of the parts—they reinforce one another. When applied together, they offer the manager a method of influencing departmental costs. Unfortunately, many times emphasis is placed on only one element (usually the manager's strong point) to the detriment of the others.

The costs of supplies and services must be controlled in much the same manner, (i.e., establish standards, review actual results, compare to standards,) and, if necessary, take corrective action. The use of a supply budget can greatly facilitate this function. In fact, development and use of a tight but realistic departmental supply budget is the single most important thing the manager can do to control supply costs. Other useful steps include:

1. Centralize the issuance of supplies.
2. Develop a procedure for requisitioning supplies that will promote their appropriate use.
3. Issue supplies in sensible quantities.

As we suggested, the control of capital investment in equipment is not as amenable to control as personnel and supplies. However, the same control procedures are used. There are several suggestions that might be useful in controlling the equipment costs in a health services organization.

1. Purchase or lease only the equipment needed. A $200 adding machine may be quite adequate for certain uses, although it is not as appealing as the fancy microcomputer system.
2. Use and maintain the equipment properly. Be certain that all employees are trained in the proper use of machines. Make comparative studies of possible use of in-house service units for repair and maintenance of machines instead of outside, contracted service agreements.
3. Standardize the equipment, because this will simplify training and maintenance and may result in quantity discounts in the original lease or purchase.
4. Replace machines whenever this will result in a real cost saving through increased productivity.

The Management Audit as a Means of Controlling Costs

Managers in health services organizations very often experience a problem common to managers in all organizations. This is the problem of being so involved in the day-to-day operation that they cannot see the opportunities for improvement all around them. The manager who has a heavy workload finds it difficult, especially where there are no obvious problems, to make changes in the present operations and procedures. However, the effective manager should have a personal objective of constantly seeking to improve utilization of those resources entrusted to him or her. This attitude spurs the manager to continuously seek better and more efficient ways of getting things done.

A tool that can be of great value to the manager in the health services organization who is trying to control costs (as well as make general improvements in departmental operations) is the management audit. This is nothing more than a *systematic analysis* of activities in the manager's department or unit. Such an audit can yield results that lead to cost control as well as general improvement in departmental operations. The objectives of a management audit are to bring into sharp focus the activities and operations of the department and to force a careful appraisal of the effectiveness and efficiency of work performance. A management audit permits the manager to review the organizational pattern, sharpen objectives, reemphasize policies, review standards, and scrutinize procedures. It is hardly possible that such a close analysis of any department or unit in a health services organization would not uncover areas where improvements can be made.

The manager will probably conduct the audit, although, if possible, an outside consultant can be of great value. After all, the performance of the manager is one of the key areas of interest in the audit. Whoever does conduct it must remember that is purpose is to gather facts, develop recommendations, and work toward implementing them. These ends should be accomplished accurately, effectively, and expeditiously. The key to an effective management audit is the thought that goes into it before it is conducted. The management audit can be very extensive or relatively simple, depending on the manager's time and the objectives he or she sets.

In essence, the management audit is conducted by analyzing in a systematic and planned way the work done in a particular department. Such a searching approach to the effectiveness and efficiency of operations will take time and effort. The results, however, make it worthwhile. Three general benefits are obtained from the management audit:

1. *Evaluation of operations.* This is an obvious benefit in that a systematic examination of all phases of operation within the department or unit is made.
2. *A means of effective control.* When the audit is made, the manager has at his or her disposal a significant tool for control. Remember that control implies establishing standards, measuring actual results, and then correcting deviations. The information obtained in the management audit goes far beyond the few pieces of quantifiable information usually used for control purposes in most health services organization departments. It provides comprehensive information on what actual performance is like in the department or unit.

3. *Improvement of relationships between managers and their subordinates.* As employees in the department learn how an audit works and how everyone benefits, a better feeling develops. Management sees its plans and directives carried out. A greater understanding arises, for employees see their particular jobs in relationship to the jobs of others, discover how each job fits into the total pattern, and learn the contributions of each job and worker to the whole departmental operation.

These benefits can only be realized if the management audit is properly conceived and carried out and if the findings are communicated to all workers in the department. Of course, the burden of responsibility falls on the manager to use the information gathered to make improvements that can lead to effective cost control and a general improvement in operations within the department.

Some authorities suggest periodic audits, usually annually. However, the scope of the management audit suggested above dictates that a more realistic approach is for the manager in the health services organization to be involved in one aspect or another of the audit on a continuing basis. What this means is that managers will always be involved in a systematic and careful examination of what is going on around them. The management audit gives them a framework within which the analysis is conducted. The end result is a constant searching for areas where improvements can be made, and for more effective control of the resources over which the manager has been given responsibility.

CONTROLLING THE QUALITY OF CARE

Few subjects in the health services field have received as much attention as the quality of care provided. This interest stems basically from the professional concern of those who deliver care to do so in the best possible manner. In recent years, more formalized interest in quality of care has come from major third-party payers (primarily the federal government and business) and, to some extent, from consumers who have begun to realize that the care they receive is subject to variations in quality. The tremendous increase in malpractice suits has served to emphasize the interest in and concern about the quality of care provided in health services organizations.

There are many aspects involved in measuring quality of medical care.[8] For example, one can measure and evaluate the structure of the setting in which care is given by looking at the characteristics of the setting that are thought to be related to quality. These might include the scope of services offered, the education of those providing the services, or any of a number of other structural characteristics thought to be related to quality. The actual *process* of providing care can be examined by looking at the interactions

Structure
Joint Commission on Accreditation of Healthcare
    Organization (JCAHO) accreditation
Staffing ratios
Staff education and qualifications
Compliance with licensure bodies

Process
Compliance with professionally defined standards of care
Compliance with defined treatment protocols
Medication errors
Critical-incident reports

Outcomes
Severity-adjusted disease-specific mortality rates
Severity-adjusted disease-specific functional health status
Patient satisfaction

Figure 9–4. Measures of quality of care.

between patients and those providing care. This is accomplished by such means as direct observation of medical practice, medical record review, and a determination of the appropriateness of treatment. A final aspect of quality that can be measured is the *outcome* of care. That is, the status of the patient after care has been provided, or the end result, can be evaluated. For the health services organization as a whole, such things as severity-adjusted disease-specific mortality rates or functional health status can provide a means of measuring outcome. Figure 9–4 suggests some typical measures of quality of care in health services organizations.

While there is no universal agreement on how to control quality in health services organizations, or even on how to measure quality, there is widespread acceptance that quality should receive considerable attention. In the case of hospitals, the Joint Commission on Accreditation of Healthcare Organizations (JCAHO) has established as one of its standards that "the hospital shall demonstrate that the quality of care provided to all patients is consistently optimal by continuously evaluating it through reliable and valid measures."* An excellent description of the JCAHO's "Performance Evaluation Procedure for Auditing and Improving Patient Care" has been developed by Jacobs, Christoffel, and Dixon.[9]

The American Hospital Association has developed a guide for use by hospitals in developing their quality assurance efforts. The basic framework of this guide is very much like the four-step control model we developed earlier in this chapter. The steps in the quality assurance program outlined by the American Hospital Association are as follows:[10]

---

* The Joint Commission on Accreditation of Healthcare Organizations periodically revises its standards, the latest being in 1988.

Step A - Criteria development
Step B - Description of the actual practice
Step C - Judgment or evaluation (does B = A?)
Step D - Corrective action (necessary if B ≠ A)
Step E - Reassessment (after D, now does B = A?)

In applying the general outline of the controlling function (setting standards, measuring actual results, comparing to standards, taking corrective action), one must first develop standards of quality. These will be characteristics of excellence against which the actual care being provided will be measured. The difficulties in setting appropriate standards make this one of the most complex issues facing health services managers.

If the professionals in the health services organization can agree on standards, measure the actual results of the provision of care, compare them to the standards, and take corrective actions when necessary, then they will be controlling the quality of care. Health services organizations are doing this to some extent. For example, hospitals typically have a utilization review program and a medical audit program in which peers evaluate the care that is given in the hospital. The fact that these procedures are peer reviews is important because peers can best determine the standards that are appropriate. Also, peer judgment is necessary in evaluation of the actual care provided, and peers can best determine the appropriate corrective action that needs to be taken.

It is fair to say that, at this point in time, controlling the quality of care provided in health services organizations is receiving a great deal of attention and effort. The complexities involved in determining appropriate standards are the major drawback. Until such time as widely accepted standards are developed and disseminated, the control of quality of care in health services organizations will not be as complete as health professionals want it to be. Currently, there is a widespread recognition that much research is needed to establish the structural and process measures that are most strongly associated with desirable outcomes of care. To date, structural and process measures have been more commonly used than outcome measures, simply because such measures are easier to develop. An important challenge remains: to develop and then use valid outcome standards of quality as managers seek to control quality in health services organizations.

CONTROLLING IS DIFFICULT

The reader can see from the examples of controlling costs and quality of care in health services organizations that this is one of the most difficult functions of the manager. The following suggestions reflect some of the most important requirements of effective controls:

1. *Controls must reflect the nature and needs of the activity.* All control systems should reflect the job they are to perform. This is merely a requirement of reflection of plans: the more controls are designed to deal with and reflect the specific nature and structure of plans, the more effectively they will serve the interests of the health services organization.

2. *Controls should report deviations promptly.* The ideal control system detects deviations soon after they actually occur. Only if information reaches the manager in a timely manner can he or she take effective action.

3. *Controls should be forward-looking.* Although ideal control is instantaneous, as in certain electronic controls, the facts of managerial life include a time lag between the deviation and corrected action. Perhaps the key point of control in ensuring achievement of objectives is that of detecting potential or actual deviation from plans early enough to permit effective corrective action. Therefore, the manager, in striving to apply this principle, would surely prefer a forecast of what will probably happen next week or next month—even though this contains a margin of error—to a report, accurate to several decimal points, on the past, about which nothing can be done.

4. *Controls should be objective.* Management necessarily has many subjective elements in it, but whether a subordinate is doing a good job should ideally not be a matter for subjective determination. Where controls are subjective, a manager's or a subordinate's personality may influence judgments of performance inaccurately. However, people have difficulty explaining away objective control of their performance, particularly if the standards and measurements are kept up to date through periodic review. Effective control requires objective, accurate, and suitable standards.

5. *Controls should be flexible.* Controls must remain workable in the face of changed plans, unforeseen circumstances, or outright failures. If they are to remain effective, despite failure or changes in plans, flexibility is required in their selection.

6. *Controls should point up exceptions at critical points.* Effective control requires attention to those factors critical to performance. Generally, the more managers concentrates their control efforts on exceptions, the more efficient will be the results of their control activities.

7. *Controls should be economical.* Controls must be worth their cost. Although this requirement is simple, its practice is often complex, for a manager may find it difficult to know what a particular control system is worth, or to know what it costs. Economy is relative, since the benefits vary with the importance of the activity, the size of the

operation, the expense that might be incurred in the absence of control, and the contribution the control system can make.

8. *Controls should be understandable.* Some control systems, especially those based upon mathematical formulas, complex break-even charts, detailed analyses, and computer simulations, are not always understandable to the managers who must use them. Managers could often understand even complex control systems if they would take the time to learn to do so; but whether the lack of understanding results from complex techniques or impatience in learning them, the effect is the same: the control system will not function.

9. *Controls should lead to corrective action.* A control system that detects deviations from plans will be little more than an interesting exercise if it does not show the way to corrective action. An adequate system will disclose where failures are occurring and who is responsible for them, so that corrective action can be taken.

10. *Controls should reflect the organization pattern.* Organization structure, being the principal vehicle for coordinating the work of people, is also a major means for maintaining control. It is the manager who is the focal point of control, just as he or she is the focal point for the assignment of tasks and the delegation of authority and responsibility.

SUMMARY

Controlling is the regulation of activities in accordance with the requirements of plans. Controlling consists of four steps: (1) establishing standards, (2) measuring performance, (3) comparing actual results with standards, and (4) correcting deviations from standards.

There are different types of standards, and there are a number of techniques that can be useful in setting them. The manager's personal observation is the best way of measuring performance. If the manager finds that corrective action is necessary, he or she should view it as a means of improving the performance of subordinates. The manager should keep in mind that, generally, the more intimately a person is involved in the control decisions that are made, the more likely it is that the person will accept them and support them.

Controlling costs is a process that managers can undertake to improve the effectiveness with which their departments utilize resources. The more complex issue of controlling the quality of care provided in the health services organization has become increasingly important in recent years, and promises to be even more important in the years ahead as quality comes under much closer scrutiny.

REFERENCES

1. Newman WH: *Constructive Control: Design and Use of Control Systems.* Englewood Cliffs, NJ, Prentice-Hall, 1975, pp 3–5.
2. Mondy RW, Sharplin A, Flippo EB: *Management: Concepts and Practices,* ed 4. Boston, Allyn & Bacon, 1988, p 509.
3. Lipson SH, Hensel MD: *Hospital Manpower Budget Preparation Manual.* Ann Arbor, Mich, Health Administration Press, 1975.
4. Stoner JAF, Wankel C: *Management,* ed 3. Englewood Cliffs, NJ, Prentice-Hall, 1986, pp 601–602.
5. Esmond T Jr: *Budgeting Procedures for Hospitals,* ed 3. Chicago, American Hospital Association, 1982.
6. McConkey, DD: *MBO for Nonprofit Organizations.* New York, AMACOM, 1975; Deegan AX, II: *Management by Objectives for Hospitals,* ed 2. Germantown, Md, Aspen Systems Corporation, 1982.
7. Kaluzny AD, Warner PM, Warner DG, Zelman WN: *Management of Health Services.* Englewood Cliffs, NJ, Prentice-Hall, 1982, p 251.
8. Dowabedian A: *Explorations in Quality Assessment and Monitoring,* vols I, II, III, Ann Arbor, Mich, Health Administration Press, 1980, 1982, 1985.
9. Jacobs CM, Christoffel TH, Dixon N: *Measuring the Quality of Patient Care: The Rationale for Outcome Audit.* Cambridge, Mass, Ballinger Publishing Co, 1976.
10. American Hospital Association: *Quality Assurance Program for Medical Care in Hospitals.* Chicago, American Hospital Association, 1972, Section 3, p 1.

*T*EN
Managing Change: The Management Imperative

September 15
2 P.M.

The president looked slowly around the lecture hall at the students. He was very pleased to have been invited to be a guest lecturer for the nursing students on the topic of "Management in the Hospital." He cleared his throat and began.

"My subject this afternoon is management. Some of you may not find it as interesting as the professional practice of nursing, but it is just as important to the well-being of the patient as any of the other skills that go into modern medical care . . ."

The president continued lecturing for almost an hour and a half before saying, "In conclusion, the single greatest challenge facing the manager is to look at the organization, or that part of it he or she manages, and think about what is—compared to what should be—and then find ways to change it."

As he watched the students file out of the lecture hall, he collected his notes and thought to himself, "Bringing about change really is the key to management—but it's so much easier to talk about than to do. That situation with Luther Fillerey pointed up half a dozen things that needed to be changed. Oh well, I'll get to them soon."

It was 3:30 P.M. as the president headed back to his office and the pile of work waiting for him.

INTRODUCTION

Change is not easy, nor has it ever been. Machiavelli wrote in *The Prince* several hundred years ago that "it must be said that there is nothing more difficult to carry out, nor more doubtful in success, than to initiate a new thing." Those of us involved in trying to improve the delivery of health services know the truth of his words. Yet if the objective of making health care available and affordable to all is to be realized, changes must occur. Bringing about change is the basic imperative faced by all managers in health services organizations.

Health services organizations are under unprecedented pressure to change—in some cases to change their methods of operation, in some cases to change their objectives, and in some cases to change both. These pressures stem from consumers and their advocates, government, leaders in the medical establishment, and a growing awareness on the part of many people (inside and outside health services organizations) that they, as institutions, are not as effective as they need to be. The force of these pressures is exacerbated by continuing progress in medical science and technology, which outstrips the system for delivering health services. It is clear to the knowledgeable observer that the delivery system is being restructured and the roles of health professionals are being redefined in modern society. Organizations usually exist, however, in a state of equilibrium. Organizations generate numerous forces and balances to perpetuate themselves and to reject changes that disturb the equilibrium.[1]

There are many types of changes that take place within health services organizations. A very important dichotomy of these changes is whether they are imposed on the organization (by a government regulation for example) or made without direct, coercive, external pressure. Both situations are organizational changes, but the latter is an *innovative* organizational change. We are more concerned here with the innovative than with the imposed change. Health services organizations do not exist in a vacuum. They interact with, react to, and influence their environments. The health services organization that only reacts to its environment (where changes are literally forced by external pressures) cannot be thought of as an innovative organization. We shall restrict our definition to innovative organizational change.

We should point out at the outset that there is not yet a universally accepted definition of innovative organizational change. Thompson defines *innovation* as "the generation, acceptance, and implementation of new ideas, processes, products, and services."[2] Becker and Whisler separate the creation of an idea from its use. They define *innovation* as "the first or early use of an idea by one of a set of organizations with similar goals."[3] The first or early user is thus the innovator, regardless of the source of the idea. Mohr separates invention from use, but does not include first or early use in his definition. He defines *innovation* as "the successful introduction into an applied situation of means or ends that are new to that situation."[4] The reader can see that these three representative definitions of innovation are quite different.

One of the best definitions is suggested by Rowe and Boise. They state: "Organizational innovation refers to the successful utilization of processes, programs, or products which are new to an organization and which are introduced as a result of decisions made within that organization."[5] Using this definition, it is possible to distinguish between organization change and innovative organizational change. When change is forced from external pressures, it can be defined as the successful utilization of processes, programs, or products new to an organization. If, on the other hand, the change comes about because of decisions made within the organization, then it is *innovative* organizational change and not merely change. Innovation and change are both important concepts for the health professional manager because they are both taking place and will continue to take place in the health services organization.

If one observes a number of organizational changes in health care settings, a variety of objectives would seem to be present. These objectives might be such things as better performance, greater motivation, reduced turnover, or any one of an almost limitless number of things. However, in health care settings organizational changes usually fit into one of two broader categories: (1) changes in the organization's level of adaptation to its environment and (2) changes in the internal behavior patterns of participants. Health services organizations are in a constant struggle to adapt themselves to their external environment. They cannot control (except to a very limited extent) the external environment; therefore, organizational changes are required to allow the organization to deal with challenges imposed from outside the organization by such things as consumer demands, government regulation, medical and scientific advances, planning agencies, third-party payers, and so forth. For the most part, health services organizations make organizational changes in reaction to these environmental pressures. In some cases, however, changes are made without outside pressure or in anticipation of future pressures. This innovative behavior characterizes organizations that lead instead of follow their industry. Such health services organizations can be seen as attempting to change their environments as well as themselves. Obviously, if an organization's level of adaptation is to be improved, the behavior patterns of a number of employees must be modified both in terms of their relationships to one another and to their jobs. Thus, the second basic category of organizational change is that which alters the behavior patterns of organization participants.

TYPES OF CHANGE

Kaluzny and Hernandez have identified three types of change as a function of whether ends or means or both are involved[6]:

[1.] *TECHNICAL CHANGE* . . . involves some modifications in the means by which the normal and usual activities of the organization are carried out. This may involve some innovative technology or some programmatic or structural alteration in the design of the organization to meet its designated objectives. Technical changes may vary in focus, cost, and impact, but they do not represent changes in the basic goals of the organization. For example, the decision of a hospital to require estrogen receptor assay tests may represent little cost beyond the laboratory fees and may have little impact on the overall organization. However, the decision by the hospital to implement computer-based information systems . . . or to install tomography, lithotripter, or angioplasty will have substantial financial impacts. Moreover, such a decision will affect many hospital functions, placing new demands on available resources and reallocating power among the existing departments.

Structural-programmatic changes are more difficult to define than techno-logical changes, but they also focus on the manner in which work is conducted within the organization, rather than on any modification of the goals of the organization itself. For example, the introduction of service-unit management, . . . nurse midwifery services, childbirth preparation classes, prenatal contraceptive counseling . . . , organizational development, . . . or quality assurance programs as a managerial innovation . . . centers on the reallocation of tasks and changes in reporting relationships among indi-viduals.

[2.] *TRANSITION* . . . means change in organizational goals but not in the essential means of achieving these goals. The provision of nontherapeutic abortions and the sale of governmental or not-for-profit community hospitals to for-profit systems are examples of transition. In these situations the technology and basic structure (the organizational means) are already avail-able within the institution; however, the intent is to apply these to achieve different objectives. These changes occur less frequently; when they occur, however, they are associated with a great deal of stress and trauma since goals are usually identified with some powerful group within the organi-zation.

[3.] *TRANSFORMATION* . . . is the most extreme form of change. Change occurs in the means the organization uses to reach its end, and also in the ends themselves. For example, hospitals replace traditional inpatient cura-tive services with provision of preventive health care programs to various employer organizations. They also may diversify their operations to include the building and management of condominiums, office buildings, shopping centers, and retirement homes. Each of these activities involves substantial changes in organizational ends and means. Transformation occurs less frequently than other forms of change, but when it does, it involves a basic modification of overall organizational direction and reflects changes in the means by which organizations accomplish these modified ends.

BRINGING ABOUT ORGANIZATIONAL CHANGE

Organizational change, whether it represents an innovation or is imposed by pressures external to the organization, can be introduced by a number of approaches. A useful dichotomy of the various approaches is to look at those that emphasize *what* is to be changed and those that emphasize the process of *how* change is introduced.

One of the most widely used delineations of the *what* approaches is that made by Leavitt.[7] He describes three approaches to organizational change: structure, technology, and people. Structural approaches to the introduction of change are such things as the organization chart, budgeting methods, and rules and regulations. The technological approaches stress changes intro-duced by such means as the introduction of new services (open-heart surgery, for example) or new technological equipment (CAT scanners, for example). The third classification, the people approaches, stresses alterations in attitudes, motivation, and behavioral skills. Changes of this type are made through such techniques as training programs, selection procedures, and performance appraisal programs.

A good illustration of *how* approaches is contained in Greiner's work identifying seven approaches to change most frequently used by managers.[8]

A. *Unilateral Power:*
1. *The Decree Approach.* A "one-way" announcement originating with a person with high formal authority and passed on to those in lower positions.
2. *The Replacement Approach.* Individuals in one or more key organizational positions are replaced by other individuals. The basic assumption is that organizational changes are a function of a key person's ability.
3. *The Structural Approach.* Instead of decreeing or injecting new blood into work relationships, management changes the required relationships of subordinates working in the situation. By changing the structure of organizational relationships, organizational behavior is also presumably affected.
B. *Shared Power:*
4. *The Group Decision Approach.* Here we have participation by group members in selecting from several alternative solutions specified in advance by superiors. This approach involves neither problem identification nor problem solving, but emphasizes the obtaining of group agreement to a particular course of action.
5. *The Group Problem Solving Approach.* Problem identification and problem solving through group discussion. Here the group has wide latitude, not only over choosing the problems to be discussed, but then in developing solutions to these problems.
C. *Delegated Power:*
6. *The Data Discussion Approach.* Presentation and feedback of relevant data to the client system either by a change catalyst or by change agents within the [health services organization]. Organizational members are encouraged to develop their own analyses of the data, presented in the form of case materials, survey findings, or data reports.
7. *The Sensitivity Training Approach.* Managers are trained in small discussion groups to be more sensitive to the underlying processes of individual and group behavior. Changes in work patterns and relationships are assumed to follow from changes in interpersonal relationships. Sensitivity approaches focus upon interpersonal relationships first, then hope for, or work toward, improvements in work performance.

It should be noted that few changes can be successfully introduced using only one of these strategies. A balanced approach carefully combining several elements is needed. For example, a health professional manager may wish to encourage a more effective communication network among her or his subordinates. To accomplish this change, the manager will need to take a "people" approach by providing the subordinates with a training program in communication skills. However, the full implementation of this change may also require "structural" changes that lead to more open communication among the subordinates.

In an analysis of 18 studies of organizational change, it was learned that successful changes utilized patterns involving sharing approaches; that is, superiors sought participation of subordinates in decision making. In the less successful attempts, the approaches were closer to either end of the continuum outlined above; five used unilateral approaches of decree, replacement, and structure, and two used sensitivity training or fact finding and discussion.[9]

Organizational change is a very complex process. The manager concerned with introducing and managing change needs a conceptual framework of the process. Most research indicates that the central concept needed to understand the process of change clearly and objectively is to think of organizational change as an evolving series of stages. It does not occur all at once. Rather, one phase sets necessary conditions for moving into subsequent stages. Lewin pioneered in identifying three phases of change: unfreezing, changing, and refreezing.[10] The unfreezing stage represents a necessary first step in stimulating people to recognize the need for change. The changing stage involves introduction and application of the change. Finally, the refreezing stage provides the necessary reinforcement to make certain that new behavior patterns are adopted on a permanent basis.

No matter what change process is used, there are several prerequisites to organizational change:[11]

1. Something has to precipitate change—a happening, development, signal, or an individual has to place the organization in a mold for change.
2. The organization itself must be ready to change, or someone within the organization, the change agent, must convince others that old, comfortable ways should be replaced by new, untried ways.
3. The proposed new ways either must mesh with or not seriously disturb the existing value system.
4. The change agent must select the approach or combination of approaches necessary to convince others of the need for change (for example, by planting seeds for change through a board/management/medical staff educational process; by using task forces and other internal devices to develop ideas and build coalitions; or both).
5. The change agent must create a shared body of values and attitudes—a new consensus where key individuals within an organization reinforce one another in selling the new way and in defending it against inertia, reluctance, or outright opposition.

THE HUMAN ELEMENT IN CHANGE

Some changes involve a new design for a form or a new machine; others involve basic behavior patterns in people. But *all* change affects people in the organization in some way. Regardless of who may institute the change, the person affected is compelled. The person's response is a function of both background, including needs and experiences, and the particular situation in which the change is introduced. One cannot predict from the technical content of the change alone the person's response. A manager may view change "logically" and feel that any resistance is irrational. But he or she will never understand or be able to predict change responses unless something is known about the person affected by the change and about that person's past experiences.

Each changed situation is interpreted by individuals according to their attitudes. The way people feel about the change then determines how they will respond to it. Attitudes, in turn, are not the result of chance: they are caused. One cause is personal history, which refers to a person's biological processes, background, and all social experiences away from work. That is what the person brings to the workplace. A second cause is the work environment itself, reflecting the fact that the person is a group member and is influenced by group codes, patterns, and attitudes.

The human element is, by its nature, complex. For the manager wishing to make a substantive change, this complexity requires a comprehensive and systematic approach to change. A variety of tools and techniques must be used. The term for such an approach is *organization development* (OD). Huse defines OD as: ". . . a process by which behavioral science knowledge and practices are used to help organizations achieve greater effectiveness, including improved quality of work life and increased productivity. . . . the focus is upon human resources and their motivation, utilization, and integration within the organization."[12]

Organizational development is a problem-solving process (with various techniques available) through which organizations can reach decisions about when and where to make useful changes. The process is more than the sum of techniques used; synergy results from combining the various techniques. Margulies describes the process.[13]

> *First,* it involves the generation and exploration of pertinent information regarding the organization's functioning. *Second,* it involves an evaluation of that information and a diagnosis of current functioning with specific emphasis on those aspects of organizational behavior that are dysfunctional. And, *finally,* it involves the formulation of an interventional strategy, based on that diagnosis, which can bring about changes so that more of the organization's behavior is functional in terms of its goals.

The term *action research* is used as an analog for the process of organizational development. As Margulies points out, "in combining action processes (planning, execution, and evaluation) with research processes (problem identification, hypothesis formation, and testing), the result is a sequence of steps and activities that identify the relevant events that must happen in the initiation and implementation of change."[14] Figure 10–1 summarizes the action research model and illustrates the problem-solving

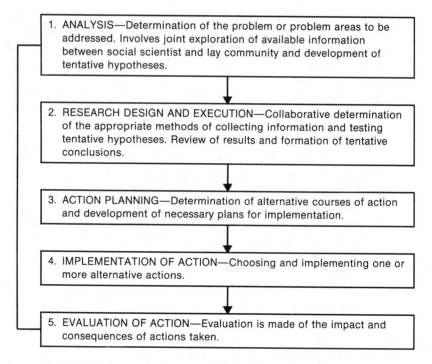

Figure 10–1. The action research process. *(From Margulies N: Managing change in health care organizations. Medical Care, August 1977, p 696. Reprinted with permission.)*

process character of a systematic and cyclical organizational development effort. As Margulies states, action research:[15]

> . . . incorporates five different but related aspects, all very significant in the process of change and development. Action research (1) is a *methodology for generating knowledge* about the processes of an organization, (2) is a *mechanism or strategy for disseminating that knowledge* and for generalizing that knowledge to other similar situations, (3) provides a *logical sequence for organizational and individual problem solving*, (4) may be thought of as a *powerful interventional strategy* in the process of organizational change, and (5) represents a *philosophical view* that strongly encompasses the need and desire for ongoing organizational review.

This systematic approach increases the likelihood that change can be successfully accomplished. Yet, even with such efforts, change is often difficult to achieve. As we shall see below, this is largely because of the human propensity to resist change.

The Human Response to Change—Resistance

One of the most persistent problems faced by a manager attempting to initiate a change is resistance. There are a number of possible sources for this often-encountered attitude. These sources include the following[16]:

1. Insecurity
2. Possible social loss
3. Economic losses
4. Historical stability
5. Unanticipated repercussions
6. Union opposition

Sources of Resistance

Perhaps a few words about each of these sources of resistance to change is in order.

Insecurity. Insecurity is usually suggested as the major source of general resistance. The present is known, understood, and has been absorbed. There is comfort in the status quo; people have worked out a relationship with it. Change introduces some degree of uncertainty. Organizations are often so complex that a seemingly simple change, such as moving the location of the water cooler, can have far-reaching repercussions. To some, such a move is a symbol of management's lack of concern for inconvenienced employees. To others, it means more traffic and interference around their workplace. And to still others, it is another bit of evidence of the autocracy of management. Change, then, could involve a reduction in a current level of satisfaction. People affected by changes often do not really know what will happen, but their past experiences have taught them to look for the worst. Change also suggests to people that either they or their methods are unsatisfactory.

Social Losses. There are various kinds of social losses that can ensue from change. The mere fact that management wishes to impose a change is evidence of the employee's lack of independence. In addition, many of the modern technological changes tend to isolate the employee from co-workers even further.

Change will also involve altering informal relationships among personnel. A close friend may now work in another room, or work materials may now be received from a person of lower status. The complex of informal relationships must inevitably be affected by the introduction of any change involving people. Established status symbols may be destroyed, or a lower-status individual may be given a high status symbol. Social acceptance will be in jeopardy if a particular employee is favorable toward a change inaugurated by management while the majority of the group is not. The individual may have to choose between cooperation with management and the friendship of co-workers. Thus, what may seem desirable from a logical and technical view may meet with heavy resistance because the price in social relationships is too high.

Economic Losses. There are some changes introduced by management that inflict economic loss upon employees. In many cases, through technological advances, more work can now be done by the same or fewer personnel. Resistance to this kind of change is entirely understandable and most difficult to overcome. Even without the loss of job or reduced earnings, the same earnings may be accompanied by an accelerated pace or increased contribution.

Stability. If the organization's past history has been highly stable, it is doubly difficult to introduce a change. When personnel have not only adjusted to the status quo, but have begun to feel that it is a permanent situation, the inauguration of even the most minor change may be considered to be revolutionary and highly disruptive. There are times, of course, when an organization that has pursued a policy of instituting changes fairly frequently has, in this manner, made change a part of the status quo.

Unanticipated Repercussions. Few if any changes can be kept completely isolated; there are usually repercussions felt by other parts of the organization. These affected areas may bring about the downfall of the proposed improvement. For example, there is often a desire to change and improve supervisory practices; supervisors are therefore given a training course in human relations. Effecting changes in supervisory attitudes and methods is difficult enough; visualize, then, the difficulties the supervisors in turn experience upon returning from the training course. Their subordinates had previously worked out a relationship with these superiors; now they do not know what to expect. The most admirable and correct action by the newly trained supervisor is likely to be met with a great deal of suspicion, particularly if it is inconsistent with the pattern of the past. Many attempts to change supervisory behavior have met with failure because other parts of the organization have been neglected.

The Union. If there is a labor union, its representatives may at times be inclined to oppose changes suggested by management. These representatives were not elected necessarily to cooperate with management and staff officials; their role is to protect the interests of the union member. The employee is usually more comfortable with a fighting union representative than with one inclined to cooperate with management on changes designed to promote the interests of the organization. Thus, it is expected that the union will produce some resistance, even in cases where union leaders recognize that proposed changes are good both for union members and the health services organization.

Looking for the Causes of Resistance

As the foregoing indicates, the causes of resistance to change are many and complex. It is much easier to be aware of the symptoms than of the underlying causes. There may be increased griping by employees and suggestions that the change will not work. Even more dangerous symptoms may show up as poor work, slowdowns, or other factors. If the health professional manager views the symptoms as fundamental problems, he or she will be at a loss in attempting to resolve the situation. For example, the many reasons given as to why the change will never work can be discussed and most, if not all, of them diminished through rational analysis. Yet it soon becomes apparent that the real source of resistance has to do less with rational analysis than with intuitive feelings. If management never attempts to ascertain the source of these feelings, it will constantly be treating the symptom rather than the causes. Figure 10–2 illustrates the manner in which individuals respond to change.

STEPS IN MAKING A CHANGE

Given the background on resistance to change described above, how can the manager implement changes? The following approach can be effective. It is a step-by-step method that includes the feature of encouraging the participation of employees who will be affected by the change.

Step 1. Recognition of the Need for Change

This step is crucial to the entire change process. It is at this point that managers decide to act. If, in the manager's judgment, the forces for change are significant, the process moves to the next step—diagnosis.

A major change is proposed	Person evaluates the impact on him/her	Response to change
	—Destructive,	—Oppose, resist,
	—Threatening,	—Tolerate,
	—Uncertain,	—Accept, support,
	—(Positive) very good	—Join

Affected by:
1. Extent of information about the change
2. Extent of participation in change decision
3. Trust in initiator of change
4. Past experience with change

Figure 10–2. An individual's response to change. *(Adapted from Fulmer RM: The New Management ed 4. New York, Macmillan, 1988, p 203. Reprinted with permission.)*

Step 2. Diagnosis of the Problem

The key decision in this step is whether the stimulus for change should be acted upon. This decision can be approached by making three related decisions. (The reader may wish to review the material on decision making in Chapter 4 at this point.)

1. What is the problem as distinct from its symptoms?
2. What must be changed to resolve the problem?
3. What outcomes are expected, and how will these outcomes be measured?

The managerial response to these questions should be stated in terms of criteria that reflect organizational effectiveness. Measurable outcomes such as production, efficiency, satisfaction, adaptiveness, and development must be linked to skill, attitudinal, behavioral, and structural changes necessitated by the problem identification. It is necessary to make changes in response to a real situation requiring a change and not on the whim of the manager or anyone else.

Step 3. Identification of Alternative Methods and Strategies

In this step, the health professional manager considers the possible approaches to change that are available to him or her. At this point the manager must take into account the needs of the employees as well as of the health services organization. The individual situation will dictate the possible approaches to take. Inherent in the situational approach is the understanding that each organization must adapt in unique ways to its particular situation. Accordingly, conditions are created that limit the range of possible methods and strategies available to the manager. The leadership style, the formal organization, and group norms all are constraints or limitations that must be considered.

Step 4. Selection of the Method and Strategy

The analysis of the problem, identification of alternatives, and recognition of constraints lead to the selection of the most promising method and strategy. At this point, the judgment of the health professional manager is the key factor. Managers must select an approach to change that they feel is most likely to yield the desired results. It is very important to let the people who will be affected by the change participate in the choice.

Step 5. Implementation of the Change

This is, of course, the critical step. It is also the most difficult because at this point one stops thinking about the change and actually makes it. The following are some suggestions that will prove helpful:

1. Make certain that employees understand the situation that makes a change necessary. If they can perceive its necessity, they are more likely to make an effort to adjust. It is often advisable for a change to be

introduced on a trial basis in order to encourage acceptance. Familiarity, through experience, with the nature of the change, as well as the assurance that one is not stuck with it, may reduce some of the insecurity. The manager must also appreciate the importance of allowing enough time for the change to be digested.

2. Disturb as little as possible the existing customs and informal relationships. The culture developed by a group has real value from the viewpoint of organizational effectiveness, and management should work in consonance with these beliefs when possible.

3. Provide information about the change in advance. Such information can include the reasons necessitating the change, its nature, timing, and impact upon the organization and the people in it.

4. Encourage employee participation in the implementation (as well as the formation) of changes. Participation in the determination and implementation of change will reduce resistance. There is a feeling of lessened pressure upon employees and greater understanding of the nature and probable impact of the change. There is also likely to be an increased sense of pride, since the change was worked out through consultative practices. It is clear that people follow their own decisions best.

5. Provide for means of releasing tensions resulting from the introduction of change. In many cases, change results in the creation of tensions among those affected by it. Management should be aware of the necessity for the release of these emotional tensions. It should not attempt to meet hostility with hostility or emotions with logic. After the resentment has been aired, it is then possible that employees may finally accept the change.

Step 6. Evaluating the Change

Evaluation is necessitated by the manager's responsibility to utilize optimally the resources entrusted to him or her and to account for their utilization. Additionally, evaluation provides feedback, which can lead to corrections where necessary or can strengthen the manager's conviction that the change was wise—or it can create the recognition that further change is necessary.

SUMMARY

This chapter examines the management imperative of change—innovative change, which is the successful utilization of processes, programs, or products that are new to an organization and are introduced as a result of decisions made within that organization.

Change is not easy. People resist it for many reasons: insecurity, the possibility of social and economic losses and other reasons. Changes can be wrought in many ways. Some are more successful than others, and these are pointed out in this chapter. The process of change can be viewed as a step-by-step approach consisting of:

1. Recognition of the need for change
2. Diagnosis of the problem
3. Identification of alternative methods and strategies
4. Selection of the method and strategy
5. Implementation of the change
6. Evaluation of the change

Change is certainly not as easy as outlining six steps might lead one to believe. But it is inevitable, and it is necessary. It might very well be that the most important skill the manager in a health services organization can possess is the skill to implement changes. When one looks at health services organizations and sees what is, compared to what could be, the importance of the manager's change skills comes into focus.

REFERENCES

1. Davis K, Newstrom JW: *Human Behavior at Work: Organizational Behavior,* ed 7. New York, McGraw-Hill, 1985, p 236.
2. Thompson VA: Bureaucracy and innovation. *Administrative Science Quarterly,* June 1966, p 2.
3. Becker SW, Whisler TL: The innovative organization: A selective view of current theory and research. *The Journal of Business,* October 1967, p 462.
4. Mohr LB: Determinants of innovation in organizations. *The American Political Science Review,* March 1967, p 112.
5. Rowe LA, Boise WB: *Organizational and Managerial Innovation: A Reader.* Pacific Palisades, Calif, The Goodyear Publishing Co, 1973, p 6.
6. Kaluzny AD, Hernandez SR: Organizational change and innovation, in Shortell SM, Kaluzny AD (eds): *Health Care Management: A Text in Organization Theory and Behavior,* ed 2. New York, Wiley, 1988, pp 380–381.
7. Leavitt HJ: Applied organization change in industry: Structural, technological, and human approaches, in Cooper WW, Leavitt HJ, Shelly MW III (eds): *New Perspectives in Organization Research.* New York, Wiley, 1964.
8. Greiner LE: Patterns of organization change. *Harvard Business Review,* May-June 1967. Copyright 1967 by the President and Fellows of Harvard College; all rights reserved.
9. Greiner: Patterns of organization change, p 125.
10. Lewin K: *Field Theory in Social Science.* New York, Harper & Row, Pub. 1951.
11. Peters JP, Tseng S: Managing strategic change. *Hospitals,* June 1, 1983, p 65.
12. Huse EF, Cummings TG: *Organization Development and Change,* ed 3. St. Paul, Minn, West Publishing Co, 1985, p 1.
13. Margulies N: Managing change in health care organizations. *Medical Care* August 1977, pp 694–695.
14. Margulies: Managing change in health care organizations, pp 695–696.
15. Margulies: Managing change in health care organizations, p 695.
16. Flippo EB, Munsinger GM: *Management,* ed 5. Boston, Allyn & Bacon, 1982, pp 406–407.

Index